Bonhoeffer and the Racialized Church

Bonhoeffer and the Racialized Church

Ross E. Halbach

BAYLOR UNIVERSITY PRESS

Cover and book design by Kasey McBeath
Cover art: Filip Kominik, Unsplash

Hardcover ISBN: 978-1-4813-1276-9
Library of Congress Control Number: 2020017778

Printed in the United States of America on acid-free paper with a minimum of thirty percent recycled content.

In loving memory of Stacy Jo Dunn

Contents

Preface

When my wife and I first started attending Irvington Covenant Church, its carpets were well worn. Scattered brown coffee stains and patterned footprints memorialized the gathering of parishioners for over twenty years. What made Irvington's carpet special was the story it told about Black and white Christians worshipping together in a historically segregated and increasingly gentrified city. A coffee stain was not just a coffee stain but a discernible memory of Black people and white people sharing a conversation, laughter, and life. Footprints were not just footprints but a visible reminder of a mosaic of bodies standing and walking in a space where prayers were spoken, songs were sung, sermons were preached, and communion was shared.

But that is not the whole story told by Irvington's well-worn carpets. While the carpeted space of Irvington had been a gathering place for people across the racial spectrum for over twenty years, the constant defiance of racial disparity and distance remained a reoccurring challenge, as it will and does in every mixed-race church. Many of our parishioners shared the sentiment that "our church was friendly, but that, at the end of the day, we weren't *really* friends." The full depth of the complex situation our mixed-race church faced came home to me personally during a series of intensive discussion groups on race. In one of these discussion groups, a number of people of color reflected on the difficulty of honestly expressing themselves in our Sunday morning services. This led a long-standing, white parishioner to ask, "Does this mean you're catering to the white people in our church?" An African American woman replied,

"We cater to you all the time, and, much of the time, we're not even fully aware we're doing it." Along with the narrative of racial reconciliation offered by our church, Irvington's well-worn carpets tell the story of how the historical contours of race set painful and violent patterns that we constantly uphold and that we are incorporated into in the Christian church of the West.

This book began existentially from within the church, and it seeks to remain present within the racial trauma haunting our local churches today. Our intensive discussions about race at Irvington, addressing the gentrification of the church's neighborhood, the inequities among the church's parishioners, the unconscious catering toward the congregation's white members, and much more, led a seemingly thriving multiracial church in the inner city to crumple to a fifth of its original size. This book is my privileged opportunity to reflect on and wrestle through the situation our church faced and faces—a situation that similarly defines every church in the United States, in one way or another, no matter its racial demographic or geographic location. My writing of this book is "privileged" in that I have been given advantages and resources unavailable to many of the people of color in my church, who nonetheless graciously supported me in the writing of this book. It is because of these dear friends, some of whom have passed away during the writing of this book, that I became better acquainted with the dynamics of racial privilege, always in play, always working in my favor. I write from and within this privilege even as I seek to work against it. I do this, as well, from the perspective that privilege is not some innocuous benefit given incidentally to those deemed white but a visceral plundering in which I have concretely participated to intentionally form my white identity. My white privilege is existential banditry.

Feeling caught in this grinding wheel of privilege, I initially found myself writing this book as an angry diatribe against white people, myself included. I was enraged with myself and with the responses of the white parishioners in my church. I wanted to know why discussing race in my church hit such a raw nerve. But more than that, I wanted to understand what happened in our shared history that makes discussions of race a land mine waiting to go off. My anger only grew as I read through the piles of books given to me by friends from church and from peers in my Ph.D. program. Listening to the voices of people of color from around the world, I discovered that my initial question was a naive one, a question that had been answered a thousand times over.

Time allowed me to slowly inhale centuries of painful wounding and exhale a new question.

This new question is the question I explore in this book. It is a question that concerns race and the church. The question is not how the church is configured by race but how the triune God, who became flesh, continues to speak within the disfigurement of the racially formed community of the Western Christian church.

Acknowledgments

Stacy Jo Dunn was a tenacious advocate of racial justice for all peoples, in all places. Her tenacity was matched by a tender compassion that called people to something more. I am simply one of the many that was fortunate enough to be forever changed by the relentless compassion of Stacy's life. She masterfully and gracefully walked me into the troubled waters of race, not knowing that her influence would later lead to my writing of this book. When I asked Stacy for a recommended reading list, in the early research stages of this book, she sent me a large portion of her own personal library. Toward the end of her struggle with breast cancer, she read initial drafts of chapters and never failed to ask me how the writing was coming. The fierce grace Stacy displayed continues to leave me in a state of wonder, and it is my hope that a fraction of that grace pierces through the pages of this book.

Along with Stacy, there are numerous others from Irvington Covenant Church who supported, encouraged, and guided me throughout this project. It was within ICC that I first discovered a group of people willing to explore the church's painful history of race, and it is this same community that sustained me at the most difficult points of this project. In Tory Campbell I found a close friend who was willing to entertain and interact with my latest theological musings and, more importantly, was always there to bring me back to earth with his warm chuckle. Phil Berlin, with his bottomless reserves to minister to others, checked in with me on almost a weekly basis and pastorally cared for my family and me during one of the most difficult stretches of writing this book.

Ife Asantewa and I became kindred spirits through facilitating an inter-group dialogue on race together almost eight years ago, and since then she has become one of my greatest teachers and closest friends. Ife's combination of wisdom, faith, and love has not only been a key source of sustenance for this project but an integral component of the engine room that propels me forward in the fight for racial justice. There are too many from Irvington to name, but to all those who sustained me and prayed for me, week in and week out, I am deeply thankful.

Of all the places I could have studied race and the American church, this project began among the cold ocean breezes of Aber-deen, Scotland. My one and a half years of research at the University of Aberdeen were a whirlwind of learning and discovery. It was in my first days there that Brian Brock introduced me to the works of Willie James Jennings and J. Kameron Carter and gently prodded me toward writing on race. Brian provided invaluable guidance that saw where I was headed before I could recognize it myself and supported me in the trembling that ensued when I did. Tom Greggs consistently supported me at crucial junctures in this project, offering perspective, sources, and critique—in precisely that order. My research on Bonhoeffer in Aberdeen would have never been the same without Michael Mawson. Mike was extremely generous with his time and spent hours discuss-ing Bonhoeffer's thought with me, whether it be in his office, after a seminar, or on our occasional walk home to our Woodside flats. There are many more professors and fellow Ph.D. students from the Univer-sity of Aberdeen who helped sharpen my argument, improve my Ger-man, influence my thought, and lighten my burden along the way. In particular, I am sincerely appreciative of the supportive community that both my peers and the faculty from the University of Aberdeen have offered beyond my doctoral studies.

It is one thing to complete a Ph.D. thesis and another thing to write a book, so I learned. I am greatly indebted to the staff at Baylor University Press, especially Cade Jarrell, for taking the time to read drafted chap-ters and offer input on earlier versions of this manuscript. I appreciate the enthusiasm that the staff at Baylor University Press have expressed in this project and for their assistance in helping me bring it to completion. Additionally, I am indebted to Michael Mawson and Jonathan Tran for reading and reviewing an earlier version of this work and for providing invaluable comments and insights that drastically changed the "still-in-process" results of this book.

I want to thank my family for the innumerable ways they have collectively contributed to this project. My parents, Peter and Marjorie, and my parents-in-law, Dan and Marsha, both provided my family with places to stay at different times during our transition home from Scotland and have unconditionally supported me with love. My sister, Shayna, allowed me to set up an office in her home to find the solitude necessary to continue my writing. My parents, also, provided their sewing room as a makeshift study, which I used for over two years with only minimal interruptions from my curious father. My brother and sister-in-law, Brad and Kari, supported my family financially early on in this project. My sisters-in-law, Chelsea and Ashley, have been an inspiration to me in how they engage with race and gender on a daily basis and have lifted my spirits on various occasions by engaging my work with detailed questions and with thorough cross-examinations. All these contributions and so many more from other family members have afforded me the will, the sustenance, and the solace to write this book.

Writing a book can be a very lonely occupation. I am grateful for the friends that have accompanied me into the dark places that this book has taken me. A good friend is one who is not afraid to inhabit the unanswerable and daunting questions before us. I had a few of these good friends accompany me on the winding journey of this book—Anthony Cornell, Ben Paulus, George Lee, Paul Utzman, Johannes Lorin, Claire Hein Blanton, Tyler Frick, Amy Erickson, Andreas Lunden, Nate Borne, and Cory Jemal—who deserve special thanks. One of my closest friends and mentors throughout my academic studies has been Paul Louis Metzger. Over the last fifteen years, Paul has consistently and compassionately supported me in every avenue of life. In Paul I have found a friend that is always willing to go there with me, whether it be into an intense discussion of race, a rehashing of painful personal matters, or a conversation about the lyrical profundity of Kurt Cobain. I am forever appreciative for the camaraderie of these close friends and others who carried me through when I felt I could not go on.

There has been no greater support for this project than that supplied by my wife, Rachel, and our three little girls, Luree, Alma, and Sunday. Alma and Sunday were born over the span of this project, and with their entrance into this tired world the strength and joy of our little family grew. Luree is already writing sentences better than her father and her inquisitiveness around questions of race gives me hope for the future. I look forward to the day when each of you girls becomes a young woman, reads this book, and thoughtfully explains to me everything wrong with it. Luree, Alma, and Sunday have the incredible gift of having one of the best teachers in the world, Rachel, as their mother. Because of Rachel, they will learn the art of fighting for racial justice and gender equality in a world that benefits them because they are white but that is stacked against them because of their gender. Throughout this project, Rachel has been an unshakable pillar of strength, an unceasing reservoir of humor, and a steady foundation of wisdom. She has provided for me, stretched me, humbled me, and kept me from breaking at my most vulnerable moments. Where this book reflects signs of courage and coherency, that is Rachel shining through. I am thankful for the ways I continue to learn each and every day from you, Rachel, about race, gender, and the importance of being a pescatarian.

Abbreviations

The following are by Dietrich Bonhoeffer and are from the *Dietrich Bonhoeffer Works*, English edition:

DBWE 1   *Sanctorum Communio: A Theological Study of the Sociol-ogy of the Church*. Edited by Clifford J. Green, translated by Reinhard Krauss and Nancy Lukens. Minneapolis: Fortress, 1998.

DBWE 2   *Act and Being: Transcendental Philosophy and Ontology in Systematic Theology*. Edited by Wayne Whitson Floyd, translated by H. Martin Rumscheidt. Minneapolis: Fortress, 1996.

DBWE 3   *Creation and Fall*. Edited by John W. de Gruchy, translated by Douglas Stephen Bax. Minneapolis: Fortress, 1997.

DBWE 4   *Discipleship*. Edited by Geffrey G. Kelly and John D. Godsey, translated by Barbara Green and Reinhard Krauss. Minne-apolis: Fortress, 2001.

DBWE 5   *Life Together and Prayerbook of the Bible*. Edited by Geffrey B. Kelly, translated by Daniel W. Bloesch and James H. Burtness. Minneapolis: Fortress, 2004.

DBWE 6   *Ethics*. Edited by Clifford J. Green, translated by Reinhard Krauss, Charles C. West, and Douglas W. Stott. Minneapo-lis: Fortress, 2005.

DBWE 8   *Letters and Papers from Prison.* Edited by John W.
          de Gruchy, translated by Isabel Best, Lisa E. Dahill, Rein-
          hard Krauss, Nancy Lukens, H. Martin Rumscheidt, and
          Douglas W. Stott. Minneapolis: Fortress, 2010.

DBWE 10   *Barcelona, Berlin, New York: 1928–1931.* Edited by Clifford
          J. Green, translated by Douglas W. Stott. Minneapolis: For-
          tress, 2008.

DBWE 11   *Ecumenical, Academic, and Pastoral Work: 1931–1932.*
          Edited by Victoria J. Barnett, Mark S. Brocker, and Michael
          Lukens, translated by Anne Schmidt-Lange, Isabel Best,
          Nicolas Humphrey, Marion Pauck, and Douglas W. Stott.
          Minneapolis: Fortress, 2012.

DBWE 12   *Berlin: 1932–1933.* Edited by Larry L. Rasmussen, trans-
          lated by Isabel Best, David Higgins, and Douglas W. Stott.
          Minneapolis: Fortress, 2009.

DBWE 13   *London: 1933–1935.* Edited by Keith Clements, translated
          by Isabel Best. Minneapolis: Fortress, 2007.

DBWE 14   *Theological Education at Finkenwalde, 1935–1937.* Edited
          by H. Gaylon Barker and Mark S. Brocker, translated by
          Douglas W. Stott. Minneapolis: Fortress, 2013.

DBWE 15   *Theological Education Underground: 1937–1940.* Edited by
          Victoria J. Barnett, translated by Victoria J. Barnett, Claudia
          D. Bergmann, Peter Frick, Scott A. Moore, and Douglas W.
          Stott. Minneapolis: Fortress, 2012.

DBWE 16   *Conspiracy and Imprisonment: 1940–1945.* Edited by Mark
          S. Brocker, translated by Lisa E. Dahill and Douglas W.
          Stott. Minneapolis: Fortress, 2006.

DBW will designate German-language editions corresponding to the
volumes above.

Introduction

There is no simple way to begin a book addressing racism in the Christian church today. The dilemma here resides not so much in the difficulty of discussing such a topic but in the creative act of beginning itself. Beginnings are always dangerous, and especially so with race in view. The trouble with beginning a book that attends to racism in the Christian church is the damage inherently caused by imagining a starting point into the discussion.

There is no simple way to begin a book addressing racism in the Christian church today, precisely, because to begin is to complicate the matter. The matter is complicated in my very speaking and writing, which are embedded within the language game of race. What is at stake here in my employment of language is not only found in the words I write on this page but also in the message interpreted between the lines. The language game of race is not merely activated through audible speech or written communication but through the infinite and intricate gestures, gazes, and reflexes given in the mundane moments of each and every day. The bulk of what we are constantly saying about race never passes through our lips or from our pens but is language just the same.

The concept of language considered here is not simply meant as a cultural or linguistic concept but as a philosophical one that describes the indelibly discursive nature of human life. Wittgenstein describes this philosophical conception of language in terms of language games coming in and out of existence, where "the *speaking* of language is part of an activity, or of a form of life."[1] Race is discussed in what follows as a language game in that race provides a specific provisional network of meaning, a form of life, which makes our speaking intelligible communication in the public sphere. This is to suggest that race is neither merely a social construct nor merely individuated acts but the interdependence of both in the power of speech acts that gain meaning through the language game of race and, at the same time, give meaning to this language game.

How the language game of race transpires in quotidian exchanges is illustrated by the philosopher George Yancy in his anecdote of "the elevator effect."[2] Yancy describes "the elevator effect" as the ensuing bodily responses he receives when he, as a Black man (dressed in a suit and tie), walks into an elevator presently occupied by a white woman:

> I walk into the elevator and she feels apprehension. Her body shifts nervously and her heart beats more quickly as she clutches her purse more closely to her. She feels anxiety in the pit of her stomach . . . there is panic, there is difficulty swallowing, and there is a slight trembling of her white torso, dry mouth, nausea.[3]

Part of the contention of this book is that these spontaneously generated gestures are a kind of theological (or at least metaphysical) speech. They reveal an affirmation of what is true, good, and beautiful, and what is not. They engender a trust in relation to what is to be feared. They say a prayer.

While the woman in this example may have a direct cognitive response that contradicts her reflexes and while she may not even be aware of the gestures she makes, the word is spoken—an enfleshed word that speaks race into existence and a language game of race that gives the word spoken its meaning. Words speak meaning onto bodies and spaces, even as bodies are forming words. In this mutual informing and forming, the meaning given to the language of race, as seen from this example, is one that advantages those deemed white and disadvantages

---

1   Ludwig Wittgenstein, *Philosophical Investigations*, trans. G. E. M. Anscombe, P. M. S. Hacker, and Joachim Schulte (Oxford: Wiley-Blackwell, 2009), 15 (emphasis original).

2   For his full account of "The Elevator Effect," see the first chapter of George Yancy's *Black Bodies, White Gazes: The Continuing Significance of Race* (Lanham: Rowman & Littlefield, 2008), 1–31.

3   Yancy, *Black Bodies, White Gazes*, 5.

the rest. To reflect this unidirectional orientation, this text specifically refers to the provisional network of meaning given to race in terms of the language game of whiteness.

Along with the public space of the elevator, the language game of whiteness manifests itself in subtle and pervasive ways within the carpeted spaces of our local churches. The language game of whiteness that informs the daily life of the Western Christian church gained its meaning from a long history dating back at least to the colonial era (beginning in the fifteenth century with the "Age of Discovery"). Within the movement of bodies in the colonial era, race emerged as a cramped theological language offered for interpreting the world and its peoples. Much of the new theological writings on race from Black theologians, discussed in this book, shed light on how Western theology, over time, subtly shifted its epicenter from God's election of Israel to the self-election of European bodies, enacting a racial scale charged with salvific seriousness.[4] The historical Christian church does not *have* a race problem; it *is* the race problem. The Western Christian church lives and moves inside a provisional network of meaning configured around and for white, male European bodies, a network of meaning the church theologically spoke and continually speaks into existence. One purpose of this project is to grapple with a thesis of this proportion and to join with the few other white theologians who have already begun to offer this challenge the proper reception it deserves.[5]

What this theological history means is that the language game of whiteness is already in play in our churches. Realizing how the Western church is intertwined with whiteness can lead to the human tendency to subtly respond with the alternative of a new beginning—a new multicultural, multiracial, or cross-cultural church that will be different

4   The three central texts this project will interact with are: Willie James Jennings, *The Christian Imagination: Theology and the Origins of Race* (New Haven: Yale University Press, 2010); J. Kameron Carter, *Race: A Theological Account* (Oxford: Oxford University Press, 2008); and Brian Bantum, *Redeeming Mulatto: A Theology of Race and Christian Hybridity* (Waco: Baylor University Press, 2010). As will be outlined in what follows, each work advances theological discourses on race in a distinct manner. What they all share is the premise that, in one way or another, race has become an organizing feature of Western theology.

5   For examples of white theologians offering receptions specifically to the works of Jennings and Carter, see Barry Harvey's chapter "A Social Economy of Whiteness" from *Taking Hold of the Real: Dietrich Bonhoeffer and the Profound Worldliness of Christianity* (Eugene: Cascade Books, 2015), 178–208; and Andrew Draper, *A Theology of Race and Place: Liberation and Reconciliation in the Works of Jennings and Carter* (Eugene: Pickwick, 2016).

this time or a new conversation that will finally bring resolution. When the past is so bleak, it becomes tempting to look for a way to reset the clock, to retell the story, to start again fresh. A new beginning may seem promising, but as a refusal of the beginning God has already given, every humanly formed new beginning only serves to evolve the language game of whiteness into more sophisticated and covert configurations.

The only beginning, it seems, I can finally offer for a book seeking to address racism in the Christian church is one marked by failure. Failure itself is a beginning of sorts, but failure alone is not a theological beginning.

The Promise of a Beginning

A genuine theological starting point, alternatively, works from the premise that the beginning has already been spoken (Gen 1) and is spoken again (John 1). This important premise functions as the hinge for all that will follow. To speak theologically, in a true sense, is a con-formed response to the Word already gifted to creation in Jesus Christ—"the Word became flesh" (John 1:14). With this given beginning as its guide, this book's primary aim is neither a final analysis of the problem of whiteness that severely troubles the contemporary Western Christian church nor a conclusive resolution for this ever-evolving problem. Examining the problem of whiteness in the context of the Christian church is certainly needed and will be addressed throughout the course of this study, principally through listening to and interacting with theologians of color. This task, however, remains secondary and tempered by the gift of a beginning, a beginning the triune God graciously and freely gifts to a rebellious world.

Beginning with God's speaking raises the question posed in this book: how does the triune God speak into and through a Christian church embedded within the language game of whiteness, and how does God do so without giving into the devastating speech of whiteness? Woven into this question is the presupposition of God's gracious gift of a beginning. Working from this given beginning helps illuminate a tension between an already held belief in the triune God's sufficiency to speak and a relative space for human beings to resist or to respond to God's speaking. Moreover, the Christian church is integral to the asking of this question, for it is in this distinct community that the tension between divine and human speech comes to a crescendo. This tension goes back to Christianity's roots in Israel, where the Hebrew prophets spoke for God: "Thus saith the Lord." It is a tension that comes to a climax in the Christian church each time someone offers the bread and wine and speaks Christ's words to another: "Your sins are forgiven" (Luke 7:48; Matt 9:5).

Because God's beginning has already been spoken, the intended purpose of this book is not to imagine a solution for the catastrophic reality of whiteness in the Christian church but to attend to the triune God's continual speaking in church and world and to how God's speaking is consistently resisted by the language game of whiteness. Placing the emphasis on God's speech leaves open a relative space for the language game of whiteness to resist God's speaking, but, more importantly, it refuses to give whiteness the power to hush God's utterances. The triune God's speaking may be resisted, but God's word is never thwarted.

Having the locus of this study on the triune God's speaking situates this text within the genre of Christian theology. The primary concern, then, is not how whiteness may be addressed generally, but how whiteness is to be understood and addressed specifically in the life of the historical Christian church for the sake of the world at large. To this end, another contention of this book is that faith in Jesus Christ finds one already joined to a historical community, in and through which God has spoken and is speaking. God speaks not through a perfected humanity but through flawed human beings gathered in history by the Holy Spirit as God's people. The distinction placed on God's people, therefore, is not to be found in an absence of resistance to God's speaking but in an acknowledged struggle against this resistance wrought from being incorporated into the triune God's gracious loquacity. The way forward through whiteness is only discovered along the way, in participation with Jesus Christ. Through God's people being incorporated into God's speaking, the language game of whiteness is shown for what it is—a continual resistance to God's gracious call to repentance.

Preparing the Way

The biblical significance of repentance is reflected in the fact that all three Synoptic Gospels (Matthew, Mark, and Luke) inaugurate the public ministry of Jesus Christ with John the Baptist's call to a baptism of repentance for the forgiveness of sins. The timing of John's call to

repentance at the beginning of Jesus' public ministry raises the important question: how does repentance relate to Jesus' coming? The answer
to this question is found in John's harkening back to the words of the
prophet Isaiah:

> In the wilderness prepare the way of the LORD,
>   make straight in the desert a highway for our God (Isa 40:3).

Preparing the way is situated between a beginning and end given in
Jesus Christ. The surprise that Jesus has come incites preparation
enacted through repentance. Simultaneously, this preparation cultivates
a readiness for the surprise of Jesus' coming. Repentance participates in
the creaturely time gifted in Jesus Christ, proceeding from God's gift of
a beginning and moving toward the surprise of God's final judgment.

Because the beginning has already been given, repentance does
not *construct* the way of the Lord; it *prepares* the way. When repentance is wrongly understood as a new beginning, a newly constructed
path, it refuses the beginning already gifted to creation and Israel
through God's speaking. As John reminds Israel, "God is able from
these stones to raise up children to Abraham" (Luke 3:8). The possibility of this miraculous act reminds Israel how God has already spoken
creation into existence of out nothing (ex nihilo) and how God formed
Israel into a distinct people in a similar fashion. God's beginning is a
gracious gift received by Israel. Rather than presenting a new beginning, repentance receives from God a beginning already spoken. And
precisely in receiving God's beginning, repentance prepares the way
for the surprise of God's speaking now.

Additionally, because the God who is from the beginning can only
speak the end, repentance does not *secure* the way of the Lord; it *prepares*
the way. The peril of making repentance into the final word is real, and
its seduction led some in the crowd to question whether John "might be
the Messiah" (Luke 3:15). John's baptism with water is not to be confused
with the coming of Christ, who comes with winnowing fork in hand
and who baptizes with the Holy Spirit and fire. Repentance gives the
final word to God, so much so that its own meaning is bound to and
drawn from this final word. Repentance is neither the beginning nor the
end but, instead, a receiving of God's beginning and end that joins with
Christ in preparing the way for God's Word to break into the immediacy
of the present moment.

This book's constructive claim is that repentance speaks in a temporal register that *directly* challenges the language game of whiteness. Repentance works between a God-given beginning and end. Whiteness is addressed through a repentance offered in the creaturely time gifted by God between beginning and end, a beginning and end spoken through God's external address. On the one hand, this claim seeks to avoid the underlying temptation of hastily employing God's direct word to abruptly extinguish whiteness. To employ God's direct word in this manner exchanges the surprise of God's speaking for mere human ideas about the possibility of a new beginning beyond whiteness or a final end to whiteness. On the other hand, associating a direct challenge of whiteness with repentance seeks to circumvent the converse temptation of untethering God's direct word from a necessary human response, here and now. In sum, it is not God's speaking of a beginning or end that directly challenges whiteness, but the human response of repentance, oriented by and open to God's external address, that directly challenges the resistant reflexes of whiteness. The directness of this challenge is given in that repentance works within the same relative space as whiteness, where human beings can resist or respond to God's speaking. By placing the challenge of whiteness here, a crucial distinction is left between the Creator's gracious speaking and the responsive speech of creaturely freedom.

Such a distinction reserves a place for the triune God to speak freely and frees human creatures to respond. While God's speaking always exceeds human language, this does not render God's speaking unintelligible. The triune God's gracious Word already given in Jesus Christ brings together divine speech and fallible human speech without removing the distinction between the two. God's people participate in God's communicative activity in and to the world as the body of Christ, and in this participation, repentance becomes intelligible as a preparing of the way for the surprise of God speaking in all times and places.[6]

6 Jennifer McBride draws from Bonhoeffer's thought to provide a similar reconsideration of repentance. She argues repentance is not simply a transformation or changing of one's mind but is confirmation to Christ and participation in the very being of Christ. See Jennifer M. McBride, *The Church for the World: A Theology of Public Witness* (Oxford: Oxford University Press, 2012), 15.

Bonhoeffer on Preparing the Way

Those familiar with the writings of the German theologian Dietrich Bonhoeffer hopefully will recognize his influence on the approach and aim already laid out for this book. In particular, John the Baptist's call to repentance as a preparing of the way is a motif that took on such great importance for the late Bonhoeffer that he considered tying together his magnum opus, *Ethics*, under the title "Preparing the Way and Arrival."[7] This potential title reflects a culmination of Bonhoeffer's lifelong concern for relating a temporal creation distorted by the fall with God's good and eternal will (Jas 1:17).

While this text draws collectively from Bonhoeffer's corpus, it harnesses his discussion of "Ultimate and Penultimate Things" from *Ethics* as a focal point for guiding the project. Bonhoeffer's description of the ultimate (the last thing) and penultimate (the things before the last) plays an important role for this study as it offers the theological grammar employed to link a repentance that directly challenges whiteness with God's ultimate address given in Jesus Christ. As stated in a provisional sense, the penultimate constitutes a relative space held open by the surprise of God's ultimate Word given in Jesus Christ. The relative space of the penultimate allows for either a *resistance* that remains *closed* to the surprise of God's ultimate word or a *repentance* that *prepares the way* for the surprise of God's ultimate word. Based on this framework, it is suggested that whiteness is a continual resistance to the surprise of God's speaking that must be challenged directly through a preparing of the way that relies on and anticipates the wonder of God speaking in history and even now.

The import of Bonhoeffer's motif of the ultimate and penultimate is that it provides a distinct space for examining the concrete complexities of whiteness in North American congregations in dependence on God's direct address heard within these same congregations. This theological framework, thus, helps shift theological discussions of race *from* a conversation about how to overcome whiteness in the church *to* a discovery of how the triune God's speaking is already challenging whiteness in the church. This proposed trajectory for theological race discourses relies on a distinct reading of Bonhoeffer's writings that undergirds this study as a whole.

7   Bonhoeffer made this suggestion to Bethge in a letter dated November 27, 1940: "Today a possible title for my book occurred to me: 'Preparing the Way and Arrival' [*Wegbereitung und Einzug*] corresponding to the division of the book (into penultimate and ultimate things)" (*DBWE* 16:92).

Reading Bonhoeffer within the Communion
of Sinners and Saints

Bonhoeffer's writings are vast and vary in content and form, a complexity that yields the problem of accounting for his developments within the continuity of his writings noted by numerous Bonhoeffer scholars.[8] Bonhoeffer's description of the ultimate and penultimate helps address this enigma, not just for his own writings but also for all theological thinking, understood as the shared memory of the church.[9] Rather than reading Bonhoeffer simply as a commentator on theology, his own theology calls us to ponder his writings as placed within a historical community of faith that transcends time and space. The presupposition of the community of saints as directly established by God in the form of a historical community is the premise that marks all of Bonhoeffer's thought.[10] It is precisely this premise that provides the basis for continuity in

8   One important example of development, or rather crystallization, in Bonhoeffer's theology is seen in his transition from speaking about "orders of creation" to "orders of preservation" and from "orders of preservation" to "divine mandates." For representative examples of this transition, see *DBWE* 1:119; 3:140; 6:68–74. An affirmation of the continuity in Bonhoeffer's thought is shared by the following influential Bonhoeffer scholars: John Godsey, *The Theology of Dietrich Bonhoeffer* (London: SCM Press, 1960); André Dumas, *Dietrich Bonhoeffer: Theologian of Reality*, trans. Robert McAfee Brown (London: SCM Press, 1971); Ernst Feil, *The Theology of Dietrich Bonhoeffer*, trans. Martin Rumscheidt (Minneapolis: Fortress, 1985); Jürgen Moltmann and Jürgen Weissbach, *Two Studies in the Theology of Bonhoeffer*, trans. Reginald H. Fuller and Ilse Fuller (New York: Charles Scribner's Sons, 1967); and Eberhard Bethge, *Dietrich Bonhoeffer: A Biography*, rev. ed., ed. Victoria Barnett (Minneapolis: Fortress, 2000).

9   In *Act and Being*, Bonhoeffer argues that "theology is a function of the church," which presupposes Christ's presence in its past and future preaching: "For there is no church without preaching, nor any preaching without remembrance. But theology is the memory of the church" (*DBWE* 2:130).

10   As with any theological figure that has been studied as rigorously as Bonhoeffer, there are different schools of thought for how he should be read. Rather than delving into these debates, the aim of these introductory remarks is to signal the reading of Bonhoeffer employed in this study. This study presents a broadly synchronic approach to Bonhoeffer's writing on the basis that his own understanding of theology endorses this method. There are many notable Bonhoeffer scholars that offer alternative approaches. As one example, Jon Phillips focuses on Bonhoeffer's Christology as the foundational locus of his thought, which Phillips suggests later led Bonhoeffer to move away from his earlier views of the church as the locus of God's revelation. See Jon Phillips, *Christ for Us in the Theology of Dietrich Bonhoeffer* (San Francisco: Harper & Row, 1967). Charles Marsh offers a similar but more nuanced argument in *Reclaiming Dietrich Bonhoeffer: The Promise of His Theology* (Oxford: Oxford University Press, 1996), 79–80.

Bonhoeffer's writings, as well as the need for continual developments within his theology and beyond it.

The dynamics of development and continuity are understood in Bonhoeffer's corpus as part of the historical church's concrete composition. The existing church is simultaneously a fully human and historical community (a communion of sinners) and a reality of God's revelation (a communion of saints). As such, the historical church preserves a body of thought (dogma) that remains open and obedient (penultimate) to the immediacy of God's Word given in Jesus Christ (ultimate). Or better, the church's memory is a theological thinking that *prepares the way* for God's ultimate Word, already given and pending, "always uttered anew beyond theology."[11] This makes theology a secondary task, a task that requires continual repentance in reference to the living person of Christ, who is present in and as the church. The immediacy of Christ as Word and sacrament leaves theology always *undone*, in both senses of the word.[12] Theological thinking is always both incomplete and inadequate on its own. Theology is a continual reflection on our desperate need for a fresh word from the living person of Jesus Christ.

Granting these limitations—that theology always remains undone and located within the community of faith—Bonhoeffer suggests that theology should be done courageously and humbly. Theology, in this sense, *is* repentance. Its goal is not to speak for God but to prepare the way for the surprise of God's speaking. With this in mind, Bonhoeffer's oeuvre is considered in this book as a limited system of thought that seeks to describe the church's inner history as split within itself "in the concepts of primal state [i.e., creation], sin, and revelation."[13] This fragmentation of the church's inner history informs how Bonhoeffer's thought does not so much coalesce around one theological doctrine (e.g., Christology or ecclesiology) as much as it holds together a tensive constellation of theological

---

11   *DBWE* 2:131.

12   Highlighting the immediacy of Christ's presence, Bonhoeffer writes, "Christ *speaks* the Word instead of *being* the Word" (*DBWE* 12:317, emphasis original).

13   *DBWE* 1:62. Michael Mawson's work on Bonhoeffer's ecclesiology highlights this "theological dialectic of creation, sin, and revelation" as integral to Bonhoeffer's understanding of the church in its concrete sociality. See Michael Mawson, *Christ Existing as Community: Bonhoeffer's Early Ecclesiology* (Oxford: Oxford University Press, 2018), 5–6. Mawson's careful reading of Bonhoeffer's ecclesiology informs this study in my own attempts to employ Bonhoeffer's theological dialectic to discuss how whiteness is to be understood and addressed from within the Christian church.

doctrines that mutually inform one another.[14] It is in these dynamic interactions between theological doctrines that Bonhoeffer's theology does the
most work. The living *Christ* addresses the concrete *church* in the midst of
the *fallen creation* that the triune God *preserves*. This allows for a repentance that brings the *church* into participation with *Christ* in *preserving*
the *fallen creation* in preparation for the triune God's direct address.
While each of Bonhoeffer's theological works may foreground a particular
theological doctrine (creation, hamartiology, Christology, ecclesiology),
a synchronic reading of his works brings out how each theological locus
gains its shape from other theological loci. In support of this synchronic
reading of Bonhoeffer, Wayne Floyd Jr. suggests the following:

> Christology in *Christ the Center*, creation in *Creation and Fall*, sin
> in *Act and Being*, and the community of the Church in *Sanctorum
> Communio*—provide a nexus of concerns within the coherence of
> which theology can be said to occur. Theology "is" neither *one* of
> the loci, nor the *totality* of them. Theology is the dynamic interac-
> tion of their particular themes, each a monad reflecting the others,
> without which the individual cannot become intelligible.[15]

Reading Bonhoeffer's theology as "the dynamic interaction" of particular themes will prove to be instrumental for this study, because it allows
one to take seriously the damaging effects of sin, including whiteness,
without giving up hope in the triune God's sufficiency to speak.

Bonhoeffer as an Interlocutor for Addressing Whiteness

The preceding preliminary remarks about Bonhoeffer still leave a fundamental question unanswered. Why Bonhoeffer? There are two main reasons for purposefully selecting Bonhoeffer as the central interlocutor of
this book. The first reason, lamentably, has to do with aesthetics. Bonhoeffer, the German, is recognizably white. Speaking with Bonhoeffer's voice
today is to speak with the authority and privilege of one who, through the

---

14   A. N. Williams carefully expounds upon this approach to systematic thinking, which
is applied to Bonhoeffer's corpus in this book. She calls this type of systematic thinking "systematicity" and describes it as "when the treatment of a single locus or issue is shaped by the
awareness of its potential to interlock with other loci, indeed in some cases, its dependence
on them for its own shape." See *The Architecture of Theology: Structure, System, and Ratio*
(Oxford: Oxford University Press, 2011), 1.

15   Wayne W. Floyd Jr., *Theology and the Dialectics of Otherness: On Reading Bonhoeffer
and Adorno* (Lanham: University Press of America, 1988), 289 (emphasis original).

turning pages of history, has been deemed white. I employ Bonhoeffer's voice, then, as a conscious recognition that I enter into a moving theological discussion about race from a given location—from the side of privilege. While a number of European theologians could have been selected to serve this purpose, Bonhoeffer's widespread and perennial appeal make him especially applicable.[16] The growing admiration for Bonhoeffer's life and work, specifically in terms of his interactions with race, makes it all the more timely to explore how contemporary theologians of race challenge aspects of his thought in significant ways, and how, in turn, together they call us all into a repentance that directly challenges whiteness.

The second reason for selecting Bonhoeffer has to do with his unrelenting attention on the concrete church as simultaneously fully human (a historical community) and a reality of God's revelation. Bonhoeffer never tries to dress the church up, nor does he ever give up on God's working through the historical Christian church as the community of Christ. In *Sanctorum Communio* he writes that it is only "as a concrete historical community, in the relativity of its forms and in its imperfect and modest appearance, that it is the body of Christ, Christ's presence on earth."[17] This distinct ecclesial approach requires an accounting of the sociohistorical fragmentations and dysfunctions in the empirical church—the very church and local congregations in which we find ourselves. At the same time, it requires that we examine how the depth and complexity of these dysfunctions are known, precisely, from within the concrete church as the paramount place where God speaks. In this way Bonhoeffer's ecclesial approach to history calls us into a thoroughgoing exploration of the complex network of meaning that whiteness bestows on the church today, not as a means for finding an exit plan but as a discovery of how God continues to speak in our resistance. This is not an easy path to travel. The white South African and Anglican priest Peter Hinchliff discusses the difficulty of walking this path in his reflections on Bonhoeffer and apartheid in South Africa:

> Perhaps one can say of Bonhoeffer at least, that as he understood the nature of sin, it is possible to find oneself in a situation where every course open to one seems sinful. In South Africa in the early 1960s that seemed a very obvious truth . . . One was burdened with

16   For a discussion of how Bonhoeffer's life and writings have appealed to a number of different audiences, see Stephen R. Haynes, *The Bonhoeffer Phenomenon: Portraits of a Protestant Saint* (Minneapolis: Fortress, 2004).

17   *DBWE* 1:209.

a terrible sense of responsibility and guilt for a society of which one
could not wash one's hands nor do very much to improve.[18]

Hinchliff articulates a common experience that paralyzes many white
Christians as we seek to address whiteness and find ourselves stuck
between guilt and helplessness. This paralysis allows the language game
of whiteness to persist. Bonhoeffer's focus on the church does not leave us
at the impenetrable impasse that Hinchliff's reflections on Bonhoeffer and
apartheid in South Africa appear to suggest. Instead, Bonhoeffer's ecclesial
approach of preparing the way exhorts the church to embrace how God's
speaking frees us from the constant self-evaluation of what "seems sinful"
and into an active responsiveness in participation with Christ.

This preliminary discussion of sin and whiteness raises the pressing need to distinguish the two. The main distinction this text proposes
between sin and whiteness is this: sin conditions all human beings in
the same manner, while the trusted language of whiteness conditions in
a *specific* and *provisional* manner to elevate some by demoting the rest.[19]
Whiteness is a particular outworking of sin. This means that, while each
human person is equally responsible for the fall into sin, white people have
a unique responsibility for creating and perpetuating the language game
of whiteness. Again, this is why repentance as a preparing of the way represents the appropriate register in which whiteness is directly addressed.
Repentance requires something from us all, but what repentance requires
differs for those benefiting from whiteness and those suffering under it.
"Every valley shall be filled, and every mountain and hill shall be made
low" (Luke 3:5). Repentance, specifically in this way, joins distinct human
beings together in preparing the way for the surprise of God's speaking.

Bringing Bonhoeffer into Dialogue with
Contemporary Theologians of Race

This book seeks to facilitate a repentance that directly challenges whiteness, but more than this, it is meant as an enactment of repentance. To
this end, the writings of contemporary theologians of color are brought
into dialogue with Bonhoeffer's writings. The approach offered is
broadly dialogical rather than comparative, allowing for a collaboration

---

18   Peter Hinchliff, *Holiness and Politics* (Grand Rapids: Eerdmans, 1979), 104–5.
19   Chapter 3 will discuss how Bonhoeffer's theological understanding of sin lays the
groundwork for clarifying a distinction between sin and whiteness.

that seeks to bring together through mutual repair.[20] To allow for this dialogical approach, this study gives less attention to Bonhoeffer's direct reflections on race and his experiences in Harlem (as important as these may be) and places more attention on his conception of the ultimate and penultimate, along with the way his theology traces dynamic interactions between different theological loci.[21] Bonhoeffer's attendance to how the triune God speaks in the midst of a fallen creation provides the point of connection with contemporary theological discussions on race. In this manner, Bonhoeffer's writings are brought into dialogue with the writings of Willie Jennings, J. Kameron Carter, and Brian Bantum to enact a repentance that prepares the way of the Lord.

Jennings, Carter, and Bantum each in their own right have helped to advance theological discourses on race into new territory in the present moment. Jennings and Carter have done this through their shared argument that modern Western theology matured within a supersessionism that exchanged God's election of Israel with a white European self-election, an exchange that leads to the continual becoming of whiteness. Jennings and Carter diverge, however, in the manner in which they make this argument. Jennings' *The Christian Imagination* levels this argument primarily from the perspective of creation, while Carter's *Race: A Theological Account* offers it through the lens of Christology. Last, Brian Bantum's *Redeeming Mulatto* has furthered these previous lines of the discussion by arguing that an embodied problem such as race requires an embodied response in the Christian church's liturgical practices. Thus, Bantum provides a unique ecclesial response to whiteness. Focused attention is given to these three theologians not only because of

20   For a discussion of the approach of repair employed primarily in chapters 3 and 4 of this study, see Nicholas Adams, "Reparative Reasoning," *Modern Theology* 24, no. 3 (2008): 447–57. Adams' description of reparative reasoning, as seen in Peter Ochs' work, resonates in many ways with Bonhoeffer's approach to theology. In distinction from an Enlightenment view that seeks foundations for thinking and from a Rationalist view that seeks to clarify the mind's innate knowledge of the world, Adams argues that reparative reasoning supposes "that the inquirer finds herself in the middle of things, and philosophy's task is to make our ideas about those things clearer" ("Reparative Reasoning," 448). As a result, Adams maintains, "reparative reasoning is historically situated, and is thus self-consciously finite and temporary" (454).

21   This distinct approach, which brings Bonhoeffer into dialogue with contemporary theologians of race, differentiates this project from previous works done on Bonhoeffer and race. See, for example, Josiah Ulysses Young, *No Difference in the Fare: Dietrich Bonhoeffer and the Problem of Racism* (Grand Rapids: Eerdmans, 1998); and Reggie L. Williams, *Bonhoeffer's Black Jesus: Harlem Renaissance Theology and an Ethic of Resistance* (Waco: Baylor University Press, 2014).

the distinct challenges each one presents for Bonhoeffer's thought but for the tense strain and dialogical synthesis they offer one another.

With that said, it should be acknowledged that this selection of interlocutors leaves various points of tension within contemporary theological discussions of race unaddressed. In particular, the growing body of theological work being done by women of color (women such as Katie Cannon, Delores Williams, Kelly Brown Douglas, and M. Shawn Copeland, to name a few) has expanded conversations about race to consider how race intersects with gender (and sexuality).[22] Not including Womanist voices in the dialogue presented here constitutes a specific limitation and a distinct risk for this study. It leaves unexplored how the interplay between whiteness and patriarchy creates a layering of inequitable configurations that mutually conceal one another.[23] To mitigate this limitation and risk, the complexities of whiteness discussed in this book should *not* be read as comprehensive but as a concentrated entry point into considering various interrelated inequities, such as those caused by patriarchy, that relentlessly distress the Christian church today.

The Structure of the Argument

The argument of this book is divided into two parts. Part 1, "Words Already Spoken," is divided into two chapters that work together to develop a theological history of whiteness through Bonhoeffer's framework of the ultimate and penultimate. Chapter 1 lays out a distinct methodology for exploring a theological history of whiteness, and chapter 2 applies this methodology to offer a theological account of the history of whiteness in the United States. The specific methodology presented in

22 See Katie Canon, *Black Womanist Ethics* (Eugene: Wipf & Stock, 1988); Delores S. Williams, *Sisters in the Wilderness: The Challenge of Womanist God-Talk* (Maryknoll: Orbis Books, 1993); Kelly Brown Douglas, *Sexuality and the Black Church: A Womanist Perspective* (Maryknoll: Orbis Books, 1999); and M. Shawn Copeland, *Enfleshing Freedom: Body, Race, and Being* (Minneapolis: Fortress, 2010).

23 The work of Delores Williams, one of the forerunners of Womanist theology, is especially helpful for exposing how race and gender are intertwined in the oppression of Black women. She challenges both Black Liberation Theology and White Feminist Theology by arguing that each acquiesces in its own way to an aspect of whiteness that facilitates the oppression of Black women. In response to this, Williams focuses on the story of Hagar, the Egyptian slave of Abram and Sarai, to highlight how African American women for centuries have not only brought liberation in the midst of oppression but also preserved a positive quality of life for themselves and their families "in the presence and care of God" (*Sisters in the Wilderness*, 175).

chapter 1 seeks to shift our theological discussions of race from the spatial categories of particular and universal to the temporal categories of penultimate and ultimate employed in Bonhoeffer's *Ethics*. This chapter argues that Bonhoeffer's temporal categories move theological debates about race from a problem/solution orientation to a discernment/surprise orientation. Chapter 2 employs this discernment/surprise orientation to attend to how the evolving language game of whiteness, already spoken in the history of the United States, reflexively resists God's gracious address. As a whole, part 1 describes the sufficiency of God's speaking as revealing our own resistance, to prepare the way for a more involved conversation about the complexities of whiteness found in the Christian church and about how we may ready ourselves, in the midst of the resistance of whiteness, for hearing God's voice today.

Having made the case for a discernment/surprise orientation to race, the book goes on in part 2, "Words between Ultimate and Penultimate," to explore the weaknesses and strengths of this approach by bringing Bonhoeffer into dialogue with Willie Jennings (chapter 3), J. Kameron Carter (chapter 4), and Brian Bantum (chapter 5). Part 2 revolves around the question of how the triune God speaks into and through a Western Christian church configured by whiteness without capitulating to whiteness. The arc of part 2 moves toward answering this question by passing through a discussion of creation in conversation with Jennings and Christology with Carter, and then ending with an examination of ecclesiology with Bantum.

Chapters 3 and 4 begin this arc by offering a dialogical unfolding that seeks to illuminate the weaknesses and strengths in Bonhoeffer's concept of an ecclesial preparing of the way. The main weakness exposed in bringing Bonhoeffer's theology into dialogues with Jennings and Carter is an ecclesial thinking that eclipses Israel with the overwhelming ethos of the Western Christian church. While many have expressed reservations about Bonhoeffer's supersessionism before, here Jennings and Carter each provide unique insights that helpfully pinpoint and describe Bonhoeffer's supersessionism as directly lending itself to a facilitation of whiteness in subtle yet potent ways.[24] The strength of Bonhoeffer's thought elucidated in these same dialogues is the nuanced manner in

24   For a discussion of Bonhoeffer's supersessionism, see chapter 5, "Bonhoeffer and Post-Holocaust Theology," in Stephen R. Haynes, *The Bonhoeffer Legacy: Post-Holocaust Perspectives* (Minneapolis: Fortress, 2006), 83–108. For a defense of Bonhoeffer's use of Scripture that seeks to exonerate Bonhoeffer from the charge of supersessionism, see chapter 7, "Reading the New in Light of the Old," in Harvey, *Taking Hold of the Real*, 178–208.

which Bonhoeffer handles the ultimate and penultimate to offer an ecclesial preparing of the way. It is suggested that Bonhoeffer's ecclesial preparing of the way avoids the tendency found in both Jennings' and Carter's theological challenges of whiteness to place God's direct word against a Western Christian church configured by whiteness. Instead, Bonhoeffer's ecclesial preparing of the way opens a temporal register that allows for a consideration of how whiteness is directly challenged through a repentance that is oriented by God's ultimate word and that prepares the way for God to speak. This distinctive approach preserves a discernment/surprise orientation that is attentive to how God continues to speak into and through a Western Christian church disfigured by whiteness.

Whereas chapters 3 and 4 lay out the case for Bonhoeffer's framework of an ecclesial preparing of the way, chapter 5 demonstrates its specific repercussions on how we understand God's direct word as given in the midst of a Christian church entrenched in whiteness. These repercussions are shown through a comparison of Brian Bantum's proposal for an ecclesial challenge of whiteness in *Redeeming Mulatto* and this text's proposal for an ecclesial challenge of whiteness as adapted from Bonhoeffer's thought. It is argued that Bantum moves in the direction of placing an ecclesial challenge of whiteness in an ultimate register that disallows consideration of or attention to how God speaks in the midst of a Christian church disfigured by whiteness. In contrast, this book's proposal is to provide an ecclesial challenge of whiteness in the temporal register of repentance, allowing for both a more detailed discussion of how whiteness is concretely challenged in the church's daily life and a description of how God continues to speak in the midst of a Christian church historically shaped by whiteness.

Rather than offering solutions for how whiteness may be addressed in the Christian church today, this study concludes that it is through living with a sustained and growing discernment of how whiteness shapes the Christian church, each and every day, that we participate with Christ in preparing the way for the surprise of God's gracious address.

I
Words Already Spoken

1

Discerning Surprise

Bonhoeffer and Theological Race Discourse in America

There are both benefits and challenges that come with relating Bonhoeffer's thought to contemporary theological race discourse in the United States. One benefit is that, in being largely removed from the American context, Bonhoeffer's writings offer an unfamiliar voice that can interrogate the underlying presuppositions present in contemporary discussions about race. The challenge, though, is how to connect Bonhoeffer's foreign thinking to the contemporary situation of race in the United States without introducing anachronism or domesticating his voice.

The question of how we are to listen to Bonhoeffer's voice today relates, in part, with the central question examined in this project: how does the triune God speak through a historical community that is sinful, and specifically inundated with the modern racial distortions of whiteness, and how does God speak through this community without capitulating to the devastating language of whiteness? Bonhoeffer's motif of the ultimate and penultimate offers a unique lens for thinking through this question, and even in bringing us to this question in the first place.

Through evaluating Bonhoeffer's understanding of the ultimate and penultimate in relation to the overarching question of this study, this chapter demonstrates how the unfamiliarity of Bonhoeffer's thought contributes novel insights for theological discourses on race in the United States today. In this way, the course will be charted for bringing Bonhoeffer's writings into dialogue with Willie Jennings, J. Kameron Carter, and Brian Bantum in part 2.

The question faced in this chapter is not how to resolve the problem of whiteness but how to discern God's working in a fallen world marked by whiteness. This framing relies on Bonhoeffer's conceptual scaffolding of the ultimate and penultimate. Bonhoeffer's account of the ultimate and penultimate works from the *surprise* that God's Word has already arrived in the living person of Jesus Christ (ultimate) and that, based on this arrival, a community of faith is publicly formed through *discerning* its contours in creaturely time as Christ's body on earth (penultimate). This approach of a discernment drawn from the surprise of Christ's arrival is developed through an examination of (1) Bonhoeffer's life in relation to race, (2) his specific account of the ultimate and penultimate from *Ethics*, and (3) how his account of the ultimate and penultimate provides a unique approach to race in comparison to two common theological approaches to race. Through these three sections, the benefits and challenges of hearing what Bonhoeffer's voice may contribute to contemporary theological race discourses are brought to the fore, beginning with his own life.

Beyond Saint or Sinner

The challenge of applying Bonhoeffer's life to the contemporary issue of race not only involves accounting for contextual differences but also how to honestly remember a life such as Bonhoeffer's that reflects a mixed portrait, with strokes both of brilliance and of bewilderment. There is an acute danger that comes with the impulse to search Bonhoeffer's life and his writings for principles for addressing racism.[1]

---

1   Many scholars from around the world have excavated Bonhoeffer's writings to discover insights for the pressing situation of race faced today. One example of this, applied to the context of South Africa, is seen in John W. de Gruchy's *Bonhoeffer and South Africa: Theology in Dialogue* (Grand Rapids: Eerdmans, 1984). Another, rooted in the context of the United States, is found in Josiah Young's *No Difference in the Fare*. The approach presented here differs from these previous studies specifically in how it applies Bonhoeffer's framework of the ultimate and penultimate to reframe contemporary theological discussions about race.

Without care, Bonhoeffer's life can be reduced to an end in itself that is formed into dead principles for either racial righteousness or racial condemnation. The following exploration presents two divergent images of Bonhoeffer's dealings with race to illuminate the limitations and dangers of applying Bonhoeffer's life and his statements on the topic of race directly to contemporary race issues. These two portraits of Bonhoeffer reveal that the motif of the ultimate and penultimate is not simply a theory to follow but a tense reality lived out in participation with Jesus Christ, allowing for the valences of saint and sinner to often appear side by side.

Bonhoeffer as Saint

The first portrait that may be drawn from Bonhoeffer's engagement with race is a saintly one. This portrait gains support from a diverse array of interpretations of Bonhoeffer's time in Harlem and his work with the renowned Abyssinian Baptist Church during his post-doctoral year at Union Theological Seminary in 1930–1931. As a prime example, the late James H. Cone suggested that Bonhoeffer "showed an existential interest in blacks" and even stands as one of the few exemplary white theologians "to empathize fully with the experience of black people."[2] Josiah Young offers a theological explanation for Cone's gleaming remarks. Young speculates that Bonhoeffer's early theological anthropology (offered in *Sanctorum Communio*) "equipped Bonhoeffer to socialize with blacks in a way that defied American racism."[3] Along similar lines, Mark Ellingsen presents Bonhoeffer as a "multi-culturist before his time" and someone whose anthropology and ecclesiology are "suggestive of the agenda of contemporary Black Liberation Theology."[4] These positive reviews of Bonhoeffer, specifically focused on his time in Harlem, are fortified by a number of biographies of Bonhoeffer's life that offer detailed accounts of

2   James H. Cone, *The Cross and the Lynching Tree* (Maryknoll: Orbis Books, 2011), 41–42.

3   Josiah Ulysses Young, "Nobody Knows but Jesus," *The Living Pulpit* 4, no. 2 (1995): 12. In another article, Young also states, "I think Bonhoeffer found Abyssinian compelling because it made his thesis in *The Communion of Saints* come alive." See Josiah Ulysses Young, "'Is the White Christ, Too, Distraught by These Dark Sins His Father Wrought?': Dietrich Bonhoeffer and the Problem of the White Christ," *Religious Studies* 26, no. 3 (1999): 328.

4   Mark Ellingsen, "Bonhoeffer, Racism, and a Communal Model for Healing," *Journal of Church and State* 43, no. 2 (2001): 235.

how he was impacted by the African American community in Harlem during his yearlong stay in New York.[5]

This documentation of Bonhoeffer's experiences in Harlem has led many to seek connections between his time in Harlem and his struggle against anti-Semitism in his homeland.[6] Clifford Green argues that "the encounter with racism in America paved the way for [Bonhoeffer's] opposition to the racist anti-Semitism of National Socialism."[7] In *Bonhoeffer's Black Jesus*, Reggie Williams offers compelling evidence that demonstrates how Harlem transformed a young intellectual and German nationalist into a concrete disciple of Christ who was prepared to address the anti-Semitism of Hitler's Germany. Williams writes, "Bonhoeffer remains the only prominent white theologian of the twentieth century to speak about racism as a Christian problem."[8] Drawing on Williams' work, Ken Wytsma, the founder of the Justice Conference, describes Bonhoeffer as an example of one who used his privilege on behalf of others.[9] Part of what contributes to a saintly portrait of Bonhoeffer, in relation to race, is the connection drawn between his time in Harlem and his actions that followed shortly after.

Thus, Bonhoeffer's rise to sainthood gains further support based on accounts of his activity in the resistance movement during the later years of his life. The saintly attributes of Bonhoeffer's life during this time have been catalogued meticulously: his bold challenge of the *Führer*;[10] his participation in the ecumenical movement;[11] his appreciation for Mohandas

5   See, for example, Bethge, *Dietrich Bonhoeffer*, 154–55; and Charles Marsh, *Strange Glory: A Life of Dietrich Bonhoeffer* (New York: Vintage, 2014), 101–35. Biographies of Bonhoeffer's life, in general, have furnished an accessible view of Bonhoeffer that is largely positive when it comes to his engagement with race.

6   Reggie Williams has offered the first full-length monograph dedicated to examining how Bonhoeffer's interactions with the African American church in Harlem influenced Bonhoeffer's later theology and participation in the resistance against National Socialism. See Williams, *Bonhoeffer's Black Jesus*.

7   Clifford J. Green, "Editor's Introduction to the English Edition," in *DBWE* 6:4.

8   Williams, *Bonhoeffer's Black Jesus*, 139.

9   See Ken Wytsma, *The Myth of Equality: Uncovering the Roots of Injustice and Privilege* (Downers Grove: InterVarsity Press, 2017), 125–27. Wytsma suggests that Bonhoeffer's "introduction to African American life helped him realize that this radical redefining [from transaction to relationship] and discipleship involved standing with others as Jesus did" (126).

10   See Bonhoeffer's essay "The Führer and the Individual in the Younger Generation" in *DBWE* 12:268–81.

11   See Bonhoeffer's lecture "On the Theological Foundation of the Work of the World Alliance" in *DBWE* 11:356–69.

Gandhi and his desire to visit him in India;[12] his outspoken Lutheran defense of Jewish Christians leading to a claim of *status confessionis*;[13] his assistance of Jewish and political refugees while pastoring in London;[14] his eulogizing of his grandmother's empathy toward Jews;[15] his description of viewing "history from below";[16] his involvement in "Operation 7" and the conspiracy against Hitler;[17] and, finally, his imprisonment and death.[18] These remarkable events and accolades form an inspirational storyline out of Bonhoeffer's life, a life that appears worthy of emulation for those seeking racial justice today.

Bonhoeffer as Sinner

There is, however, a second, less charitable portrait of Bonhoeffer's dealings with race that may also be sketched. This second image of Bonhoeffer's life raises problematic features surrounding many of the same events accounted for above. Take Bonhoeffer's time in Harlem, for instance. Ruth Zerner points out that Bonhoeffer himself claimed that he learned more during his one-month stay in America in 1939 than he had during his yearlong stint in 1930–1931,[19] the very year intensely focused on by biographers to highlight Bonhoeffer's transformative change in Harlem. To cement her point, Zerner reports that, during this second short visit to the United States in 1939, Bonhoeffer "did not visit a black church."[20] Josiah Young, offering both perspectives of Bonhoeffer, takes this line of argument one step further when he suggests that Bonhoeffer's attraction to Black people in America was not rooted in their connection to Africa but

12   Josiah Young highlights Bonhoeffer's appreciation for Gandhi and his desire to study with him. See Young, *No Difference in the Fare*, 28–29.

13   See Bonhoeffer's paper "The Church and the Jewish Question" in *DBWE* 12:361–70.

14   See Bethge, *Dietrich Bonhoeffer*, 325–417.

15   See *DBWE* 14:911. Because of these appreciative comments toward the Jews, Bethge reports that Bonhoeffer's cousin refused to shake his hand after his eulogy for his grandmother. See Bethge, *Dietrich Bonhoeffer*, 505.

16   See *DBWE* 8:52.

17   See Marsh, *Strange Glory*, 317–59.

18   Marsh provides a detailed and disturbing account of Bonhoeffer's death. See Marsh, *Strange Glory*, 382–94.

19   Ruth Zerner, "Dietrich Bonhoeffer's American Experiences: People, Letters, and Papers from Union Seminary," *Union Seminary Quarterly Review* 31, no. 4 (1976): 279.

20   Zerner, "Dietrich Bonhoeffer's American Experiences," 280. Bonhoeffer's main struggle during this second trip to the United States was predominately with himself as he discerned whether he should stay in America or return to a war-torn Germany.

to the extent that they "bore the impress of the West."[21] This suggestion opens up another view of Bonhoeffer that locates his interactions abroad more firmly within a restricted Eurocentric perspective of the world.

From within this more critical portrait of Bonhoeffer's life, there are a number of reasons for arguing that Bonhoeffer never broke free from the Eurocentric and nationalistic sensibilities so clearly observed in his early Barcelona lectures.[22] Thomas Day, for example, sees an elitist view at work in Bonhoeffer's essay "Heritage and Decay" from his *Ethics*.[23] Young makes a similar argument with race in mind by pointing out how Bonhoeffer's reflections from prison on the "world come of age" blindly move forward without any consideration of the far-reaching effects of colonialism or the racial fissures inherent in Bonhoeffer's account of this brave new world.[24] Young substantiates this claim by referencing a number of comments from Bonhoeffer's later writings and speeches that wholly neglect Africa and that quickly dismiss those from the East.[25] This alternative view of Bonhoeffer lends itself to another examination of the racial struggles Bonhoeffer faced at home against Aryanism for the sake of the Jews.

Post-Holocaust Jewish scholars have led the charge in establishing this more suspect view of Bonhoeffer's defense of the Jews.[26] In an article published in 1981, Stanley Rosenbaum reports that he searched Bonhoeffer's works in vain for references about the Jews that are not "ignorantly patronizing or dogmatically conversionist."[27] In Bonhoeffer's attempts to help the Jews, Rosenbaum contends that Bonhoeffer was a tragic victim of his time. Bonhoeffer's efforts to help the Jews, in the end, capitulated to Christian polemics against Jews. For a Jew, Rosenbaum concludes, "Bonhoeffer is no saint" but "the best of a bad lot."[28] The Jewish scholar Albert Friedlander extends this argument to place the Western Christian

21   Young, *No Difference in the Fare*, 5.

22   See especially Bonhoeffer's lecture "Basic Questions of a Christian Ethic" in *DBWE* 10:359–78.

23   See Thomas Day, "Conviviality and Common Sense: The Meaning of Christian Community for Dietrich Bonhoeffer" (Ph.D. diss., Union Theological Seminary, 1975), 372. For Bonhoeffer's essay "Heritage and Decay," see *DBWE* 6:103–33.

24   See Young, *No Difference in the Fare*, 4.

25   See Young, *No Difference in the Fare*, 5–6.

26   For a full account of Jewish responses to Bonhoeffer's theology, see Haynes, *The Bonhoeffer Legacy*, 19–28.

27   Stanley R. Rosenbaum, "Dietrich Bonhoeffer: A Jewish View," *Journal of Ecumenical Studies* 18, no. 2 (1981): 306.

28   Rosenbaum, "Dietrich Bonhoeffer," 307.

Church as a whole into question. Friedlander suggests that the myth of Bonhoeffer's sainthood was "created because the Church wanted reassurance that it, the Institution, was not a sinner."[29]

On the heels of these Jewish criticisms of Bonhoeffer, Christian scholars have provided similar interpretations of his life. Kenneth Barnes argues that one cannot deny that Bonhoeffer fell into the very demeanor and biases of the Nazi party despite his intentions to oppose Nazism and defend the Jews.[30] Stephen Ray Jr. offers an explanation of Barnes' claim by suggesting that Bonhoeffer found himself in an "anti-Semitic language loop."[31] Additionally, Stephen Haynes provides a more damning critique of Bonhoeffer when he contends that the majority of Christian interpreters of Bonhoeffer fail to observe the continuity of traditional Christian views of anti-Semitism running throughout his corpus.[32] Haynes argues that this anti-Semitism is seen in a theology riddled with expressions of deicide and supersessionism, present even in Bonhoeffer's later works.[33] Based on these critical accounts, the mystique of Bonhoeffer's sainthood is tarnished with the flaws of a privileged individual, negatively shaped by the racial proclivities of his own time and place.

Bonhoeffer as Witness

Having both a positive and negative portrait of Bonhoeffer's interactions with race in view helps demonstrate the difficulty of attempting to apply his life directly to the complex and ever-evolving problem of race. Possibly the only direct application that we may draw from his life is that dealing with race, as with any complex issue, is bound to receive praise from some and disapproval from others. Simply entering into a discussion about race is filled with tension and volatility, requiring a firmer foundation than success or failure, praise or disapproval, saint or sinner. When viewed in isolation, each interpretation of Bonhoeffer's life is

29   Albert H. Friedlander, "Bonhoeffer and Baeck: Theology after Auschwitz," *European Judaism* 14 (1980): 31.

30   Kenneth C. Barnes, "Dietrich Bonhoeffer and Hitler's Persecution of the Jews," in *Betrayal: German Churches and the Holocaust*, ed. Robert Ericksen and Susannah Heschel (Minneapolis: Fortress, 1999), 116.

31   Stephen G. Ray Jr., *Do No Harm: Social Sin and Christian Responsibility* (Minneapolis: Fortress, 2003), 91.

32   See Haynes, *The Bonhoeffer Legacy*, 83–85.

33   For Haynes' presentation of Bonhoeffer's deicide and supersessionism in his later works, see chapter 5, "Bonhoeffer and Post-Holocaust Theology," in *The Bonhoeffer Legacy*, 83–108.

shortsighted. A positive reading of Bonhoeffer's engagement with race lends itself to heartbreak, confusion, and anger as a person enters into the painful and repentant work of unraveling whiteness. On the other hand, a negative reading of Bonhoeffer's dealings with race can foster helplessness and apathy as a person wrestles with the systemic breadth of whiteness. Each isolated approach, in its own way, allows the pervasive powers of whiteness to continue unabated.

This is why Bonhoeffer's life should not be read as an end in itself but as a window into Christ's call that pulls one into the messiness of addressing complex issues (such as whiteness) in the present moment. As Bonhoeffer himself wrote at the end of his life:

> If one has completely renounced making something of oneself—whether it be a saint or converted sinner . . .—then one throws oneself completely into the arms of God, and this is what I call this-worldliness: living fully in the midst of life's tasks, questions, successes and failures, experiences, and perplexities.[34]

If Bonhoeffer's life and theology offer any claim, it is that faith in Christ drives one beyond speculations of saint or sinner and into participation with the living Christ. Faith looks only to Jesus Christ: "I no longer cast even a single glance on my own life, on the new image I bear," Bonhoeffer writes. "For in the same moment that I would desire to see it, I would lose it."[35] The externality of Christ's call expels every glance toward one's own self-justification or self-condemnation, freeing one to enter with Christ into the muddled turmoil of world history from one's particular place in it.[36]

Bonhoeffer's own reflections demonstrate his struggle to enter the messiness of world history from his particular place of privilege. As he looked back on his life while in prison, Bonhoeffer wrote, "I wonder whether my excessive scrupulousness is not a negative side of bourgeois existence—simply that part of our lack of faith that remains hidden in times of security."[37] It is important to note that Bonhoeffer's main concern in this reflection is not whether his privilege makes him

---

34 *DBWE* 8:486.

35 *DBWE* 4:287–88. This statement is taken from the conclusion of *Discipleship*, where Bonhoeffer discusses sanctification in terms of a growing dependence on Christ.

36 In *Ethics* Bonhoeffer explains, "Faith means to base life on a foundation outside myself, on an eternal and holy foundation, on Christ" (*DBWE* 6:147).

37 *DBWE* 8:303.

a saint or a sinner but how it resists the response of faith that finds security solely in Christ. The call of Jesus Christ resituates one's whole life beyond mere self-description and into a passive response to God's already spoken word.

Bonhoeffer poignantly depicts how faith is a passive response to God's call in a sermon from 1934 on the life of Jeremiah.[38] Commenting on Jeremiah 20:7, "You have overpowered me, and you have prevailed," Bonhoeffer suggests that God's gracious call overpowers Jeremiah's own active resistance to this same call. Resistance is both recognizable and futile when through faith one is "seized by the word, by the call."[39] Bonhoeffer suggests that it is God's overwhelming love that leads Jeremiah—by faith—down a path toward suffering, scorn, and danger. In this call and response, however, the concern is no longer for Jeremiah's own suffering or wellbeing but God's suffering love and care for God's creation.

This same call from God given to Jeremiah is the call Bonhoeffer testifies to hearing in his own life. Bonhoeffer proclaims, "I had to follow the way of suffering, I could no longer resist."[40] It is this same call that Bonhoeffer hears coming to the church as a whole, the church in Germany in 1934 and the church near and far today. Bonhoeffer claims that the community of faith may resist God with its will and with its "own flesh and blood" (a reference to National Socialism's loyalty to blood and soil), but the faith community can "no longer go back beyond the point where they received the word, the call, the command of God."[41] What defines the church is not its perceived purity but its continued struggle to discern and respond to God's call—already given.[42]

Bonhoeffer's admonishments turn us from an analysis that stands over his life (or our own) to an active participation in discerning the concrete and historical church's own resistance to Christ's call. This discernment is on display in Bonhoeffer's most intimate writings that

38   Bonhoeffer delivered this sermon on January 21, 1934 to the German congregation he was pastoring in London. See *DBWE* 13:349–51.

39   *DBWE* 13:349.

40   *DBWE* 13:351.

41   *DBWE* 13:352.

42   Keith Clements recalls that Bonhoeffer prepared this sermon on Jeremiah 20:7 in "the tense days before Hitler's reception for the church leaders" of Germany. Clements also notes that Bonhoeffer made various appeals to intervene in the outcome of this event. See Clements' comments in *DBWE* 13:349, n. 1; see also Bethge's account in Bethge, *Dietrich Bonhoeffer*, 325–45.

wrestle with his own self-knowledge in relation to God, others, and creation. In his famous poem "Who Am I?," written in 1944 from Tegel Prison, Bonhoeffer wavers between his fellow prisoners' claims of what they see when they see him and what he knows of himself.[43] "They often tell me," Bonhoeffer writes, "I bear days of calamity serenely, smiling and proud."[44] But the image in his mind of himself is that of "a caged bird, struggling for life breath, as if I were being strangled, starving for colors, for birdsong, thirsting for kind words, human closeness . . ."[45] Bonhoeffer questions whether his identity is bound to the memory of what people have said of him or what he imagines of himself, or whether he is hypocritically both. In this questioning, Bonhoeffer's poem evidences the rhythm of a psalm, traveling between competing voices and between lament and praise.[46] His own internal struggles are situated within the invocation of God in the worshipping community that offers "kind words" and "human closeness" and within God's speaking through all of creation in the vibrancy of "colors" and "birdsong."[47] Bonhoeffer views himself within the broader struggle of an empirical community that both hears the call of God and must rely on God's call in the midst of its own questioning and resistance.

The final line of Bonhoeffer's poem relies on God's knowing and calling precisely in his questioning: "Whoever I am, thou knowest me; O God, I am thine!"[48] Faith in God's call does not resolve Bonhoeffer's questioning seen in his statement "Whoever I am." Bonhoeffer never claims full knowledge of himself; nor can we, when who we are has been distorted with creation's fall. Bonhoeffer's life bears witness to a

43   For slightly different interpretations of Bonhoeffer's poem "Who Am I?," see Michael Northcott, "'Who Am I?' Human Identity and the Spiritual Disciplines in the Witness of Dietrich Bonhoeffer" in *Who Am I?: Bonhoeffer's Theology through His Poetry*, ed. Bernd Wannenwetsch (London: T&T Clark, 2009), 11–30; and Bernd Wannenwetsch, *Political Worship: Ethics for Christian Citizens*, trans. Margaret Kohl (Oxford: Oxford University Press, 2004), 290–92.

44   *DBWE* 8:459.

45   *DBWE* 8:459.

46   Bernd Wannenwetsch offers a similar reading of this poem. See Wannenwetsch, *Political Worship*, 290–92.

47   Throughout Bonhoeffer's *Letters and Papers from Prison*, he speaks of his longing to participate in "worship, confession, and the Lord's Supper" within the consolation of Christ's gathered community. See *DBWE* 8:179. As will be discussed in what follows, it is God's call heard in the church's proclamation of word and sacrament that opens the church to discerning God's speaking in all of creation, in the colors of fall or the chirping of a bird outside the window of Bonhoeffer's prison cell.

48   *DBWE* 8:460.

dependence on the externality and contingency of God's call. The externality of God's call suggests that it is a claim that is received passively through faith—"you know me"; the contingency of God's call means that it is not a truth that we hold but a truth that holds us—"I am yours!" This understanding of God's call, reflected in Bonhoeffer's life, moves us beyond perceptions of success and failure and into the turmoil of a community of faith that discerns the living Christ pressing into it to prepare the way for God's invocation to be heard.

What is on display in Bonhoeffer's own life is how the historical Christian church, as a whole, lives in the penultimate through faith in God's ultimate call. Bonhoeffer testifies to as much in a letter to Bethge from December 5, 1943: "We are living in the penultimate and believe the ultimate, isn't that so?"[49] Bonhoeffer proposes that God's ultimate word does not give the community of faith a final solution but a discernment that lives into life's perplexities to prepare the way for the surprise of God's final word. Rather than holding special insights for overcoming whiteness, Bonhoeffer's life guides us beyond the paralysis of self-justification (or self-condemnation) that perpetuates whiteness and, thus, into a more concrete struggle with whiteness. God's call in Jesus Christ does not give the Christian church a resolution to the complex problem of whiteness but leads the church into a discernment that struggles against the way whiteness subdues the surprise of Christ's coming. Bonhoeffer's life, in this manner, invites the community of faith into discerning the contours of Christ's body in the fallen world, for it is in Christ that the ultimate and penultimate are properly related to one another. To explore what this means, we turn next to Bonhoeffer's account of the ultimate and penultimate.

"Ultimate and Penultimate Things"

Bonhoeffer's motif of the ultimate and penultimate assists in addressing the burning question posed in this book: how does God speak to and through a church undeniably marked by whiteness without submitting to the effects of whiteness? Bonhoeffer's discussion of the ultimate and penultimate speaks to this question by attending to a broader inquiry: how does God work through a sinful church without capitulating to sin?

49   *DBWE* 8:213. The German reads: "*Wir leben im Vorletzten* [before the last] *und glauben das Letzte* [the last], *ist es nicht so?*" (*DBW* 8:266). The terms of "penultimate" and "ultimate" offer an English gloss on the more direct translation of "before the last" and "the last."

Bonhoeffer's terminology of the ultimate addresses how God speaks into a world and church riddled with sin, and his explanation of the penultimate addresses how God's speaking refuses to capitulate to sin. The ultimate is the surprise of God's gracious speaking that gifts human beings with temporal life as a creaturely response to Jesus Christ. The penultimate is the temporal space held open by the surprise of God's gracious speaking, allowing for either a *resistance* that is closed to or a *repentance* that prepares the way for the surprise of God's speaking. The connection between these two, ultimate and penultimate, is a living connection found in Christ, as observed above in the witness of Bonhoeffer's life. This living connection suggests that the terms ultimate and penultimate do not represent quantifiable things to be humanly grasped but a renewed posture of human creatures grasped by their Creator. The surprise of God's gracious speaking opens human beings to respond to God, neighbor, and the earth, and, at the same time, God's gracious speaking holds open a space to address hindrances, such as those formed through an allegiance to whiteness, that muffle the surprise of God's arrival in the living person of Jesus Christ.

To show the distinct connection Bonhoeffer observes between the ultimate and penultimate, attention is drawn, first, to his understanding of the ultimate and, second, to his description of the penultimate. After exploring the ultimate and penultimate separately, consideration is given to how Bonhoeffer relates the two in Jesus Christ. The value that each concept suggests for theological race discourse will be considered in turn.

The Ultimate

The ordering of the "ultimate" before the "penultimate" in the title of his essay "Ultimate and Penultimate Things" is no incidental move on Bonhoeffer's part.[50] Listing the eschatological end first hints not only at the priority of the ultimate but also at the manner in which God's external and contingent word upholds all of life in opposition to the downward spiral of sin and death after the fall. All of life begins and ends with the ultimate of God's word. The ultimate, however, is not a beginning and end to be thought of within sequential time but that which comes from outside of time to give us the temporal moments of everyday life. The ultimate is the surprise of God's gracious speaking that breaks into a

---

50   One of Bonhoeffer's *Ethics* working notes demonstrates that he had considered listing the penultimate first. See *DBWE* 6:146, n. 1.

sinful world to give time itself meaning in Jesus Christ. Bonhoeffer summarizes this concept of the ultimate in traditional Reformation fashion as the "one happening" of God's "justification of the sinner by grace alone."[51] This concise definition of the ultimate describes the surprise of God's speaking through four key terms: (1) event, (2) justification, (3) sinner, and (4) grace. Evaluating these terms in Bonhoeffer's essay "Ultimate and Penultimate Things" and in his broader thought assists in articulating how God speaks into a fallen world without capitulating to sinful enclosures, including the modern occurrence of whiteness.

First, the "one happening" (or one event) of the ultimate frames "the justification of the sinner by grace alone" as encompassing all of life in relation to God's direct address in Jesus Christ. [52] There are not multiple happenings, just *one*. This one happening concentrates "the length and breadth of human life," as a whole, "in one moment."[53] The ultimate is only ultimate in relating each person to all of temporal life. "All this happens," Bonhoeffer contends, "when Christ comes to each person."[54] When Christ is received through a person's response of faith, the individual is incorporated into the whole of human life received and narrated in Jesus Christ. In *Act and Being*, Bonhoeffer describes this "happening" as enfolding all of time in the immediacy of the *actus directus*, the direct act of faith. He explains,

> The essence of the *actus directus* does not lie in its timelessness, but in its intentionality toward Christ, which is not repeatable because it is freely given by God. Its essence, that is to say, lies in the way Christ touches upon existence, in its historical, temporal totality.[55]

The direct act of faith opens a distinct person to the free gift of life in Christ, who touches all of human history, all of human life, sin and all, simultaneously in each moment. As a "happening," the ultimate

---

51   *DBWE* 6:146.

52   *DBWE* 6:146. The English translation offers the phrase "in the one event" for Bonhoeffer's German phrase "*in dem einen Geschehen*" (*DBW* 6:137). Bonhoeffer could have used the German noun "*das Ereignis*" to describe the ultimate as an event, but instead here he uses the German phrase "*in dem einen Geschehen*," which injects the idea of a "happening," something that comes to pass in the immediate moment. The translation of "happening" offered here is used to highlight the immediacy communicated in Bonhoeffer's German phrase "*in dem einen Geschehen*."

53   *DBWE* 6:146.

54   *DBWE* 6:147.

55   *DBWE* 2:100.

remains a surprise beyond fallen human beings' grasp. This does not mean the direct act of faith offers no content for material reflection, but that the *intention* itself is not available for reflection or for recreation. The content of human reflection that the direct act of faith provides is a collective recognition given by each member already found in Christ's community of faith, a conclusion Bonhoeffer reaffirms in his chapter on the ultimate and penultimate.[56] The happening of the ultimate, Bonhoeffer writes, "cannot be grasped by anything we are, or do, or suffer."[57] Instead, the one event of the ultimate defines a person's whole life in relation to God, others, and creation. This is why Bonhoeffer will argue that it is through the ultimate that "people recognize God and their neighbors for the first time."[58] Time itself begins and ends with the ultimate. Life itself is known as temporal life in relation to the surprise of God's ultimate word: "God said, 'Let there be light' . . . And there was evening and there was morning, the first day" (Gen 1:3, 5).

Second, when Bonhoeffer speaks of *justification*, he is not merely referring to a legal declaration on God's part but to a communicative *event* that incorporates the whole of life, human and nonhuman, into Christ, manifested in the worship of the empirical church.[59] Bonhoeffer describes this communicative event in *Lectures on Christology* as involving an address between persons: "The word in the form of address is only possible as word between two persons, as speaking and response,

56   This crucial place of the church in Bonhoeffer's considerations of the ultimate and penultimate is absent in most essays assessing "Ultimate and Penultimate Things" from *Ethics*. For example, in his essay "Ultimate, Penultimate and Their Impact," Ján Liguš fails to address the significance of the church for Bonhoeffer's conception of the ultimate and penultimate. See Liguš, "Dietrich Bonhoeffer: Ultimate, Penultimate and Their Impact. The Origin and the Essence of Ethics," in *Bonhoeffer's Ethics: Old Europe and New Frontiers*, ed. Guy Christopher Carter et al. (Kampen: Kok Pharos, 1991), 59–72. In contrast, the theologian John Manoussakis picks up this strand in Bonhoeffer's thought when he argues that, for Bonhoeffer, "the ethical assumes also a eucharistic dimension." See Manoussakis, "'At the Recurrent End of the Unending': Bonhoeffer's Eschatology of the Penultimate" in *Bonhoeffer and Continental Thought: Cruciform Philosophy*, ed. Brian Gregor and Jens Zimmermann (Bloomington: Indiana University Press, 2009), 228–29.

57   *DBWE* 6:146.

58   *DBWE* 6:146.

59   Bernd Wannenwetsch helpfully points out this distinction between a forensic understanding of justification and one that is closer to Luther's understanding of justification in his comparison of Richard Niebuhr and Bonhoeffer; see Wannenwetsch, "'Responsible Living' or 'Responsible Self'? Bonhoefferian Reflections on a Vexed Moral Notion," *Studies in Christian Ethics* 18, no. 3 (2005): 125–40. See also Barry Harvey's discussion of justification in Bonhoeffer's thought in Harvey, *Taking Hold of the Real*, 40–41.

responsibility."[60] God's word of address, unlike the imagery conjured up in a static idea, has an immediacy to it. Justification is a call and response that is lived into rather than an idea that is left open to human interpretation and distortion. Thus, Bonhoeffer will argue that the ultimate is found in a life that "knows itself as a member of a church and of a creation that sings the praises of the triune God."[61] The ultimate places the human being in creaturely time as a creature that lives before God through praise, primarily given in the church's proclamation of word and sacrament. At one important juncture in *Creation and Fall*, Bonhoeffer connects the realization of creatureliness and church membership by arguing that it is precisely in the event of receiving the body and the blood of the Lord's Supper that the creature in its bodily nature is once again related properly to a piece of the fallen earth claimed through God's speaking over it.[62] The communicative event of the church's proclamation of word and sacrament serves as a microcosm of God's incorporation of all of life into God's just activity.

Third, Bonhoeffer's naming of the *sinner* speaks to how God does not deal with human sin by reversing time but by being the storyteller that creates time through the gracious gift of Jesus Christ, who bears sin. In God's narrating of time through Christ, "the past and future of the whole of life flow together in God's presence."[63] This is how the triune God addresses a fallen world: God tells the story of humanity by bearing the world's sin at all points in time through Jesus Christ. Bonhoeffer presents this idea with his understanding of the "image of Christ" from *Discipleship*.[64] Whereas the "image of God" is bestowed on human beings in a world without sin (before the fall), "the image of Christ" is God's image borne, now, within a rebellious world that rejects its Creator (after the fall). "Out of sheer mercy," Bonhoeffer claims, God assumes "the image and form of the lost human being."[65] What hides Jesus Christ, for Bonhoeffer, is not Jesus' humanity but Jesus' coming in the likeness of sinful flesh (Rom 8:3)—Jesus' humiliation is found in his bearing of

60   *DBWE* 12:316.

61   *DBWE* 6:147.

62   See *DBWE* 3:79 and also *DBWE* 12:318. Linking Bonhoeffer's *Ethics* to his earlier writings is crucial for perceiving how his conception of the ultimate and penultimate fits within his ecclesial approach, developed to a greater extent in his earlier works.

63   *DBWE* 6:147.

64   See Bonhoeffer's final chapter, "The Image of Christ," in *DBWE* 4:281–88.

65   *DBWE* 4:282.

the image of sinful humanity.[66] This means that past sin is not forgotten and ignored but remembered and addressed in God's simultaneous declaration of judgment and forgiveness in Jesus Christ's bearing of sin. The church as a whole participates in this bearing of sin as it suffers with one another and the world in our collective rejection of and resistance to God's gracious speaking. This leaves faith alone as the posture oriented by and toward God's surprise. God's word in Jesus Christ has already been spoken in history, and yet this word comes home to the sinner in the contingent surprise of God's grace.

Fourth, the surprise of the ultimate is the surprise of God's *grace*. Grace is the surprise of Jesus Christ's coming to the whole creation and the whole individual in the same moment. Part of the surprise of grace is that God's address in Jesus Christ is to all, spread out over time. The individual person grasped by the surprise of God's grace stands with "others whom God loves equally."[67] Along with this, the ultimate lies always in the future as a surprise that gives human beings the gift of each present moment. In the final section of *Act and Being*, Bonhoeffer describes this gracious gift of a future in terms of the "eschatological possibility of the child."[68] The child does not live in the present by grasping for it (or for the past) but by living in the surprise of God's future. Bonhoeffer poignantly states,

> The echoless cries from solitude into the solitude of self, the protest against violation of any sort, have *unexpectedly* received a reply and gradually melt into the quiet, prayerful conversation of the child with the father in the Word of Jesus Christ.[69]

The ultimate opens a posture of worshipful conversation and discovery, not only with God but with neighbor and creation as well. The adult lives as a perpetual child in the wonder of God's surprising grace. That is why Bonhoeffer will say, "Not all time is a time of grace; but now—precisely now and finally now—is the 'day of salvation' (2 Cor. 6:2)."[70] The "day of salvation" is the absolute now of God's contingent address to the sinner, which makes the sinner present to the present moment.

---

66   Bonhoeffer differentiates between Christ's humanity and humiliation in his *Christology Lectures*. See *DBWE* 12:313–14, 356–60. This distinction will be discussed further when Bonhoeffer's Christology is presented in chapter 4.

67   *DBWE* 6:146.

68   *DBWE* 2:159.

69   *DBWE* 2:161 (emphasis added).

70   *DBWE* 6:151.

Bonhoeffer's conception of the ultimate provides a unique way of expressing how God's ultimate word touches all of life while refusing to degrade God's word into "something calculable, a commodity," robbing it "of its essential divinity."[71] This delineation of the ultimate as God's external and contingent word provides a specific intervention into contemporary discourses on race. As will be seen in the final section of this chapter and the subsequent chapters, there is a temptation either to elevate racial designations to the level of God's ultimate word or to degrade God's ultimate word into a commodity. In both cases, the well-meaning desire is to provide a *direct* challenge to the violence of whiteness. But this direct challenge comes at the cost of inadvertently divinizing racial designations or racializing God. The importance of Bonhoeffer's description of the ultimate is that it avoids both of these temptations by suggesting that God's ultimate word comes as an external and contingent surprise beyond human definitions (of race or otherwise). It is actually in retaining the externality and contingency of God's ultimate word that whiteness is more thoroughly challenged through relegating it to its proper location in temporal history. Whiteness presents a relative obstruction to the hearing of God's word, and this obstruction is directly addressed through a temporal struggle that counters the resistance of whiteness with a daily readiness that prepares the way for the surprise of God's speaking in all places and times. Bonhoeffer describes the nature of this struggle in his account of the penultimate as a preparing of the way.

The Penultimate

If Bonhoeffer's conception of the ultimate reflects the analogy of the child, living in the wonder of the future, then his description of the penultimate resembles the learned prudence of an adult, living from a reflection on the past. The two, child and adult, are held in tension for Bonhoeffer in what Joshua Kaiser insightfully calls *Becoming Simple and Wise*.[72] This harkens back to Jesus' summons to be as wise as a serpent and as innocent as a dove (Matt 10:16). While the imagery of the child in juxtaposition with the adult offers an initial glance into Bonhoeffer's terms of ultimate and penultimate, the image is an individualistic one

---

71   *DBWE* 6:151.

72   Joshua A. Kaiser, *Becoming Simple and Wise: Moral Discernment in Dietrich Bonhoeffer's Vision of Christian Ethics* (Eugene: Pickwick, 2015).

that fails to fully capture the corporate and cosmic elements residing in his framework of the ultimate and penultimate.

The penultimate is temporal life itself (human and nonhuman) as that which has an open posture to Christ's gracious coming. Bonhoeffer's concept of the penultimate describes how a good creation distorted by sin after the fall is understood "as the world preserved and maintained by God for the coming of Christ."[73] Attending to God's fallen creation, its history and its life, from one's specific place in it is to participate with Christ in refusing the destruction of the penultimate. This battle to preserve the penultimate is a relative struggle, because the destruction of the penultimate *may only hinder* the coming of the ultimate and can *never outright refuse* this coming.[74] Thus, Bonhoeffer claims that the "ultimate holds open a certain space for the penultimate"[75]—a relative space for either a hindering of or a preparing for the surprise of God's gracious speaking in Jesus Christ. The penultimate describes the preparatory side of this relative struggle as determined and sustained by God's ultimate word. In this struggle history is remembered and the human being is known through the community of faith's repentant acknowledgment of God's preservation of all creation. By penultimate, then, Bonhoeffer has in mind an ecclesial discerning of the church and world's refusal to listen to God's speaking in history, bound up with a repentant response that attends to historical hindrances to hearing God today.

In terms of knowing and remembering, Bonhoeffer explains that the penultimate is a preparing of the way already determined and sustained by the ultimate. While the penultimate includes everything that precedes the ultimate (the justification of the sinner by grace alone), the penultimate only *knows* it is penultimate in relation to the ultimate. The penultimate, he writes, "is addressed as penultimate after finding the ultimate."[76] That the penultimate is determined and upheld by the ultimate means the penultimate is without self-sufficiency or autonomy. The penultimate is what it is because the ultimate judges it to be so. Whereas Bonhoeffer describes the ultimate in terms of the absolute moment of

73   *DBWE* 6:165. Bonhoeffer stipulates that this is how the world becomes understandable "from a Christian perspective."

74   In his chapter "Natural Life," Bonhoeffer explains, "The natural [preservation of the penultimate] does not compel the coming of Christ, nor does the unnatural [destruction of the penultimate] make it impossible; in both cases the real coming is an act of grace" (*DBWE* 6:173).

75   *DBWE* 6:159.

76   *DBWE* 6:159.

"one happening," the penultimate is never something present but a judgment made by the "ultimate on what has gone before,"[77] and in this way is *remembered*. Therefore, Bonhoeffer stipulates that the penultimate is not a condition (of worldly reform or otherwise); it is a judgment spoken by the ultimate over what has already taken place.

What this understanding of the penultimate means in practical terms is demonstrated in Bonhoeffer's subsequent discussion of humanness as known from within God's act of justification. Humanness precedes God's justification, yet humanness remains defined by what God has already done in the gracious surprise of justifying the sinner. For this reason Bonhoeffer will argue that it is a "violation of the ultimate" to call "being human a precondition for justification by grace," because being human is not a condition but a judgment "based on and determined by being justified."[78] As a judgment on the past, Bonhoeffer will argue that there is a being human that precedes being justified, precisely because Jesus Christ comes not to perfect human beings but to fallen ones. The ultimate enfolds a being human that is understood retrospectively as God's judgment over the penultimate. Based on this external judgment, the ultimate always places the penultimate into question in such a way that it does not destroy the penultimate but makes it what it is—that which is preserved for the sake of Christ's coming.

Recognizing the penultimate for what it is, Bonhoeffer suggests, is to prepare the way for Christ's coming through repenting of every hindrance that remains closed to this coming. Repentance is an obedience given through concrete deeds that prepare the way for the response of faith.[79] The life of faith orients itself toward Christ in the penultimate by actively and visibly working to prepare the way of the Lord, so that "all flesh shall see the salvation of God" (Luke 3:6).[80] In reference to John the Baptist's call to repentance, Bonhoeffer suggests that there are historical conditions of human degradation and willful neglect that place a special hindrance before

---

77 *DBWE* 6:159.

78 *DBWE* 6:160.

79 In an earlier discussion of the penultimate from *Discipleship*, Bonhoeffer draws a close connection between repentant obedience and faith. The connection between repentance and faith is observed in his explanation of his statement "*Only the believers obey*, and *only the obedient believe*" (*DBWE* 4:63). He further explains, "In exactly the same way that obedience is called a consequence of faith, it is also called a prerequisite of faith" (*DBWE* 4:64). Later, in *Ethics*, Bonhoeffer makes a similar point by stating that the penultimate is both everything that comes before the ultimate and "everything that follows the ultimate, in order again to precede it" (*DBWE* 6:159).

80 *DBWE* 6:161.

Christ's coming. As an example Bonhoeffer offers the instance of slaves that are deprived of time to hear God's word, specifically in terms of the church's preaching.[81] In this case the first concern is not the church's preaching but addressing violent constraints that hinder the hearing of God's word for particular persons. Repentant acts do not replace the church's response of faith given in its proclamation of Word and sacrament but are necessary for making "it outwardly possible for people to hear and follow the call to where the word is proclaimed."[82] The visible deeds of repentance have worth precisely because they are penultimate things, things that precede the last thing already here in Jesus Christ. The last thing (the ultimate) is contingently given, for Bonhoeffer, chiefly in the existing church's proclamation of Word and sacrament, and this is why he will say that "going to church is as far as one can go in the context of what the penultimate commands."[83] Bonhoeffer's concern here is with a potential confusion between the ultimate and penultimate. Preparing the way has ultimate consequences, but it is not the ultimate itself, which only God speaks.

What distinguishes Bonhoeffer's proposal of preparing the way is a faith in God's speaking through the living Christ, who is present in and as the church. For Bonhoeffer the direct act of faith received in the church is required for the conscious activity of preparing the way for two reasons. First, it is only by faith that "the fallen world becomes understandable as the world preserved and maintained by God for the coming of Christ."[84] Second, preparing the way recognizes that "Christ alone prepares the way of Christ's coming."[85] Bonhoeffer's approach of preparing the way, then, is an ecclesial approach of participation with Christ. At the same time, the nuanced manner in which Bonhoeffer discusses the penultimate as preceding the ultimate, only to recognize itself later as penultimate, suggests that every person is faced with the relative possibility of preparing the way. While the church through its encounter with Christ may have unique insights into the relative space of the penultimate, the task of preparing the way is bestowed on the whole world through Christ.[86] The church is not sealed off from the world but rather

81   *DBWE* 6:162.
82   *DBWE* 6:166.
83   *DBWE* 6:166.
84   *DBWE* 6:165.
85   *DBWE* 6:167.
86   Support for Bonhoeffer's espousal of this view can be found through a careful analysis of his chapter on the "Natural Life," as will be done in chapter 3. For Bonhoeffer's account of the "Natural Life," see *DBWE* 6:171–218.

representative of the world as a whole. The irruption of God's ultimate word into the community of faith reveals God's speaking in the fallen world at all times and in all places.

Bonhoeffer's understanding of the penultimate affords the Christian church a unique role in *remembering* the history of whiteness in the United States as the church's own resistance to God's continual call. To remember whiteness in this way is to acknowledge God's preservation of the fallen creation for the sake of Christ. The canopy of God's preservation calls for a memory of the devastating violence perpetrated by whiteness and, at the same time, shelters this memory from having a totalizing effect.[87] Furthermore, the church is called not only to remember but also to *respond* to this memory of whiteness through addressing the particular ways whiteness hinders a hearing of God's word. Preservation of the penultimate requires repentance, expressed through concrete reparations that account for the compounding inequities facilitated by whiteness that serve to destroy the penultimate. The work of reparations, from this perspective, is not meant as resolution to the problem of whiteness but as a readying of ears to hear and eyes to see precisely in the midst of the muffling and shrouding of whiteness. Reparations enact a repentance that follows from and anticipates God's promise that "all flesh shall see the salvation of God" (Luke 3:6).

The Relation between the Ultimate and Penultimate

The distinctiveness between the surprise of the ultimate and the temporal life of the penultimate raises the question of how to relate the two, childhood and adulthood. How does one live simultaneously as a child in the wonder of a future spoken by God and as an adult in the discernment of a past preserved by God? Bonhoeffer addresses this question through the pastoral example of comforting someone after the death of a loved one.[88] In such a case, he cautiously warns against the temptation of grasping for God's ultimate word to bring a sense of resolution to

---

87 While not dealing directly with race, Jonathan Tran's work on the Vietnam War and memory captures a similar concept to the one presented here. Jonathan Tran does not shy away from the horrendous acts perpetrated in the Vietnam War but explores how the church might consider these events in relation to its worship of Jesus Christ. He writes, "Christians worship the one who has saved history and thus rendered unnecessary attempts to make it come out right. Time *as creation*, then, is not meant to be controlled. Rather, time *as creation* is meant for worship." Jonathan Tran, *The Vietnam War and Theologies of Memory: Time and Eternity in the Far Country* (West Sussex: Wiley-Blackwell, 2010), 8.

88 See *DBWE* 6:152–53.

the situation. This form of cheap grace is to be avoided because, one, it can wrongly domesticate the ultimate into something at one's disposal and, two, it may serve as an evasion of actually being with someone in the temporal moments of his or her pain.[89] Based on these warnings, Bonhoeffer concludes that at times it is better to remain consciously in the penultimate, because it gives a "more genuine reference to the ultimate."[90] The ultimate is not an evasion of temporal life but that which opens one to the multifaceted texture of everyday life—what Bonhoeffer will call the polyphonic life in *Letters and Papers from Prison*.[91]

The ultimate has simultaneity with the penultimate in that, as emphasized above, God's ultimate liberation of the fallen creation requires a preservation of the fallen creation as penultimate. Bonhoeffer observes this simultaneity when he states that the Christian must "walk the long way through the penultimate for the sake of the ultimate."[92] The relation between the ultimate and penultimate is not a graspable doctrinal claim that serves to avoid temporal life but a living faith in Christ that makes one present to the struggles and joys of others, experienced in daily sicknesses and healings, deaths and births, oppressions and liberations. The relation between the ultimate and penultimate is resolved in the living Christ into which the church is incorporated in its daily life.

To clarify this proper relation between the ultimate and penultimate, Bonhoeffer considers two incorrect approaches for relating the ultimate and penultimate. He calls these approaches the radical solution and the solution of compromise.[93] Bonhoeffer argues that both solutions are extremes in that they absolutize one truth at the cost of another truth. Radicalism absolutizes the end; compromise absolutizes what exists.[94] By making absolute claims, each approach dissolves the distinct unity between the ultimate and penultimate revealed in Jesus Christ: "The radical solution approaches things from the end of all things, from God the judge and redeemer; the compromise solution approaches things from

---

89   *DBWE* 6:152.

90   *DBWE* 6:152.

91   In speaking of the polyphonic life, Bonhoeffer suggests that Christianity "puts us into many different dimensions of life at the same time; in a way we accommodate God and the whole world within us. We weep with those who weep at the same time as we rejoice with those who rejoice . . . One has to dislodge people from their one-track thinking—as it were, in 'preparation for' or 'enabling' faith, though in truth it is only faith itself that makes multidimensional life possible" (*DBWE* 8:405).

92   *DBWE* 6:152.

93   See *DBWE* 6:153–57.

94   *DBWE* 6:154.

the creator and preserver."[95] These solutions are flawed because they do not attend to how Jesus Christ as the reconciler reveals God as both judge and redeemer *and* creator and preserver and so resolves the relationship between the ultimate and penultimate. In Jesus Christ's life, death, and resurrection, the doctrinal categories of creation and preservation intersect with the doctrinal categories of reconciliation and redemption, and mutually inform one another. The church is bound to Christ in preserving the world (creation and preservation) in preparation for the surprise of God's contingent address (reconciliation and redemption).

While Bonhoeffer's accounts of the radical and compromise solutions may seem to participate in straw man tactics, the fundamental import of his insights concern the ever-present temptation to sever the ultimate from the penultimate or to confuse the two. In his essay from 1932, "Thy Kingdom Come! The Prayer of the Church-Community for God's Kingdom on Earth," he portrays the church as participating in both otherworldliness (radicalism) and secularism (compromise).[96] Otherworldliness faces the temptation of claiming "eternal victories that are so easily achieved" when one runs up against continual "temporal defeats."[97] Secularism faces the temptation of becoming self-appointed victors within earthly struggle: "Who does not wish for human beings to assume his role on earth in loud, boastful strength—just as the strong acquire the weak."[98] The inherent danger in both radicalism and compromise is the evasion of God's speaking in the midst of the fallen world. Radicalism avoids God's speaking by disengaging worldly struggle through a hasty application of God's ultimate word. Compromise avoids God's speaking by taking on worldly struggles in such a way that God's ultimate word is circumvented.

In contrast to these solutions, the community of faith brings together these two opposing views by participating with Christ in living on the cursed ground, the cursed ground that "the flesh of Christ bore" and on which he walked, the cursed ground on which "the tree of the curse stood," and the cursed ground on which Christ establishes God's kingdom through resurrection.[99] The Christian church partakes in "Christ's encounter with the world," which is an encounter, Bonhoeffer states,

95   *DBWE* 6:154.
96   For the full devotion on the second line of the Lord's Prayer, which Bonhoeffer presented at a women's retreat, see *DBWE* 12:286–97.
97   *DBWE* 12:288.
98   *DBWE* 12:288.
99   *DBWE* 12:288.

"beyond all radicalism and compromise."[100] Moreover, Bonhoeffer's relation between the ultimate and penultimate incorporates the church into God's speaking through praying with Christ on the cursed earth that hides God's countenance. He exclaims,

> The hour in which we pray today for God's kingdom is the hour of the most profound solidarity with the world, an hour of clenched teeth and trembling fists. It is not a time for solitary whispering, "Oh, that I might be saved." Rather, it is a time for mutual silence and screaming, that this world which has forced us into distress together might pass away and Your kingdom come to us.[101]

In praying with Christ, the temptations of radicalism and compromise are refuted in a "mutual silence and screaming," silence before God's ultimate word and a screaming that participates with Christ in preparing the way for God's kingdom on earth. The relation between the ultimate and penultimate is not a two-step process but simultaneous in Jesus Christ.

Bonhoeffer's emphasis on the simultaneity of the ultimate and penultimate in Jesus Christ leaves no room for a struggle with whiteness to be separated from God's ultimate word—the justification of the sinner by grace alone. Both the struggle to prepare the way through addressing hindrances such as whiteness and the hearing of God's ultimate word are encompassed in the life, death, and resurrection of Jesus Christ. Christ is both the call and the response into which the church here and now is incorporated. This means, on the one hand, that whiteness does not need to be completely extinguished from the local church before God's ultimate word can be received. On the other hand, this means that hearing God's ultimate word necessitates a daily struggle against every hindrance, including whiteness, which diminishes the opportunity to hear God's word clearly. The simultaneity of the ultimate and penultimate in Jesus Christ beckons the church to join a struggle against whiteness already being waged. The church joins with Christ in this struggle by living fully in the pains and joys of life as a whole to prepare the way for Christ's coming. The challenge, as we will see in the next section, is the continual struggle to distinguish the ultimate from the penultimate while holding the two together.

100 *DBWE* 6:159.
101 *DBWE* 12:289.

Reconfiguring Theological Race Discourse
with Bonhoeffer

In North America, contemporary theological discourses on race are generally divided between two camps: a *particularist* or contextual approach that specifically addresses whiteness and a *universalist* approach that addresses racial divisions more broadly.[102] The particularist approach accentuates a struggle within creation through offering reparations to address concrete racial inequities in history. The universalist approach emphasizes an eschatological vision of the reconciliation of all persons through the unity found in Jesus Christ. The difficulty faced by these two orientations is how to connect the particularist and the universalist approaches in a meaningful way that simultaneously addresses particular histories and the universal truth of the gospel without bifurcating or confusing the two. Bonhoeffer's motif of the ultimate and penultimate helps coordinate the particularist and universalist approaches to race through introducing the temporality of a historical community into the discussion. Spatially configured, the universal and particular function as a zero-sum game, but temporally configured, the ultimate speaks of the contingency of God's call that upholds all of life in the penultimate through participation with Christ in the community of faith. Thus, Bonhoeffer's ecclesial approach of preparing the way provides a promising recalibration of theological discourses on race and whiteness by shifting the dialogue from the commonly used spatial terms of a "universal" and a "particular" to the temporal terms of "ultimate" and "penultimate."

The assistance provided by Bonhoeffer's motif of the ultimate and penultimate in the ongoing search for a proper response to whiteness is brought out by considering the preceding discussion in conjunction with representative expressions of the particularist and universalist approaches to race. Jennifer Harvey's argument for reparations in *Dear White Christians* offers a representative example of the particularist approach,[103] and

102 For a presentation of these broad divisions in theological race discourse, see Jennifer Harvey's discussion of a universal versus a particular ethic in *Dear White Christians: For Those Still Longing for Racial Reconciliation* (Grand Rapids: Eerdmans, 2014), 57–62. For a more nuanced discussion of the topic, see J. Deotis Roberts, *A Black Political Theology* (Philadelphia: Westminster, 1974), 133–35.

103 Other theologians, along with Harvey, that generally follow the particularist approach, with various nuances, include: James H. Cone, *Black Theology and Black Power* (Maryknoll: Orbis Books, 1969); James W. Perkinson, *White Theology: Outing Supremacy in Modernity* (New York: Palgrave Macmillan, 2004); Victor Anderson, *Beyond Ontological Blackness: An Essay on African American Religious and Cultural Criticism* (New York: Continuum, 1995); and Vine Deloria Jr., *Custer Died for Your Sins: An Indian Manifesto* (New York: Macmillan, 1969).

Miroslav Volf's argument for reconciliation in *Exclusion and Embrace* provides a representative example of the universalist approach.[104] These two works are not meant to be exhaustive but expressive of the two most common North American approaches to a theology of race.[105] As representative examples, Harvey and Volf exhibit the respective strengths of the particularist and universalist approaches to race. These strengths, however, move in the direction of severing the ultimate from the penultimate (in Harvey's case) or confusing the two (in Volf's case). In contrast, by refusing to place the universal and particular against one another, Bonhoeffer assists in coordinating the strengths of these two approaches to race in terms of an ecclesial preparing of the way.

The Particularist Approach: Jennifer Harvey and Reparations

Jennifer Harvey's *Dear White Christians: For Those Still Longing for Racial Reconciliation* is a book dedicated to a particular audience—white Christians. Coming out of her doctoral studies with the late James H. Cone at Union Theological Seminary, Harvey's work is sensitive to the importance of context for evaluating and seeking to address race, or more specifically whiteness.[106] This is why her book is not addressed to people of color but to "white Christians." Harvey argues that generally white Christians, of the more progressive stripe, have rightly sought to address race but have done so through a problematic methodology.

104 Miroslav Volf, *Exclusion and Embrace: A Theological Exploration of Identity, Otherness, and Reconciliation* (Nashville: Abingdon Press, 1996). Other books that generally follow the universal approach, with various nuances, include: Paul Louis Metzger, *Consuming Jesus: Beyond Race and Class Divisions in a Consumer Church* (Grand Rapids: Eerdmans, 2007); David E. Stevens, *God's New Humanity: A Biblical Theology of Multiethnicity for the Church* (Eugene: Wipf & Stock, 2012); Gerardo Marti, *A Mosaic of Believers: Diversity and Innovation in a Multiethnic Church* (Bloomington: Indiana University Press, 2005); and John Piper, *Bloodlines: Race, Cross, and the Christian Church* (Wheaton: Crossway, 2011). These books represent a new focus found in the multiethnic church movement that seeks to address race through breaking down walls of division in the Christian church.

105 The theological approaches of Jennings, Carter, and Bantum, discussed in the proceeding chapters, do not easily fit into either of the two approaches listed here. With that said, there are still remnants of the universal/particular divide in each of their unique approaches.

106 James H. Cone, one of Harvey's teachers at Union Theological Seminary, is considered the forbearer of the views that Harvey adapts and espouses in *Dear White Christians*. See, for example, Cone's two earliest works, *Black Theology and Black Power* and *A Black Theology of Liberation* (Maryknoll: Orbis Books, 1970). Following Cone, there was a proliferation of similar approaches to race from a contextual viewpoint that located the racial problem between the oppressed and the oppressors.

White Christians have approached race through a *reconciliation paradigm* that prioritizes bringing together divergent racial groups before addressing how whiteness structures unjust disparities between these groups. Harvey suggests that this prioritization of racial diversity before attending to racial disparity obscures the systemic problem of whiteness. As a result, the reconciliation paradigm allows racial inequity to persist under the guise of a diversity covertly facilitated by whiteness.[107] White Christians continue to hold the reins of power and the bulk of the resources. Harvey's proposal is that white Christians and predominately white churches must address this power imbalance through shifting from a *reconciliation paradigm* to a *reparations paradigm*. The promise of the reparations paradigm is found in how it directly addresses the history and reality of whiteness largely neglected by white Christians working within a reconciliation paradigm.

Harvey's argument is largely based on the distinction she draws between a universalist ethic and a particularist one.[108] The universalist ethic frames conversations about race within the categories of sameness and otherness, focusing its efforts on integration and emphasizing the equality of all human beings. Alternatively, the particularist ethic frames conversations about race within the categories of oppressed and oppressor, focusing its efforts on justice and emphasizing the inequalities handed down through a particular history that creates structural differences between racial groups. Harvey pits these two frameworks against one another to show how a particularist ethic is better suited to expose and challenge whiteness.

She explains that a universalist ethic is problematic for conceptualizing matters of race, because its affirmation of sameness "has virtually no meaningful impact on day-to-day lives."[109] This is not only problematic, Harvey contends, but also wrongheaded. It seeks to relate to others through a sameness that is already defined by whiteness rather than observing that what really connects us are the histories and social structures that shape concrete identities along a sharp divide. Harvey concludes that a particularist ethic offers "more adequate ways of engaging race that take seriously

---

107 The reconciliation paradigm, Harvey claims, embraces Martin Luther King Jr.'s message of integration but largely disregards his call for justice. The result is a detached method for addressing race that forces people of color into "white dominated settings to allow for diversity." Harvey, *Dear White Christians*, 36.

108 For her full discussion on a universalist ethic versus a particularist one, see Harvey, *Dear White Christians*, 57–62.

109 Harvey, *Dear White Christians*, 59.

the structures, histories, violence, and other concrete realities that create our moral crisis and cause interracial alienation."[110]

Harvey holds that a particularist ethic can properly address "the actual state of things" through the redistribution of resources and power.[111] Her appeal is not to give up on racial reconciliation but to offer a more genuine form of reconciliation through attending to racial repair. The reparations approach attends to the historically disparate structures upheld and perpetuated by whiteness, requiring a specific response from white people. Harvey summarizes this view by arguing that the church needs to take the counterintuitive risk of letting go of reconciliation for now, so that the church's first priority becomes addressing the historical disparities that continue to tangibly segregate the church as well as the broader society.[112] Reparations and repair must pave the way, Harvey suggests, for realizing the reconciliation that white Christians seek.

Harvey's description of the reparations paradigm shares a certain resonance with Bonhoeffer's account of the penultimate. Both Harvey and Bonhoeffer emphasize the need to account for historical disparities through concrete action. Challenging whiteness requires historical structures to be addressed directly with a particular response—reparations. While Harvey's emphasis on reparations is sorely needed in the Christian church today, presenting the need for reparations based on a contrast between the particularist approach and the universalist approach to race raises some possible risks. The main risk in making this comparison is that it inadvertently moves in the direction of a problem/solution orientation for addressing race. Harvey presents a shift from diversity to disparity (which is significant), but she offers this shift from within a contrasting framework that structures both the reparations and reconciliation paradigms. The underlying structure for both the reparations and reconciliation paradigms remains an attempt to diagnose the problem with a corresponding solution. In other words, the reparations paradigm is more of a change in strategy than it is a shift in foundational theological assumptions. This leaves the reparations paradigm vulnerable to many of the same weaknesses Harvey indicates for the reconciliation paradigm. Pinpointing racial disparity as the underlying problem lends

110 Harvey, *Dear White Christians*, 63.

111 Harvey, *Dear White Christians*, 4.

112 Harvey, *Dear White Christians*, 4.

itself to giving us (specifically white Christians) the sense of bringing a solution that we can orchestrate. This is not meant as an argument against reparations but an argument for finding a deeper source for offering reparations that avoids the hamster wheel of the ever-evolving defenses of whiteness. To this end, it is important to consider how Bonhoeffer's understanding of the ultimate and penultimate may assist in placing Harvey's call for reparations onto a broader theological foundation.

Rather than wedging a spatial divide between the universalist and particularist approaches to race, Bonhoeffer's understanding of the ultimate and penultimate presents a temporal framework. Every temporal moment in the penultimate is upheld and threatened by the ultimate. This allows for a particular response of reparations in historical time (as stressed by Harvey) that remains connected to God's contingent and external word through faith. Since the *penultimate* is only recognized in relation to the ultimate, reparations have value specifically in addressing how whiteness obscures God's ultimate call from being heard (a call that stands before and after reparations). Reparations thus can represent *particular* responses of repentance in the penultimate that prepare the way for God's ultimate call, in which *all* of history is enfolded. Bonhoeffer's temporal framework of the ultimate and penultimate, in this way, sets Harvey's reparations paradigm on the surer foundation of the singular reality of God's working, found through the church's participation in Christ's real encounter with the fallen creation. The surprise of God's external and contingent claim over all of history incorporates the community of faith into the repentant response of reparations, so as to confront unjust racial hierarchies in preparation for the Christ who has come and is ever coming.

The shift here is not to a divergent strategy but of who is in control—God is in control rather than white people. White Christians are invited to join with Christ in offering concrete repairs for the historical disparities caused by whiteness, precisely in light of God's speaking and in preparation of God's pending word. Framing reparations in this way avoids the risk of turning reparations into a solution and instead offers reparation as a discernment that prepares for the surprise of God's pending advent.

The Universalist Approach: Miroslav Volf and Reconciliation

Whereas the particularist approach to race has the strength of directly addressing historical racial disparities with concrete action, the universalist approach has the strength of offering an eschatological hope that can guide and support the Christian church in the difficult work of enacting racial justice. One of the paramount expressions of how this eschatological hope undergirds the universalist approach is found in Miroslav Volf's influential book *Exclusion and Embrace*. Coming out of the context of the Croat-Bosniak war, Volf's work seeks a theological ethic for addressing social conflict that deflects a mere rehashing of racial animosity. He asks, "How does one remain loyal both to the demand of the oppressed for justice and to the gift of forgiveness that the Crucified offered to the perpetrators?"[113] In addressing this question, Volf relies on a Trinitarian theology that has become an integral part of the best expressions of the universalist approach to race.[114] The Trinity provides a non-homogeneous model that grounds relational personhood in the distinct persons of Father, Son, and Spirit. The church participates in this divine communion through its union with Christ, who, as both the oppressed and the oppressor, creates unity among distinct persons. This eschatological vision provides an external hope, lived into through the reconciliation of different people groups in a shared struggle against racial divisions.

For Volf, the eschatological hope that Jesus embodies is not the hope of *better* social arrangements but that of a new social agency that works within *any* given social arrangement. While social arrangements should be accounted for in that they shape the identity of particular persons, including Jesus Christ, Volf argues that Christ's self-donation constructs a relational identity within the social conditioning of enmity to combat enmity.[115] Christians are not primarily defined by which side of history they fall on but how they give their lives to address historical enmity in the power of God's self-giving love. A unique eschatological identity given in Jesus Christ holds together a diversity of particulars within the oppositional struggles of history.

Volf describes this new social agency of the Christian in terms of a multicultural sensibility that recognizes the limits of one's own cultural

113 Volf, *Exclusion and Embrace*, 9.

114 For another paramount example of a distinct Trinitarian approach to race, see Metzger, *Consuming Jesus*.

115 See Volf, *Exclusion and Embrace*, 9.

perspective as one seeks to embrace one's enemies. God's self-giving love in Jesus Christ offers a "spirituality of faith" that moves one from "the particularity of 'peoplehood' to the universality of multiculturality, from the locality of a land to the globality of the world,"[116] allowing one to see other perspectives through the eyes of faith in a sort of double vision.[117] Volf accounts for this trajectory from the particular to the universal in his presentation of Paul's missionary work and Jesus' interactions with Gentiles. The missionary work of Paul traces how the particular people of Israel are opened to "become the one universal multicultural family of peoples."[118] Similarly, Jesus' encounter with the Canaanite woman (Matt 15:21–28), which begins with a harsh rebuke of a Gentile woman and ends with her daughter's healing, reveals how Jesus' own vision expands from Israel to include the Gentile nations, visited by Jesus directly after this encounter (Matt 15:29–39). Through Jesus' interactions with the Canaanite woman, Volf explains that "Jesus' understanding of mission was enlarged; he saw the key concept of his message—unbiased grace—in a new light."[119] This creating of space for others and otherness forms the central thrust of Volf's thesis. Jesus' life of including others is encapsulated within the inner logic of the cross: "on the cross God made space in God's very self for others, godless others, and opened arms to invite them in."[120] For Volf, the distinction between the oppressed and the oppressor must be situated within the primary distinction between a God without sin and the whole of sinful humanity.

The strength of Volf's reconciliation approach is found in the transcendent place it seeks to reserve for Christ as the second person of the Trinity. Without this transcendent limit, Volf suggests, the reparations approach that seeks to bring justice through addressing inequities

116 Volf, *Exclusion and Embrace*, 43. Volf tries to hold the Christian faith together with its roots in Israel through his interpretation of Paul. Shortly following the cited quotation, he writes, "Paul's solution to the tension between universality and particularity is ingenious. Its logic is simple: the oneness of God requires God's universality; God's universality entails human equality; human equality implies equal access by all to the blessings of the one God; equal access is incompatible with ascription of religious significance to genealogy; Christ, the seed of Abraham, is both the fulfillment of the genealogical promise to Abraham and the end of genealogy as a privileged locus of access to God; faith in Christ replaces birth into a people" (*Exclusion and Embrace*, 45). This explanation reveals how Volf is working within a spatial contrast between the universal and particular, forcing him into a universalizing of the scandal of Israel's particularity.

117 Volf, *Exclusion and Embrace*, 213.

118 Volf, *Exclusion and Embrace*, 50.

119 Volf, *Exclusion and Embrace*, 214.

120 Volf, *Exclusion and Embrace*, 214.

only embroils divided groups in new injustices.[121] Volf's reconciliation approach offers an external hope that meets one from beyond the historical encasement of race, a transcendence bearing similarities with Bonhoeffer's understanding of the ultimate as God's external and contingent address. Faith responds to God's call by discerning a particular response to unjust social arrangements. Still, there remains an important difference between Volf's transcendent claim and Bonhoeffer's understanding of the ultimate.

Volf examines the historical inequities of particular peoples from the perspective of God's self-giving love in Jesus Christ for all peoples. The danger in this connection is in how Volf generally situates the universal of God's self-giving love directly against particular inequities—human exclusion is addressed with God's embrace. The ultimate of God's embrace is merged with the penultimate challenge of addressing historical inequities. This universalist approach runs into the peril, expressed by Harvey, of creating a diversity facilitated by whiteness. A multicultural diversity is imagined and offered from within the already assumed parameters of whiteness.

Volf's interpretation of Jesus and the Canaanite woman, in particular, raises this concern. The historical and religious difference of Jesus' Jewish identity, highlighted by his harsh rebuke, is surpassed with a new multicultural vision of the future. As will be seen in chapter 3, Willie Jennings warns that such an interpretation of this passage minimizes the scandal of God's election of Israel and the corresponding prohibition placed on Gentile outsiders.[122] Parallels drawn between multiculturalism and Jewish/Gentile relations work to remove the scandal of Israel's particularity, allowing the self-election of whiteness to covertly replace Israel's election.[123]

121 Volf writes that "neither revenge nor reparations can redress old injustices without creating new ones" (*Exclusion and Embrace*, 223).

122 Volf's reading of this pericope stands in stark contrast to Willie Jennings' interpretation of it as an intensification of the prohibition placed on Gentile outsiders and as a signaling of Israel's election fixed by an undomesticated God. For Jennings' reading of this gospel narrative, see Jennings, *The Christian Imagination*, 262–63. Jennings' account of this narrative is reflected upon in chapter 3.

123 Much of the writings within the multiethnic church movement make the mistake of hastily associating the religious differences between Jew and Gentile with the racial differences between white and nonwhite. For example, the authors of *United by Faith* write, "When individuals were baptized into the church they were informed that in Christ there were no divisions based on *race*, class, or gender (Galatians 3:28)." See Curtiss Paul DeYoung et al., *United by Faith: The Multiracial Congregation as an Answer to the Problem of*

The problem is not simply Volf's account of Israel but, more specifically, a universalizing that translates the surprise of Jesus' person into an idea. Thus, as with Harvey, Volf's approach moves in the direction of a problem/solution orientation. Jesus' *multicultural vision* of the future subtly becomes the central driving force in Volf's proposal rather than the surprise of Jesus Christ himself as a dynamic and living Word and as Israel's Messiah. As much as Volf labors to provide a way into addressing past injustices, his universalist approach already presents an eschatological ideal that distances one from fully grappling with past injustices. The ultimate becomes a resolution that lends itself to closing past chapters with an already defined universal ending.[124]

Bonhoeffer refrains from turning the ultimate into an idea or a solution by presenting the ultimate as God's external and contingent address, which is concretely heard within the church's proclamation of Word and sacrament. There is a temporal aspect to the contingency of God's address that prevents Bonhoeffer from applying the universal onto the particular as in Volf's universalist approach. The transcendent limit of Christ is not an idea but an embodied address that confronts the community of faith in the waters of baptism, in the bread and wine of communion, and in the neighbor. Bonhoeffer presents the church as the concrete place of God's address that incorporates the community of faith into Christ's preparation of the way for God's contingent address, which stands both before and after human preparation. This divine contingency leaves the ultimate beyond the reach of direct human reflection and, at the same time, incorporates the community of faith into the continuity of God's activity in the fallen creation.[125] The Christian church

---

Race (Oxford: Oxford University Press, 2003), 158. The danger here in making this connection to race is that it can result in mapping white people onto Israel as the elected people of God, inadvertently designating people of color as Gentile outsiders to God's covenant. This is one reason why the religious differences between Jews and Gentiles must be considered carefully in distinction to the racial differences constructed in the modern world.

124 This distancing from the past is reflected in Volf's argument for forgetting. See Volf, *The End of Memory: Remembering Rightly in a Violent World* (Grand Rapids: Eerdmans, 2006). For a critique of Volf's allowance for forgetting, see Tran, *The Vietnam War*, 125–35. Tran states that "Volf's allowance for forgetting rejects the notion that God's goodness harmonizes evil. Instead, evil and suffering will be 'driven out' once justice has been restored" (128).

125 As addressed above and will be discussed further in chapter 3, Bonhoeffer pairs the contingency of God's call with the continuity of the community of faith. The direct act of faith speaks to the contingency of God's call, while the act of reflection is oriented from within the church toward how all of history lies between God's beginning and end.

lives from and toward the ultimate without claiming the ultimate directly. This leaves the Christian church in the precarious position of discerning the temptation to offer a final solution (including itself) to whiteness. Space is left for past injustices and particular histories to be remembered as enfolded in the surprise of God's speaking in all times and places. Whiteness must be concretely struggled against inside and outside of the church, but this struggle is not to be regarded as a solution; it is a preparation for the pending redemption of the fallen creation that is presently preserved by God for Christ's coming.

A Temporal Coordination of the Spatial Divide

Both the particularist and the universalist approaches to race offer important insights for addressing the historical reality of race in the Christian church. The particularist approach to race, represented in Harvey's *Dear White Christians*, highlights the need for concrete reparations that address the historical imbalances of power and resources set up through the systemic structures of whiteness. This particularist approach reflects the general move in popular culture toward antiracist work as integral to building shared space.[126] The universalist approach to race, represented in Volf's *Exclusion and Embrace*, accentuates the need for an ultimate claim that can uphold an earthly struggle for justice with the external hope of God's word. The universalist approach reflects the movement toward diversity and integration offered generally by white Christians on the heels of the Civil Rights Movement. While both approaches provide important insights for addressing race, inherent to each is a problem/solution dichotomy that curtails the discernment/surprise orientation drawn from Bonhoeffer's temporal framework of the ultimate and penultimate. In the end, the particularist and universalist approaches to race represent two sides of the same coin. They both succumb to the temptation of placing faith in one's own strength or knowledge rather than constantly looking to the living Christ to prepare the way.

Bonhoeffer's expression of the ultimate and penultimate provides a temporal coordination of the strengths of the particularist and universalist approaches to race through his proposal of an ecclesial preparing

126 For a discussion of antiracist work, see Ibram X. Kendi, *How to Be an Antiracist* (New York: Random House, 2019). For a historical discussion supporting the need for antiracist work in the Christian church, see Jemar Tisby, *The Color of Compromise: The Truth about the American Church's Complicity in Racism* (Grand Rapids: Zondervan, 2019).

of the way. Particularity is accounted for within Christ's preservation of creaturely time in the penultimate as preparation for the last thing—the justification of the sinner by grace alone. This preparation demands a particular response (reparations) from particular persons to concretely address the violent power imbalance of whiteness, and so upholds the need for antiracist work. Simultaneously, universality is accounted for in how all of creaturely time is enfolded within the surprise of God's external and contingent address. God's ultimate call humbles us to remember that even the work of an antiracist is susceptible to succumbing to the powerful inclinations of whiteness. It is Bonhoeffer's attention to the historical church itself as a fully human community and a reality of God's revelation that allows for this temporal coordination of the universalist and particularist approaches to race. The community of faith bows before God's surprising grace as it continually does the work of antiracism with Christ in temporal history to challenge a whiteness that remains closed to the surprise of God's grace.

Rather than looking for a solution to the problem of whiteness, Bonhoeffer's ecclesial preparing of the way invites us to explore how God is at work in the midst of a historical Christian church and broader society undeniably marked by whiteness. To struggle against whiteness through enacting reparations is to embrace creaturely time in the penultimate as a gift received in "silence before the inexpressible"[127]—the living Word, who has come and is coming.

Conclusion

There are many potential ways to relate Bonhoeffer's life and thought to contemporary theological race discourse in the United States. The approach charted in this opening chapter was to offer Bonhoeffer's proposal of an ecclesial preparing of the way as a method for reconfiguring theological discussions of race. It was suggested that Bonhoeffer's concept of an ecclesial preparing of the way shifts discussions about race from the spatial categories of particular and universal to the temporal categories of ultimate and penultimate. Based on this shift, it was argued that Bonhoeffer's motif of the ultimate and penultimate assists in moving theological discussion of race beyond problem/solution orientations to a discernment/surprise approach. Because the triune God has already spoken in and through the living Christ, the Christian

127 *DBWE* 12:300.

church participates with Christ in preparing the way through discerning how whiteness resists hearing and responding to God's external and contingent call.

Bonhoeffer's proposal of an ecclesial preparing of the way resituates theological discussions of race from looking for solutions to whiteness to discerning God's call in the midst of the resistance of whiteness. The goal is not to find a resolution, or to say that one party has it right and the other has it wrong, but to enter into a dialogue that is discerning of God's speaking within the complexities of whiteness. With this in mind, bringing Bonhoeffer into dialogue with contemporary theologians of color serves both to expand upon the above proposal of an ecclesial preparing of the way and to explore some of its limitations. Before we enter into this dialogue, the next chapter pauses to examine how whiteness has historically functioned as an evolving reflex that resists hearing and responding to God's contingent call. Thus, the next chapter ponders how we might *remember* the history of white people in the United States in a manner that adheres to Bonhoeffer's understanding of the ultimate and penultimate.

2

The Space of Remembering

Whiteness as an Evolving Language Game

History is a reoccurring theme throughout Bonhoeffer's corpus. He talks about the "Jesus of history" in *Lectures on Christology*,[1] European history in his chapter in *Ethics* "Heritage and Decay,"[2] and even the history of the African American church in his essay "Protestantism without Reformation."[3] In these writings, Bonhoeffer considers history not simply as an academic exercise but as a living memory drawn from the surprise of Jesus Christ's arrival. All history is messianic

1   Bonhoeffer writes, "The Christ who is present today is the historical Jesus" (*DBWE* 12:328). In making this statement, Bonhoeffer seeks to counter the idea that the Jesus discovered in the Synoptic Gospels is somehow to be distinguished from the Christ that the apostle Paul proclaims in his epistles. Similarly, Bonhoeffer draws a strong connection between the Synoptic Gospels and Paul's epistles in *Discipleship*. In this later writing, Bonhoeffer relates Jesus' verbal call to follow him recorded in the Synoptic Gospels with the church's call to be baptized as presented in Paul's epistles. Both Jesus' call and the church's call to baptism share the same immediacy of a direct call, which can only be accepted or rejected.

2   See Bonhoeffer's essay "Heritage and Decay" in *DBWE* 6:103–33.

3   See Bonhoeffer's very brief historical considerations of the African American church in his paper "Protestantism without Reformation" in *DBWE* 15:456–58.

history, which means all history gains its continuity and meaning in Jesus Christ. Or, as Bonhoeffer puts it, "History lives between promise and fulfillment."[4] The following chapter applies this framing of history to offer a theological account of the history of white people in the United States. It does this by pondering the question: how does the Christian church remember the history of white people in the United States as a time spanned between promise and fulfillment? Asking this question moves the discussion from Bonhoeffer's conception of an ecclesial preparing of the way to a contemporary application of it. The exercise of remembering our history prepares the way for hearing and responding to God's voice today.

And yet it is only because the triune God has already spoken in history that this preparation through remembering may be given. The surprise of Jesus Christ enfolds history between promise and fulfillment, carving out a distinct space for remembering the history of white people as partaking either in a *resistance to* or a *readiness for* the advent of God's speaking. God has already spoken in Jesus Christ, and we have already given a response. History, from this perspective, is understood as a reflection on the responses given to God's address, both past and present. This means that to talk about history involves more than a simple review of past occurrences. Discussing history is to be found within it.[5] It is to discover all of life, and every individual life, as drawn into the life of the Jewish Messiah—Jesus Christ.

The history discussed here focuses on white people in the United States. This concentration on white people is an intentional move that seeks to address how the history of the United States has often been remembered through a white lens that removes white people from view. To be white is to be the all-seeing eye while never being seen. White people are stripped of this fabricated privilege of omnipresence by flipping the viewing lens back onto the particularity of white people. In sum, the history presented here decenters white people *from* the role of the subject doing the examining (which is God's role alone) *to* the role of the object under examination.

This examination of white people in the United States can help us remember what has been forgotten—the evolving language game of

4   *DBWE* 12:325.
5   To reflect this orientation of being found in history, the first-person plural pronouns of "we" and "us" are used at crucial points in this chapter rather than the third person plural pronouns of "they" and "them." This use of "we" and "us" may feel disjunctive to some, which is the very purpose for employing it.

whiteness that conditions us and configures the landscapes of our daily encounters with neighbors and the earth. To regain a memory of whiteness, two broad movements in the history of the United States will be traced. These two broad movements are showcased to illuminate how the language game of whiteness evolves with time, making whiteness ever more covert and insidious. Act one recounts how the struggle to define whiteness was foundational for the formation of the United States as a nation. Act two examines recent attempts to unravel and remove the designation of whiteness from white people, only to actually further capitulate to a more subtle and subversive form of whiteness. The question up for discussion in both of these acts is how the language game of whiteness impacts the ways we hear and respond to God's word given in Jesus Christ today.

Act One: The Language Game of Becoming White

The first act of the history of white people in the United States requires an exploration of how various European people groups became identified collectively as "white" in the American context. If we are to understand what it means to be white in the United States, we must remember the history of how the racial identifier of "white" came into existence in our own specific time and place. Remembering this history from a theological perspective involves a reliance on the persistence of God's address throughout history. Based on the presupposition of God's address, the theological question that arises is this: how did the shift to a "white" identity during America's origins impact the ways we (white people) listen to God, others, and the earth? Beginning with God's address is what makes the history considered in this chapter distinct from the significant research underway in the new field of whiteness studies in the American academy.

Whiteness Studies

The new field of whiteness studies was born in the 1990s with the intent of connecting white people to the history that gave us the appellation of "white." This field of study has contributed to a recent trend among white historians to flip our historical viewing lens back onto white people. White historians such as David R. Roediger, Theodore W. Allen, Noel Ignatiev, and Matthew Frye Jacobson have produced a selection of monographs that address how European ethnicities were exchanged for the racial designation of "white" early on in the formation of the United States.[6] Reviewing the history recounted by these historians serves as an introduction to both the historical materialization of whiteness and the limitations of whiteness studies as a whole.

There is a broader history of whiteness that extends well before and far beyond the colonization of the Americas.[7] While this broader history flows into the specific history of race in the United States, whiteness studies begins its examinations of race, by and large, with the early British colonies on the soil of North America. The historians working in the field of whiteness studies trace the journey into whiteness as an intrinsic component of the United States' formation as a distinct nation on the global stage. Immigration patterns from Europe to the Americas formed a collection of different European groups struggling to make sense of their identities in a new place among new peoples. As a result, the early years of the United States were dedicated to the contest over whiteness—who would fit its definition, who would gain its power by being found within its boundaries. "Caucasians are not born," comments Jacobson, "they are made."[8]

The making of white persons in the United States was a fairly untidy business. The racial designation of "white" arose as poor European immigrants from places such as Ireland and Italy joined with Africans in rebelling against their slave owners. The method for dealing with

6   The two books attributed with defining the field of whiteness studies are David R. Roediger's *The Wages of Whiteness: Race and the Making of the American Working Class* (New York: Verso Books, 1991) and Theodore Allen's two-volume set, *The Invention of the White Race*, 2 vols. (New York: Verso Books, 1994, 1997). Noel Ignatiev's *How the Irish Became White* (New York: Routledge, 1995) deals specifically with the history of Irish immigrants in the United States and their journey into whiteness. Matthew Frye Jacobson's books present a more complex historical study of whiteness in comparison to these other three historians. While Roediger, Allen, and Ignatiev focus broadly on the economic conditions undergirding whiteness, Jacobson's books look more broadly to political and cultural aspects of whiteness. Jacobson's *Whiteness of a Different Color: European Immigrants and the Alchemy of Race* (Cambridge: Harvard University Press, 1998) tells the story of how European immigrants became white, and his follow-on book *Roots Too: White Ethnic Revival in Post-Civil Rights America* (Cambridge: Harvard University Press, 2006) extends this narrative to examine how there was a white ethnic revival that developed in response to the Civil Rights era.

7   For a broader survey of the history of white people on the world stage, see Nell Irvin Painter, *The History of White People* (New York: W. W. Norton, 2010). This broader history will be considered with the assistance of Willie Jennings' *The Christian Imagination* in chapter 3.

8   Jacobson, *Whiteness of a Different Color*, 3.

these uprisings was to establish laws that allowed the slaves who shared the lighter hues of their owners to work their way out of slavery. Thus, the Naturalization Law of 1790 declared,

> All *free white* persons who have, or shall migrate into the United States, and shall give satisfactory proof, before a magistrate, by oath, that they intend to reside therein, and shall take an oath of allegiance, and shall have resided in the United State for one whole year, shall be entitled to the rights of citizenship.[9]

The designation "free white persons" in this declaration implies that there were white people employed in servitude in 1790. Only later would the attribute "free" become a useless redundancy.[10]

The Naturalization Law of 1790 opened the door for widespread European immigration to the United States. While the initial waves of Irish, Jewish, and Italian immigrants were perceived as "white," they were not instantly seen as "free" or on the same social level as the White Anglo-Saxon Protestants, who shared the prestige of being some of the first immigrants to what would later become the United States. The British immigrants viewed the second and third waves of European immigrants as "white undesirables" who served the function of providing cheap labor. The need for cheap labor, however, competed with the desire to retain Anglo-Saxon democratic control, which was threatened by the camaraderie found between "white undesirables" and the Africans they worked alongside.

The growing threat of "white undesirables" following the Naturalization Law of 1790 was catalogued a century later in William Z. Ripley's influential 624-page text *The Races of Europe* (1899).[11] Ripley wrote *The Races of Europe* by sifting through mounds of data compiled by European anthropologists who had been compulsively measuring their populations for decades. Synthesizing this data, Ripley proposed and described three European racial types, ordered hierarchically: the Teutonic race, categorized as tall and blond; the Alpine (Celtic) race, categorized as medium in stature and with darker features; and the

---

9   *Abridgements of the Debates of Congress, 1789–1856*, vol. 1 of *Annals of Congress* (New York: D. Appleton, 1857), 184. Quoted in Jacobson, *Whiteness of a Different Color*, 22 (emphasis original).

10   Painter, *The History of White People*, 106.

11   William Z. Ripley, *The Races of Europe: A Sociological Study* (New York: D. Appleton, 1899).

Mediterranean race, categorized as short and with the darkest features. *The Races of Europe* illustrates the nineteenth-century sentiment among white Anglo-Saxons (now also grouped with Germans and Scandinavians in the Teutonic race) that the greatness of the United States was under the threat of inferior Europeans. Ripley expressed this concern by contrasting his own Anglo-Saxon ancestry with that of "the motley throng now pouring in upon us."[12]

The internal divisions among European immigrants in the United States only contributed to the reinforcement of the more pronounced barrier between "white" Europeans and those already established as nonwhite. Ripley's classifications pitted differing hues of white Europeans against the threat of darker-skinned Africans and Native Americans, associating citizenship itself with an idealized form of whiteness. Those closer to this ideal, the Celtics for example, presented a more palatable resource for carrying out the cheap labor needed in industrializing America. Still, these "second-class whites" were seen as unpalatable enough, at times, to become a political threat to Anglo-Saxon supremacy. When perceived as a threat, "white undesirables" were polemically associated with the greater threat of those clearly outside the fold of whiteness. For example, the New York *Tribune* characterized the Irish, during the uprising of the New York draft riots in 1863, as a "savage mob," as a "pack of savages," and as "savage foes."[13] The parameters for the vicissitudes of whiteness were preset and kept in place by the permanent boundary of racial otherness codified in the exclusion of Native Americans, in the alienation of Asian immigrants, and in the slavery and lynching of African Americans. Thus, the contest for whiteness only further reinforced the demarcation between white and nonwhite.

These conditions forced lower-class white people to choose a side. Would they side with the nonwhite "other" with whom they were often associated, or would they give their allegiance to the nation-state that offered them the potential power of whiteness? The greatest danger that "second-class whites" presented to the nation-state was their siding with the nonwhite "other." When solidarity between distinct European enclaves and nonwhites formed, the response was a resetting of the boundaries of whiteness to hide the contradiction of American democracy. Bacon's

12   William Z. Ripley, "Race Progress and Immigration," *Annals of the American Academy of Political and Social Science* 34, no. 1 (1909): 130.
13   Richard Henry Dana Jr., *Two Years before the Mast* (1840, 1859; repr., New York: Signet, 1964), 139, 161, 316. Quoted in Jacobson, *Whiteness of a Different Color*, 41.

Rebellion in 1676, for instance, led to the passing of the Virginia Slave Codes of 1705, which hardened the racial caste of slavery by narrowing lifelong servitude to Africans. Similarly, John Brown's attack on Harper's Ferry in 1859 presents the contradiction of a white man who fought against America for the sake of a more democratic America.[14] The hanging of John Brown demonstrated the violence necessary to protect whiteness. Violence goes to the heart of what, ultimately, made "white undesirables" a working part of whiteness in the history of the United States. Whiteness was secured through frontier settlement and ensured through slaveholding. The allegiance to the United States that baptized "white undesirables" into whiteness functioned on the violence that perceived nonwhite bodies as a constant threat to be subdued.[15]

Historians within whiteness studies trace this story of the journey from different European places and ethnic identities into the monolithic tribe of whiteness in the United States with incredible granularity, as seen in books such as Noel Ignatiev's *How the Irish Became White* or Karen Brodkin's *How the Jews Became White Folks*.[16] Even with all this granularity, whiteness studies run up against two major limitations when recounting the language game of becoming white.

The first limitation of whiteness studies is associated with the aim of purely historical research: the historian's task in whiteness studies is to recount the evolution of whiteness, not the theological meaning of this journey. If from a theological perspective all of history lives between promise and fulfillment, then reading the history of white people theologically must involve reflecting on it as transpiring between God's promise and fulfillment in Jesus Christ. The presupposition of theology is that God has spoken and continues to speak in history through Jesus Christ. The question then is: what type of response does the history of whiteness offer to God's address?

The second limitation is that the field of whiteness studies can inadvertently reduce whiteness to a historical or social construct. Whiteness, in a sense, becomes something that happened and happens to white people

14 For a detailed theological appraisal of the anomaly of John Brown and the corresponding ethical implications, see Ted A. Smith, *Weird John Brown: Divine Violence and the Limits of Ethics* (Stanford: Stanford University Press, 2015).

15 Jennifer Harvey makes a similar argument when she suggests that light-skinned peoples were actually racialized as white through violence. "White racial identity itself," she claims, "meant complicity in violence" (*Dear White Christians*, 52).

16 See Ignatiev, *How the Irish Became White*; and Karen Brodkin, *How Jews Became White Folks and What That Says about Race in America* (New Brunswick: Rutgers University Press, 1998).

and, therefore, it is something from which we can imagine our way out. The historical description of "whiteness" in whiteness studies invokes a *static* construct that can obscure the evolving *dynamism* of whiteness as both personal and corporate.[17] Rather than considering whiteness as merely a historical/social *construct*, the approach here is to consider whiteness as a language game that we continually draw from and *conjure* into existence as an ever-changing canvas on which to write. We are always and already participating in the language game of whiteness whether we cognitively recognize it or not. As demonstrated from George Yancy's example of "the elevator effect," discussed in this book's introduction, one *conjures* the language of whiteness through bodily reflexes and microaggressions that arise during everyday exchanges. The woman who clutches her purse and whose white torso trembles because of the approach of Yancy's Black body speaks a language that buffers her from the particularity of encountering another person. Whiteness is an idol repeatedly worshipped for its power to lift us out of the nerve-racking conflicts of daily racial struggles. These acts of worshipping whiteness percolate continually like impromptu prayers to God in the midst of crisis. But unlike the prayers found in the Psalms that thrust us into the pains and hardships of daily life in a fallen creation, the prayers of whiteness mimic the private prayer of the Pharisee: "God, I thank you that I am not like that other sinful person."[18] This is a prayer that closes us to God, neighbor, and earth. It refuses a doxological response of gratitude to God's gracious address.

Because the grammar of social construction found in whiteness studies lends itself to a consideration of whiteness as rationally located beyond the persons upholding and enacting it,[19] whiteness studies can-

17   The African American philosopher Cleavis Headley is suspicious of research like Ignatiev's (and whiteness studies in general), because, he argues, it is inherently reductionist in its description of white people as victims. He writes, "In so viewing whiteness as victimized, that is, in democratizing oppression and placing whiteness and blackness as symmetrically disadvantaged identities, whiteness' true state of being is obscured." See Headley, "Delegitimizing the Normativity of 'Whiteness': A Critical Africana Philosophical Study of the Metaphoricity of 'Whiteness,'" in *What White Looks Like: African-American Philosophers on the Whiteness Question*, ed. George Yancy (New York: Routledge, 2004), 100.

18   In view here is Jesus' teaching on prayer from Luke 18:9–14. Jesus' parable contrasts the tax collector's desperate request for forgiveness with the Pharisee's self-righteous assurance. Jesus concludes that is the tax collector that went "to his home justified rather than the other" (Luke 18:14).

19   Rather than breaking us out of whiteness, Cleavis Headley contends whiteness studies results in creating a formal "notion of equality that serves as a camouflage for whiteness" ("Delegitimizing the Normativity of 'Whiteness,'" 102).

not be relied upon to provide a theological remembering of whiteness as an idol. In contrast, discussing whiteness as a language game exposes how whiteness is an ingrained reflex that is conjured again and again as a deadening response, deafening us to the surprise of the triune God's speaking. The following two sections trace the historical language game of whiteness through examining it through the perspectives of (1) place and (2) time. Place and time are brought together through the surprise of God's gracious address that creates space to theologically remember the history of white people in the United States.

The Spatial Game of Whiteness: From Place to Race

The lands that European explorers stumbled upon and the diversity of peoples living in those lands presented the unprecedented opportunity of listening and responding to God afresh. It is within this promise of God's speaking to Europeans in the "discovery" of peoples and lands that the gravity of the history of white people in the United States comes into full view.

Rather than listening to the peoples and the lands of the Americas, much of the history of early European settlers demonstrates a reflex that resisted a posture of receptivity to God's address through neighbors and the earth. Willie Jennings (whose work will be directly explored in the next chapter) has drawn attention to the theological implications of the movement of bodies across the globe during the colonial era. With the movement of Europeans from Europe to Africa and then from Africa to the Americas, Jennings contends that *place* was exchanged for *race* as the foundational marker of identity. This exchange was facilitated not primarily through racial ideas but through disembodied, reflexive acts that reshaped space around white bodies. The creation of race, then, is not a suspension of relations between human bodies and places but a new facilitation of these relations indexed to white Europeans. As Jennings explains, "Racial being is an act of continual conference in which mutual interdependence is not suspended, but placed on a trajectory toward endless becoming organized around white bodies."[20]

Jennings illustrates how this continual conference shapes space through his discussion of Christopher Columbus' "discovery" of the Americas. He notes how the reflections recorded in Columbus' journals

---

20 Jennings, *The Christian Imagination*, 61.

offer a description of the Americas in reference to other lands being discovered by Europeans at the same time. Jennings comments,

> The power of Columbus's description lies in its comparative range. It connects the bodies of the new land (Africa) to the bodies of the other new land (the Americas), through the exercise of an aesthetic with breathtaking geographic flexibility. The aesthetic is of the land but not the land, of the people but not of the people.[21]

Columbus connects the two lands and peoples (Africa and the Americas) based on his own formulation of space. Jennings suggests that this formulation of space gives reference to different lands and peoples as given through Columbus' European overarching purview of these lands and peoples. This is how Columbus' judgment is "of the land but not the land, of the people but not the people." Columbus observes his own identity and the identity of those he encounters through a broad comparison rather than from within the intricate webs of language, geography, and memory shared by the peoples in these new lands. As Jennings sharply puts it, "European colonialists in acts of breathtaking hubris imagined the interlocking nature of all people and things with their own independence of those very people and things."[22] A new translation of space writes itself over place, and this new translation of space finds itself confined within the shifting vernacular of race.

Europeans who moved across the globe lived between the promise of God's speaking in history and the fulfillment of receiving the surprise of God's grace through encountering new places and peoples. This was a missed opportunity, as the new vernacular of race embodied by European colonialists dictated what was to be heard rather than listening and preparing to hear the surprise of God's address. The reflexive stance of the European immigrants toward the newly encountered peoples and lands is observed in the Third Charter of Virginia (1611–1612), which dedicated the territory of Virginia to "the propagation of the Christian Religion, and Reclaiming of People barbarous, to Civility and Humanity." Or, as announced in the Declaration of Proposals of the Lord Proprietor of Carolina (1663), the settlers came with "a pious and good intention for the propagation of the Christian faith amongst the barbarous and ignorant

---

21 Jennings, *The Christian Imagination*, 30.
22 Jennings, *The Christian Imagination*, 61.

Indians."[23] The new lands and peoples were not seen as consisting of webs of meaning held together by memory, language, and place but as vacant and unconditioned spaces to be written over. The land was interpreted as wilderness to be civilized and the peoples as barbarians to be humanized.

Behind these "pious and good intentions" was a theological translation of the creation disconnected from place, disconnected from the persons, rivers, valleys, mountains, and animals—which coalesce into the constitutive composition of an interconnected community. The movement of Europeans facilitated a reordering of animals (human and nonhuman) and lands. With this movement, European settlers also forcefully moved and displaced other peoples (Africans and Native Americans), reflecting a growing deafness to God's speaking in history through peoples and lands. In his essay "The Coming of the People," Vine Deloria Jr. observes this deafening effect in a description of the white settlers who came to occupy the land:

> He is continually moving about, and his restless nature cannot seem to find peace. Yet he does not *listen* to the land and so cannot find a place for himself. He has few relatives and seems to believe that the domestic animals that have always relied upon him constitute his only link with the other people of the universe. Yet he does not treat these animals as friends but only as objects to be exploited.[24]

The transformation of peoples and lands from perceived chaos to stability signifies the continual progression and organization necessitated by whiteness and underwritten by Christian missionary efforts. To make way for this transformation, the land itself had to be stripped of its meaning, and in the process the creature's intrinsic relation to the creation was displaced. Jennings shares, "It is a loss almost imperceptible except to the bodies of those for whom specific geography and animals continue to gesture to them deep links of identity."[25] The loss of creation escapes those perpetrating this destruction but is felt keenly by those, such as Vine Deloria Jr., who sense a strong connection to the land.

The deafening of whiteness to God's speaking through a loss of place is far reaching. Wendell Berry expands our memories of this loss of place when he argues that Europeans employed African slaves to free

23   Francis Newton Thorpe, *The Federal and State Constitutions, Colonial Charters, and Other Organic Laws of the States, Territories, and Colonies* (Washington: Government Printing Office, 1909), vol. 7, 3802; vol. 5, 2753. Quoted in Jacobson, *Whiteness of a Different Color*, 23.

24   Vine Deloria Jr., *For This Land: Writings on Religion in America* (New York: Routledge, 1999), 241.

25   Jennings, *The Christian Imagination*, 58.

themselves from the burden of stewarding the land.[26] As a result, Europeans were further decoupled from the land they owned. They were freed from the toil of tilling the earth and thus relinquished from partaking in a close connection to the soil—from place. The hidden wound buried in America's racial history is a wound that debilitates our ability to listen to neighbors and the earth, precisely in our forgetting of the interconnection between the two. The concrete result of this loss of place today is a continued degradation of animals (human and nonhuman) and a persistent disdain for the laborious jobs of caretaking. In short, the identity gained through whiteness renders us homeless—we remain vagabonds wandering in a land rendered mute.

The Memory Game of Whiteness: From European to White

The spatial game of whiteness created through the movement of peoples in the colonial era fosters a corresponding memory game. How do we remember our distinct histories—Irish, German, or Italian—when we are no longer connected to the land in which these histories were formed? Each geographic movement represents another layer of distance from the memories of distinctly held histories. The migration across the Atlantic was not the only such move. The loss of a connection to place as a marker of identity continued as Europeans, in large numbers, moved from American cities into newly formed suburbs in the 1900s. This move to the suburbs stripped European ethnic groups of the cultural memories we shared within our enclaves in the city. The food, the language, and the places that tethered us together evaporated in the suburbs, where a blander form of whiteness developed its own social cohesion.

As an example of this loss of memory, the Italian literary critic Louise DeSalvo recalls her mother's refusal to prepare or eat her immigrant grandmother's "peasant bread." DeSalvo's grandmother's traditional food was scorned by her mother because it represented everything her mother, in 1950s suburban New Jersey, was trying not to be.[27] In the suburbs, Italians found refuge from being called "wops" and "dagoes" as they came to share more in common with their new suburban neighbors than with their historical ancestors. Italians, along with other "white undesirables," were able to buy homes and go to college through federally funded programs that strictly benefited those found within the

26   Wendell Berry, *The Hidden Wound* (Farrar: North Point Press, 1989), 112.
27   See Louise DeSalvo, *Crazy in the Kitchen: Foods, Feuds, and Forgiveness in an Italian American Family* (New York: Bloomsbury, 2004), 9–13.

boundaries of whiteness. Thus, again, privilege and power were offered to European ethnic groups through an alignment with American whiteness. This allegiance came with a cost. James Baldwin called it "the price of the white ticket," which in part "is to delude" oneself into believing one is white.[28] As Nell Painter summarizes Baldwin's claim, "Embracing white supremacy and losing their ethnic identities—the price the second generation paid for the ticket to American whiteness."[29]

The space of the suburbs fostered a new memory among white Americans in the well-known imagery of the melting pot. The melting pot narrative pivoted the memory among European ethnics *from* the struggle to be found within whiteness *to* the struggle to build prosperity on whiteness. Inherent in this new struggle for prosperity was the assumption of nonwhite exclusion. For example, the Federal Housing Authority, along with the Veterans Mortgage Guarantee program, financed more than $120 billion in housing between 1934 and 1964, allotted unevenly to European ethnics moving to the suburbs.[30] This financing assisted in building new suburbs like Levittown in Nassau County on Long Island outside of New York City, where each homeowner's contract included a clause that read, "No dwelling shall be used or occupied by members of other than the Caucasian race."[31] Levittown consisted of 82,000 new inhabitants, every one of which, Painter writes, was "lily white."[32] The federal investments that financed the building of these suburbs gave white people the illusion of building our own wealth. In reality, the very basis of this wealth was harnessed from historical inequities that distanced European immigrants from the land and, as a result, from our own historical identities.

The cost of this new memory of whiteness was not only the loss of European historical rootedness but also, more importantly, the missed opportunity, yet again, to hear God speak through the migration of persons. European ethnic groups in the northern parts of the United States had the opportunity to join with and listen to our African American sisters and brothers who moved into cities like Chicago and Detroit as they

28   James Baldwin, *The Price of the Ticket: Collected Nonfiction, 1948–1985* (New York: St. Martin's Press, 1985), xiv.

29   Painter, *The History of White People*, 216.

30   See Ira Katznelson, *When Affirmative Action Was White: An Untold History of Racial Inequality in Twentieth-Century America* (New York: W. W. Norton, 2005), 112–15.

31   Harvie M. Conn, *The American City and the Evangelical Church: A Historical Overview* (Grand Rapids: Baker Books, 1994), 85.

32   Painter, *The History of White People*, 372.

fled from the oppressive conditions of the South. Rather than joining with and listening to African Americans moving into the cities, most white people retreated to the suburbs. As a result, the cities were left to decay under the withdrawal of federal support, which was channeled to build the white suburbs.[33] People of color moved into the cities to work low-paying industrial jobs and were given governmental housing units without the opportunity for ownership. American white Protestants were complicit in this abandonment of the city and forfeited the opportunity to listen as their congregations left the cities to build new community churches in the suburbs. As one example of this, in the late 1970s mainline Presbyterians were abandoning two churches in the city for each one organized in the suburbs.[34]

The migration of white churches out of the city represents countless missed interactions and opportunities to listen to and learn from those who were moving into the cities. One high-profile example of this is observed in the response of white churches to the "Black Manifesto" presented by James Forman on April 26, 1969. The manifesto came out of the Black Economic Development Conference (BEDC) and requested $500 million in reparations to be paid by white churches and Jewish synagogues for losses exacted through the Middle Passage, imperialism, slavery, and colonialism.[35] The white churches that remained in the cities (predominately mainline churches) entertained conversations with Forman and other Black church leaders but largely dismissed the need for paying reparations.[36] The white churches that had more aggressively abandoned the cities (predominately evangelical churches) gave very little thought to the BEDC's demand for reparations. For example, Jennifer Harvey shares how the editors of *Christianity Today* claimed that "liberal Protestants were reaping what they had sown when they confused the work of the gospel with social issues" and that their own evangelical response to the "Black Manifesto" was to dismiss it as an expression

---

33   As an example of this disparity in federal spending, Painter shares that "per capita lending by the FHA for mortgages was eleven times higher on Long Island than in Brooklyn and sixty times more than in the working-class Bronx" (*The History of White People*, 372).

34   Carl Dudley, "Churches in Changing Communities," in *Metro-Ministry: Ways and Means for the Urban Church*, ed. David Frenchak and Sharrel Keyes (Eglin: David C. Cook, 1979), 78–79.

35   Harvey, *Dear White Christians*, 128.

36   For an example of how mainline churches reacted to the "Black Manifesto," see Harvey's account of the response of the Episcopal Church to the "Black Manifesto" in *Dear White Christians*, 126–27.

of an "implicit repudiation of biblical revelation" coming out of liberal schools such as Union Seminary.[37]

This dismissal of the "Black Manifesto" represents how whiteness has served as a buffer that insulates the white church from listening to people of color about our joint history with the land. The migration of Black people to American cities offered the opportunity for white churches to listen to the challenges faced by Black people, the challenge of being removed from the land that they had cultivated for white people shortly after gaining the freedom to steward it for themselves. This loss of land is observed in the fact that the number of Black-owned farms fell from 916,000 in 1920 to 30,000 by 1988.[38] During the lynching era, the lives and livelihoods of Black people became increasingly threatened by white violence in more rural areas.[39] White Europeans of various shades were finding safety in the very places that threatened the lives of those deemed nonwhite. This safety reflected an insulation from the many layers of history written onto the land itself as a new memory formed within whiteness.

The language game of whiteness evolved into new spaces with the global migration patterns from Europe to Africa and from Africa to the Americas, and evolved again with the domestic migration patterns from the cities to the suburbs. These shifting migrations hinder us from remembering how God has spoken in history and how our historical lives remain bound to God's promise and fulfillment in Jesus Christ. Our inability to recollect, repair, and lament this history impacts our ability to listen and respond to God's address today. As will be discussed in act two, these migrations and losses of memory continue into the present, making the language game of whiteness ever more covert.

Act Two: The Language Game of Camouflaging Whiteness

The second act of the history of white people in the United States is a follow-up to the first. As a second act, its power is derived from the

37   Harvey, *Dear White Christians*, 120. For the article that Harvey references, see Editors, "Union Seminary: An Ethical Dilemma," *Christianity Today* 13 (June 6, 1969): 27.

38   See Berry, *The Hidden Wound*, 117.

39   In *The Cross and the Lynching Tree*, Cone describes how it was only after the abolition of slavery that lynching became a commonly used tactic to control Black people. This is because lynching no longer presented a financial loss of property for white slaveholders. As a result, the lynching era became the nightmare introduced within the hope of Reconstruction. See *The Cross and the Lynching Tree*, 4–11.

history preceding it and the absence of remembering this history. The same reflexes of whiteness observed in the United States' earlier history informs a reflex that continues to hinder our sensitivity to God's speaking today. The aim in exploring our present situation in this manner is not to condemn white people but to foster our responsiveness to God's speaking in the midst of the evolving ecosystem of whiteness that defines the present. The second act of the history of white people in the United States has changed the rules of the game, making the language of whiteness increasingly subtle and covert. While the manner in which we conjure whiteness may change with time, God's speaking through Jesus Christ remains constant. It is God's relentless call that moves us to explore the hindrances caused by whiteness today. These hindrances must not only be made known but also challenged as we seek to prepare the way for the God revealed in Jesus Christ, who beckons God's people to respond here and now.

The Rocky Balboa Effect: Changing the Rules of the Game through the Return to Ethnicity

The language game of whiteness evolved following the Civil Rights Movement. Whereas America's origins in whiteness required a relinquishing of European ethnicity, the progress brought on by the Civil Rights Movement led to an impulse among white people to reclaim European ethnicity. The foundational source of this impulse, ironically, was a jealousy among white people toward the vibrant identities of people of color that showed forth in the struggle for civil rights. These jealous intentions are often missed, as the jealousy of white people is filtered through a retelling of history that allows us to evade the problem of whiteness. The forces of jealousy and evasion combine to offer a white pushback on the progress achieved through the Civil Rights Movement.

The public discourse arising from the Civil Rights Movement illuminated the salience of whiteness and the resilience of Black Americans in the struggle for equal rights. Rather than submitting to this growing awareness of whiteness as God's call to prepare the way for God's coming, white people, by and large, discovered new methods for securing whiteness. This self-securing of whiteness manifested itself through a reflexive pushback that sought to recapture and retell the struggles faced by different white ethnic groups. The African American historian Nell Painter comments on this reflexive response among white people:

> Now the most fascinating racial identity was black, not white, a flip certain to disturb those who had struggled so hard to measure up to Anglo-Saxon standards. Working class whites who resented being ignored, Catholics who felt vulnerable in academia, and Jews who were used to having the last word were all deeply offended. And white people pushed back.[40]

The effective way in which white people pushed back was not primarily through an explicit challenge of civil rights for African Americans but through a nostalgic reclaiming of our European heritages. As a reflexive response, white people embraced the European roots of our ancestors—the same historical roots that our parents and grandparents attempted to leave behind for a ticket into American whiteness. The return to ethnicity allowed white people to overlap our own histories with the distinct struggle waged by African Americans for civil rights, thereby reshaping the narrative. The contest for Black lives was muffled by the contention that all lives matter.

The covetous desire among white people to recover our ethnic roots was bolstered through the budding narrative of the United States as a nation of immigrants. In the telling of this narrative, the mythical origins of the United States shifted from the coastlines of Plymouth Rock to the shores of Ellis Island. The landing of the Mayflower on Plymouth Rock invokes the dark memories of conquest, the middle passage, and slavery. In contrast, the arrival of "huddled masses" on Ellis Island with yearnings "to breathe free" furnishes the nostalgic image of poor Europeans gathered together to make the United States into one great nation "under God." This nostalgic recreation of the United States as a nation of immigrants asserts white supremacy "draped in a celebratory rhetoric of diversity and inclusion."[41] The narrative of an immigrant nation is a white narrative that eclipses Black slavery and disenfranchisement, Native American slaughter and removal, Chinese exclusion and forced labor, Mexican defeat and annexation, and Japanese imprisonment in internment camps. White people assume the power of whiteness enshrined in the "melting pot" narrative through the narrative's inherent exclusion of people of color, who did not enter America through Ellis

---

40 Painter, *The History of White People*, 377.
41 Jacobson, *Roots Too*, 9.

Island. Telling this narrative, again and again, exhibits a reflex that buffers white people from listening to God's continual call in the midst of the changing language game of whiteness.

The Civil Rights Movement presented white Americans with the opportunity to process and lament the racial nightmare of our history. It was at this key point in our history, however, that the idea of an immigrant nation gained a new formulation in books such as Michael Novak's *Unmeltable Ethnics* (1972). Rather than gaining power through whiteness, Novak presents white ethnics as the neglected American underdog. He shares the sentiments of many white immigrants in responding to the accusations of a Native American man by reminding him, "*my* grandparents . . . never *saw* an Indian. They came to this country after that. Nor were they responsible for enslaving the blacks (or anyone else). They themselves escaped serfdom barely four generations ago."[42] This claim of the "newcomer" provides not only a self-distancing from white privilege but also a more sinister covetousness that flips the script of the United States' history to establish white supremacy under the guise of ethnicity. As seen in Novak's book, the return to ethnicity implies that, instead of being seen as the oppressors, white ethnics are actually the continual underdogs fighting against disadvantage.

This underdog narrative of the white ethnic went mainstream through the combination of a California Supreme Court decision in 1976 and the release of the blockbuster film *Rocky* in the same year. The California Supreme Court ruled in favor of Allan Bakke, who sued UC Davis Medical School on the basis that he had been racially discriminated against as a white man because of affirmative action. On September 16, 1976, the California Supreme Court ruled that UC Davis Medical School's affirmative action policy was unconstitutional for denying Bakke's application.[43] This ruling limited the scope of affirmative action for the next several decades. The legislation of affirmative action, birthed from the Civil Rights Movement, was stillborn. As one African American newspaper summed it up, "Bakke—We Lose."[44]

A few weeks after the California Supreme Court's decision in favor of Bakke, Sylvester Stallone's cult classic *Rocky* opened in theaters across

---

42   Michael Novak, *The Rise of the Unmeltable Ethnics: Politics and Culture in the Seventies* (New York: Macmillan, 1971), xx.

43   Jacobson, *Roots Too*, 98.

44   Bernard Schwartz, *Behind Bakke: Affirmative Action and the Supreme Court* (New York: New York University Press, 1988), 148.

America. The historian Matthew Frye Jacobson comments on the connection between the Bakke case and Stallone's first motion picture:

> The Bakke case and the boxing film shared more than a historical
> moment: they shared an ethos, a way of understanding the respec-
> tive meanings of "whiteness" and "blackness" in post-Civil Rights
> America. If the white applicant had unjustly become an underdog
> under Title VI admissions practices, as the California court held,
> Rocky Balboa dramatized precisely that underdog status in his
> titanic struggle to unseat the flashy and arrogant black champion,
> Apollo Creed.[45]

The story line of *Rocky* flips the script of America's racial history by
placing the unassuming, friendly, and humble Italian American Rocky
Balboa, an obscure fighter from one of Philadelphia's roughest working-
class neighborhoods, against the "flashy and arrogant" reigning champion Apollo Creed. The film rests decidedly upon the racial lines of
Black advantage and white disadvantage. The film depicts the position
of advantage and power in the hands of Apollo Creed, who demands
a "snow white" opponent, whom he has the power to handpick. While
Rocky Balboa is the white competitor that Creed selects, the film subtly
proposes that the "Italian Stallion" is a different shade of white. Rocky
is a powerless Italian immigrant struggling to make a living under the
gritty conditions of white squalor. In stark contrast, Apollo Creed is a
demigod with all the glitz and glamour of a flamboyant celebrity.

Following this storyline, "the real discrimination," we often com-
plain, "is not against Black people but the poor white people who are
neglected in the struggle for civil rights." This grievance is inculcated
through our reflexive identification with the underdog status of Rocky
Balboa. Inculcating this storyline subtly convolutes our nation's history
by equating the valid struggles faced by individual white people with
the systemic violence perpetrated against people of color over centuries
up until today. As with Columbus, we offer a broad comparison that
inherently places Black people against white people instead of seeking
to listen to another person's pain without pondering one's own rebuttal.

This convolution of America's racial history only intensifies in
the racial contrast drawn out between the two fighters in *Rocky 2*. In
a television interview, Creed publicly humiliates and insults Rocky's

45   Jacobson, *Roots Too*, 98.

masculinity by switching his name from "the Italian Stallion" to "the Italian Chicken." Rocky, on the other hand, is hesitant about coming out of retirement, and when prodded by a reporter to say something derogatory about Apollo Creed, he responds, "Derogatory? Yeah, he's great." This simple-minded and confused answer illustrates Balboa's innocent character and humble decency. Through Creed's flamboyance and Rocky's humility, the narrative of the two *Rocky* films cunningly inverts the white-over-Black power dynamics to depict white people as the victims and Black people as the oppressors. The film generates an inherent identification with Rocky's well-deserving cause and likable character. Rocky is not a white supremacist. He is not even interested in being a representative for overlooked white people. As the film portrays him, Rocky is not even to be seen as white; Balboa is Italian. And yet Rocky symbolizes the ethos of white backlash. He embodies the grievances of white ethnics in the 1970s and has become the poster boy of the fallacy of white victimization.

The Bakke legal case and the legendary tale of *Rocky* have become so intertwined in our collective memories of white grievance and victimization that few can remember their divergent outcomes. Allan Bakke, who was labeled in a headline from the *New York Times* as "White/Caucasian and Rejected," *won* his case, while Rocky Balboa, the icon of white ethnic victimization, *lost* the fight.[46] Rocky's bloody brawl with Creed went all fifteen rounds, proving the stamina and power of the underdog to persist in the fight. In the end, however, the victory was given to the reigning champion in a split decision that the film depicts as another injustice done to Rocky. This injustice done to Rocky overshadows the split decision of the Supreme Court justices who ultimately decided on behalf of Bakke, a win for white people everywhere. The triumphal image of Rocky raising his fists in victory, with all the subtle connotations it represents, has been memorialized in the statue erected in his honor on the steps of the Philadelphia Art Museum and in the countless Rocky posters in bedrooms and offices throughout the country. The film earned $225 million in global box office sales, making it the highest-grossing film of 1976, and it won three Oscars, including Best Picture. While the *Rocky* film portrayed Apollo Creed with the control and power to select his white competitor, the film's popularity demonstrates the pervasive power inherited by white people to write our own history and to rewrite this history as a denial of our privileged inheritance.

46   Jacobson, *Roots Too*, 98.

The Bakke case and the *Rocky* film are exemplary instances of the profound ways white people "pushed back" following the Civil Rights Movement.[47] Our method for pushing back was not given in a direct challenge of African Americans but through the subtle means of telling a new narrative—evolving the language game of whiteness. The shrewd power in this newest iteration of whiteness is found in how it portrays itself as correcting historical racial disparities. If whiteness is the problem, should we not seek to eradicate it through returning to our various white ethnicities? The problem with such an approach is that it moves past the painful history of the United States through a selective recovery of white ethnic heritage. Rather than waiting for the surprise of God's address, whiteness leaves us in an enclosed echo chamber. From this echo chamber of our own making, we offer reflexive solutions to the problem of whiteness.

The only way back to our European ethnic roots is through the painful history that exchanged ethnicity for race. To travel this path requires that we carefully attend to how we remember our past today and how we spatially view the present. It requires an open responsiveness that waits for the surprise of God's address rather than rushing into reflexive solutions.

The Memory Game of Ethnicity: White Mediation of Diversity

The difficulty of returning to our white ethnic roots is that by the 1960s and 1970s, much of the cultural heritage of our European ancestors had already been forfeited in the process of becoming white. We no longer spoke our ancestors' language, ate their food, or wore their clothes. This still did not stop many of us from seeking to regain a memory of our long-lost European lineages. We sought to return to a "better" time rather than listening to how God addresses us today through the tragedy of our racial past. This yearning for a "better" time fuels the search for our ethnic identities and our nostalgic aspirations to reclaim them on our own terms.

Nowhere has this yearning for our past been fulfilled as powerfully as through the medium of film. The films and television shows that many of us grew up with gained potency through harnessing our longing to reconnect with our white ethnic roots. *The Sopranos*, *The Godfather I* and *II*, and *Fiddler on the Roof* are examples of popular

---

47   Painter, *The History of White People*, 377.

movies that sought to recast our imaginations into specific ethnic traditions. Even a movie such as *Grease*, which may not directly deal with
ethnic traditions, works subtly to support a reclaiming of ethnic identity. *Grease* features immigrants like Betty Rizzo and Danny Zuko,
who are cast as the "true" Americans. The ethnic vibrancy of Rizzo
and Zuko present the image to which, in the end, a lily-white Sandy
Alston must conform by sporting a new perm, black leather pants,
and a cigarette. Similarly, more recent films such as *Titanic* clean up
the filth of early immigrant images by casting white ethnics as those
who embrace life by drinking beer and dancing in the hull of the ship
while the cultured, wealthy white people gloomily eat their fine meals
quietly on the main deck. Jacobson argues that the American film
industry has helped to recast the normative American social location
from "simple whiteness to a distinct brand of Ellis Island whiteness."[48]
The once "undesirable" white ethnic is now remembered as an icon of
American success rather than representing the violent struggle into
whiteness that inherently excluded people of color. Thus, the history of
white ethnicity offers a specific selection of what we remember. With
this selective history comes the risk that we will miss how God has
spoken in the past and continues to speak today.

The memory of white ethnicity is not only selective but also
reduces history to a commodity for our own leisurely consumption.
Painter explains that "the white ethnicity of the late twentieth century was little more than a leisure activity, one that American entre-
preneurs embraced. Ethnic consumers could buy T-shirts imprinted
with European flags, take tours of the old country, and parade in the
street on ethnic holidays."[49] American corporations built an onslaught
of marketing campaigns around connecting their brands to their
consumers' desires to relive the simpler times of our ethnic prede-
cessors. In 1984 *Fortune* magazine proclaimed that the "ethnic sell"
was informing the advertising of big business: "Thirteen corporations,
including Coca-Cola, Eastman Kodak, and Kellogg, have launched ad
campaigns tied to the 1986 Statue of Liberty centennial celebration."[50]
The immigrant narrative offered corporations a friendly and family-
oriented message that resonated with white Americans. Ethnicity was

---

48   Jacobson, *Roots Too*, 74.
49   Painter, *The History of White People*, 377.
50   *Fortune*, August 20, 1984, 10. Quoted in Jacobson, *Roots Too*, 51.

not simply something a person was; ethnicity became something one could brand, sell, explore, and buy.

Political branding followed a similar trend in 2004 when the Republican Party kicked off its national convention on the sacred ground of Ellis Island. The gesture towards Ellis Island "represented the Republican Party's commitment to diversity," a party for "the people" made up of immigrants like the Bushes, Cheneys, Patakis, and Giulianis, whose names are enshrined on the site's "wall of honor."[51] This memorializing of Ellis Island suggests how the Civil Rights Movement itself has been drawn into a more inclusive, national narrative of "white" progression toward multiculturalism. The actions later taken by the Bush administration to induct Rosa Parks into the pantheon of our national heroes makes this clear. "Proclaiming her to be a national hero," the Black activist Angela Davis decries, "was tantamount to declaring the struggle against racism to have ended in ultimate triumph." Davis continues, "Rosa Park's body has been transmuted into a symbol of victory over racial injustice and inequality."[52] While certainly the Civil Rights Movement created progress for people of color through desegregation and the Civil Right Act of 1964 and the Voting Rights Act of 1965, it was followed by a response that made whiteness more covert and more palatable for mass consumption.

Along with the film industry, the market, and politics, theology also has taken up the challenge of remembering ethnicity within the racial landscape of the United States. The theological side of this endeavor is seen in books such as Miroslav Volf's *Exclusion and Embrace*, which serves to subtly shift theological race discussions from a conversation about whiteness and oppression to one about ethnic identity and otherness. As mentioned in the previous chapter, Volf's *Exclusion and Embrace* was written based on his experiences coming out of the Croat-Bosniak war. Nonetheless, as a professor at Fuller Theological Seminary and at Yale University, his writings are connected immediately to the racial context of America. Similar to how the narrative presented in *Rocky* subtly proposes that Balboa is a different shade of white, the reception of Volf's work in the United States

---

51   Sheng-Mei Ma, *The Deathly Embrace: Orientalism and Asian American Identity* (Minneapolis: University of Minnesota Press, 2000), 155.

52   Angela Y. Davis, *The Meaning of Freedom* (San Francisco: City Light Books, 2012), 117.

can delicately elude whiteness through his speaking as a Croatian.[53] As a first-generation immigrant, Volf's connection is to his homeland in Croatia and the memories of oppression faced there. When brought into the American context, however, Volf's reflections on identity and otherness can have the unattended effect of feeding into the resurgence of white ethnicity. Volf's broadening of the context from his new home in the United States to his previous home abroad in Croatia follows a similar shift among white ethnics at the conclusion of the Civil Rights Movement. Jacobson comments, "Soviet domination in the nations of the Eastern Bloc, the 'Troubles' in Northern Ireland, the Israeli wars of 1967 and 1973, the 'Prague Spring' of 1968, and the workers' movement in Poland all captured the attention and sympathy of overseas ethnic compatriots."[54] Race is overcome, in a sense, within the more palatable language of ethnicity—a language that, in the present moment, has been used to mask the historical disparities birthed through whiteness in the particular history of the United States. These are not the ideas that Volf presents in *Exclusion and Embrace* but the possible consequences of how our words fit into the web of meaning upheld by the evolving language game of whiteness. The danger is that our longings for a multiethnic diversity that addresses race can easily evade the history of whiteness handed down to us.

Downstream from the theological academy, the American church has faced similar struggles in navigating the complexities of distinguishing between ethnicity and race. The multiethnic church movement represents one example of how the Protestant church has dealt with these complexities. In an attempt to provide a positive response to racial segregation, the multiethnic church movement, in general, has steered away from the language of race toward the language of ethnicity. This is seen in how the very name of the movement uses the term "multiethnic" rather than "multiracial." The Cuban American pastor Gerardo Marti gives the reasoning for this altered vernacular in his book *A Mosaic of Believers: Diversity and Innovation in a Multiethnic Church*. Marti explains that his church avoids the language of race out of "fear that use of the term 'multiracial' could unintentionally reinforce

---

53   In the introduction of *Exclusion and Embrace*, Volf speaks explicitly as a Croatian in his framing of the book. He switches quickly between discussing the "genocidal aftermath" of the discovery of America and his memory of the many houses that "bore the scars of Serbian shelling." Volf draws these together to argue that "various kinds of cultural 'cleansing' demand of us *to place identity and otherness at the center of theological reflection* on social realities." See Volf, *Exclusion and Embrace*, 17 (emphasis original).

54   Jacobson, *Roots Too*, 26.

socially constructed racial boundaries."[55] There is wisdom in this statement in that it shows a healthy awareness of the potency of race that lives on today, but the short-term gains of not directly addressing race leave the power of whiteness uninterrupted and unchallenged. Left to fester, whiteness grows into more pervasive and subversive configurations of power imbalances.

David Stevens, another pastor, offers a more nuanced approach toward the language of ethnicity. He uses the language of race to discuss race as a problem that confronts the church but turns to the language of ethnicity in discussing the solution to this problem in terms of the church's corporate identity in Christ.[56] While this shift in language may seem trivial, its power is in changing the rules of the game from a racial grid that illuminates the salience of whiteness to an ethnic grid that allows for a diversity covertly facilitated by whiteness. It is often African Americans, who have lived through centuries of oppression in America, that are the first to sense this unequal playing field in churches that claim to be inclusive of all. Marti honestly points to some of these complexities when he shares that many "African Americans equate Mosaic [his church] with assimilated 'white' culture."[57] Language matters, especially when a conflation or confusion of the terms "race" and "ethnicity" inhibits the church's access to the historical problem of race and, with it, God's call to the church in history.

The memory game of whiteness in the United States is a remembering entrenched in the desire to rise above one's own historical conditioning. This yearning has led white people into a selective narration of history, a commodification of identity, and an evasion of the truth of who we are. In short, God's speaking in history is muffled through the loquaciousness of our own voices. Whiteness affords us with a false sense of control over our past, which hinders us from listening to our past as God's call waiting to be heard. Nonwhite participants have been inducted into this memory game as whiteness has evolved to include a diversity of voices mediated by whiteness. What connects this new configuration of whiteness to its earlier iterations is a selective amnesia of the past that disconnects one from history and God's active working at

55 Marti, *A Mosaic of Believers*, 29.
56 For his discussion of race, see Stevens, *God's New Humanity*, 54–55; and for his discussion of ethnic diversity gathered in the corporate identity of Christ, see *God's New Humanity*, 125.
57 Marti, *A Mosaic of Believers*, 161.

all times and in every place. God speaks at every point in history, especially the points in history we would rather soon forget.

The Spatial Game of Ethnicity: Gentrification as a "More Pleasing Name for White Supremacy"

The spatial game of *ethnicity* perpetuates the transference from place
to race through the recent return of white people back to American
cities. The relocation of white people to America's cities represents a
deep longing to recover an identity already forfeited. This desire for
identity and belonging presents the occasion either for a listening to
God's call through an open responsiveness to history and neighbors or
for an obscuring of God's call through a predisposed reflex to history
and neighbors. In the movement of bodies into new spaces, our sensitivity to God's call is revealed. Thus, the gentrification of cities across
America is not only a social and political issue but also a spiritual pre-
dicament with which the Christian church must grapple with ears to
hear and eyes to see.

Gentrification refers to the transformation of a neighborhood that
takes place under the influence of an influx of affluent newcomers. The
arrival of new residents not only increases home prices and rents; it also
reshapes the landscape of the neighborhood around the preferences of
the incoming gentry—the landowners. This transformation incurs both
a *physical* displacement of the neighborhood's lower-income residents
and a *social* displacement of the historical residents who remain in the
neighborhood. Theologically read, gentrification is to be understood as
a loss of land and identity, both for those moving in and for those displaced physically and socially. The loss of land and identity impacts both
parties, although in very different ways.

Those who debate the impacts of gentrification often weigh the
benefits versus the costs. The upside to gentrification is that it brings
investment and development into disinvested parts of a city, making
these places more livable. The downside to gentrification is that these
developments, most often, benefit those moving into the city to a greater
proportion than those previously residing there. This simple weighing
of gentrification ignores the historical inequities of race, and how these
play into the strategic plans that go into "revitalizing" a city. When
considering gentrification, we must ask how cities in the United States
were formed as places of disinvestment and as pipelines for America's

Industrial Prison Complex in the first place.[58] Attending to the history of white peoples' evacuation and return to the city reveals gentrification to be a contemporary outworking of a long racial history of migration and displacement. This history is what Ta-Nehisi Coates accounts for in his definition of the term:

> I know that "gentrification" is but a more pleasing name for white supremacy, is the interest on enslavement, the interest on Jim Crow, the interest on redlining, compounding across the years, and these new urbanites living off of that interest are, all of them, exulting in a crime.[59]

Coates goes on to sympathize with white people as profoundly caught within the wheels of history. This sentiment, however, is not meant to excuse white people but to make us all the more keenly aware of our historical culpability.

Because of the racial disparity formed over generations, the return to the city represents an affordable investment opportunity for young white professionals supported by the wealth of our parents, gained in the suburbs. Starting in the late sixties and early seventies, federal and local governments offered funds to middle- and upper-class pioneers who moved into the central city. The urban geographer Loretta Lees contends that the government justified these funds by arguing these places were "too risky for the private sector."[60] Gentrification began with individual pioneers and homesteaders (much like the early colonies), who were later followed by developers who made capital investments shaped around

---

58   For a discussion of the various pipelines that flow into American prisons to create an unequal representation of people of color in incarceration, see Dominique Dubois Gillard, *Rethinking Incarceration: Advocating for Justice That Restores* (Downers Grove: InterVarsity Press, 2018). In particular, Gillard's chapter on "The School-to-Prison Pipeline" addresses how the disinvestment of inner-city schools has contributed to a disproportionate number of people of color in America's prisons.

59   Ta-Nehisi Coates, *We Were Eight Years in Power: An American Tragedy* (New York: One World Publishing, 2017), 86.

60   Loretta Lees, Tom Slater, and Elvin K. Wyly, *Gentrification* (New York: Routledge, 2007), 175. Examples of how the government supported gentrification during this time include the 1954 housing act that provided federal funds for the redevelopment of blighted areas in the USA. Developers and investors were busy building the suburbs during this time. It was not until the global economic recession starting in 1973 that the private sector's involvement was drawn to the inner city. As property values dropped during the recession, developers and investors began to purchase large portions of neighborhoods in the central city.

providing amenities for this new social class within the city. Ironically, the urban development constructed for this new social class offered an approximation of the city's historical diversity. The younger generation of white people moving back into America's cities had become disillusioned by the sterile suburbs and saw the city as a place that embodied the multifaceted beauty of greater diversity and globalism.[61] The paradox is that this appetite for a new place in the city, apart from an awareness of persisting historical inequities, created a commodification of the "minority" experience for privileged white people.

This paradox is expressed in what some have called the "gentrification aesthetic."[62] The gentrification aesthetic is an architectural and social character patterned after a nostalgic yet disconnected embrace of the past. The paramount example of this is the transformation of warehouses, found in former industrial districts, into lofts. The sociologist Sharon Zukin argues loft living is attractive to a younger generation that holds a romanticized picture of the industrial past.[63] The apparent disconnect found here is captured succinctly by Zukin when she states, "Only people who do not know the steam and sweat of a real factory can find industrial space romantic or interesting."[64] So whereas the possessive power of whiteness channeled the previous generation of white people into the suburbs, the newest iteration of whiteness that celebrates diversity has channeled the present generation of white people back into the city. The great irony in all of this is that neither generation has ended up with what they originally intended. As people of color are pushed out of the city and into the surrounding suburbs, younger white people in the city are found in increasingly homogenous

61   Matthew Rofe found that in Australia many of the young professionals moving into the city "lamented a growing backlash of bigotry and xenophobia perceived to arise from a fear of global integration," and thus moved to the city to distance "themselves further from a myopic mainstream Australian culture." See Matthew Rofe, "'I Want to Be Global': Theorising the Gentrifying Class as an Emergent Elite Global Community," *Urban Studies* 40, no. 12 (2003): 2520. Many of the young white professionals moving into American cities share these same sensibilities of cherishing diversity and globalism.

62   For a discussion of the gentrification aesthetic, see Michael Jager, "Class Definition and the Esthetics of Gentrification: Victoriana in Melbourne," in *Gentrification of the City*, ed. Neil Smith and Peter Williams (Boston: Allen and Unwin, 1986), 78–91.

63   Zukin traces how derelict manufacturing spaces in the SoHo district of New York City first attracted artists, which later created the cultural catalyst for the commercial redevelopment of lower Manhattan. Sharon Zukin, *Loft Living: Culture and Capital in Urban Change* (New Brunswick: Rutgers University Press, 1989).

64   Zukin, *Loft Living*, 59.

spaces, while older white people in the suburbs are found in increasingly diverse spaces. The younger sought diversity and got homogeneity; the older sought homogeneity and got diversity. God continues to speak in the midst of our waywardness. We restlessly search for God; all the while God is calling out waiting to be heard, here and now.

This is not to suggest that gentrification is some kind of divine joke. It represents a new orchestration of racial violence through more covert means. Gentrification demonstrates how whiteness continues to be conjured up in the new wrapping of "a progressive liberal cloak of equality, impartiality, and equal treatment."[65] Moreover, gentrification reveals how whiteness has metastasized from the colonial moment to the present moment, from place "to race to status to property as a progression historically rooted in white supremacy."[66] There remains the opportunity to learn from this history in acknowledging it as an impairment of our ability to hear God's call. Whiteness creates a loss of place and identity as it creates new spaces that insulate white people from neighbor and land. The Christian church must wrestle with this loss of place and identity as it prepares for God's word to be spoken. Unfortunately, in its own move from the suburbs back into the city, the Christian church has struggled to locate itself among the people and the land as it searches for its own vitality within America's changing landscapes.

A view into the evolving shape of Christian congregations in American cities is given in the sociological research of Richard Cimino, carried out in the lower east side of New York City. In a paper published in 2011, Cimino describes his observations of thirty Christian churches from 2007 to 2009 in the gentrifying neighborhoods of Williamsburg and Greenpoint in Brooklyn.[67] In observing the attendance in these different churches, Camino found that younger and more transient newcomers to the neighborhood gravitated toward the more "missional" churches, such as Resurrection Presbyterian Church (an offshoot of Tim Keller's Redeemer Presbyterian Church) and North Brooklyn Vineyard Church. These "missional" churches are the ones in which Camino charts the most growth in attendance. In contrast, the "neighborhood-social center" congregations with a long-standing presence in the neighborhood and the "ethnic enclave" churches that ministered to non-English speakers saw

65   Headley, "Delegitimizing the Normativity of 'Whiteness,'" 96.

66   Cheryl Harris, "Whiteness as Property," *Harvard Law Review* 106, no. 8 (1993): 1713.

67   Richard Cimino, "Neighborhoods, Niches, and Networks: The Religious Ecology of Gentrification," *City & Community* 10, no. 2 (2011): 157–81.

diminished attendance. Based on his research Cimino concludes that gentrification can result in a "religious revitalization . . . expressed in congregations competing for members on a limited basis as they seek out and exploit niches in order to survive and meet the needs brought on by neighborhood change."[68] He argues that gentrification in Brooklyn has fragmented neighborhoods into an increased number of niches and networks around which different congregations tailor their identities. As younger white professionals move into the city, new churches form around these new arrivals. While the longer-standing churches seek to retain members through providing transportation and affordable housing, the identities of the "missional" churches coalesce around a sort of "gentrification aesthetic" that celebrates diversity in spaces becoming predominately white.

The real struggle that gentrification presents is how it occurs through the good intentions of white Christians to connect with the past and to live into a concrete expression of the gospel. White Christians have often moved to the city as an opportunity to reconnect to a richer history than the one we grew up with in the white suburbs. Christian author Sean Benesh discusses the appeal of gentrification as a means of reconnecting to the past. He offers the city as a way for Christians to make a break from modernism through a reconnection to history and place. He writes, "The appeal of these neighborhoods and such things as loft living is the attempt to reconnect with the past, carve out a sense of identity, [and] cultivate a deeper sense of place."[69] The desire that Benesh taps into is one that seeks to "reconnect" to the past rather than finding ourselves intrinsically knit into it. This slight alteration in our approach to history and place lends itself to an endorsement of loft living along the lines of what Zukin describes as a romanticized picture of the industrial past. The ability to tell our own story and history allows white Christians today to live out the racial disparities of previous generations, often without recognizing it. Anthony Smith, an African American leader, claims, "There needs to be recognition that the emerging church is still a child of larger North American Christianity. This lack of awareness leads to some unconscious racial habits."[70] Through these unconscious racial habits,

68   Cimino, "Neighborhoods, Niches, and Networks," 157–58.

69   Sean Benesh, "The Appeal of Gentrification," in *Vespas, Cafes, Singlespeed Bikes, and Urban Hipsters: Gentrification, Urban Mission, and Church Planting*, ed. Sean Banesh (Portland: Urban Loft Publishers, 2014), 102.

70   Soong-Chan Rah offers this quote based on a phone conversation he had with Smith. See Soong-Chan Rah, *The Next Evangelicalism: Freeing the Church from Western Cultural Captivity* (Downers Grove: InterVarsity Press, 2009), 119.

the majority of white church planters and white parishioners (especially within Evangelical denominations) have unknowingly accommodated themselves to the de-coloring of cities across the United States. The land has again been displaced, precisely in our distorted desire to make our own connections with history and place rather than seeing ourselves as already part of a racial history in motion and as already connected to the land in strange and violent ways.

Conclusion

The history of white people in the United States is, in many ways, a lost history. The term "white" is a familiar racial designation today, but what "white" means is often difficult to pin down. This incoherence around the term "white" is revealed when one asks a racially mixed group of people to list five unique characteristics associated with their racial identity.[71] While those of European ancestry (or those racially designated as white) usually struggle to come up with one or two unique characteristics associated with being white, people of color can often quickly list a handful of unique characteristics associated with their race. Part of the difficulty of remembering our history as white people is that reflections on race conjure memories of inequity and violence that leave us feeling guilty and lead us into the common occurrence of white fragility.[72] The buffer of whiteness formed throughout our history is the very thing that makes it difficult to recollect our history. While the history of our white identity may escape our collective memory, it remains a history that conditions us and configures the spaces within which we live and move. White people suffer from an amnesia that hinders our ability to relate to God, neighbor, and the earth. What we have lost is not simply our connection

71   Jennifer Harvey shares her experiences of asking this question to diverse audiences. See Harvey, *Dear White Christians*, 43–45. My own mixed-race church experienced this exercise by placing sticky notes on the wall listing unique characteristics associated with our race. The number of sticky notes placed on the wall by people of color far outnumbered those placed on the wall by white congregants.

72   The term "white fragility" refers to the defensive posture often triggered in white people in discussing race. Robin DiAngelo develops this concept in her book *White Fragility: Why It's So Hard for White People to Talk about Racism* (Boston: Beacon Press, 2018). DiAngelo explains, "Though white fragility is triggered by discomfort and anxiety, it is born of superiority and entitlement. White fragility is not weakness per se. In fact, it is a powerful means of white racial control and protection of white advantage" (*White Fragility*, 2).

to history but, at bottom, our sensitivity to God's continual speaking in history through Jesus Christ.

The goal of remembering the history of white people in the United States is not to find our way out of it but to find our place in it. As the language game of whiteness has developed with time, our dependency on it increases while our awareness of it wanes. We speak the language so well that we no longer grasp its inner grammar—how it functions on a daily basis to insulate us from God, neighbor, and the earth. Reviewing the history of white people in the United States helps reveal this inner grammar and how it has evolved throughout our country's history. Act one traced how a loss of land and place transpired through our migration from Europe and European ethnicity to the suburbs and a monolithic tribe of white people. Unfortunately, most accounts of the history of white people end here, failing to connect this history to our lives today. It is safer to leave our painful racial history in the past rather than attending to the ways this history lives on—in and through us. Act two examined how our painful racial history has evolved into an ethnically camouflaged form of whiteness. This act addressed how the language game of whiteness persists today through white people's reclaiming of white ethnicity and of America's inner cities. These more recent movements have often been interpreted as progress or as a challenging of whiteness, but the claim made here is that these movements rearticulate the language game of whiteness into ever-evolving and more insidious webs of reflexive meaning. Rather than seeking to challenge our own whiteness with a restlessness that capitulates to it, we must foster an attentiveness to how God already speaks in history to reveal the resistant reflexes of whiteness. The opportunity that stands before us is the opportunity to hear God's gracious address as a loving yet terrifying call that meets white people today as it has, again and again, throughout our history.

II

Words between Ultimate and Penultimate

3

Creation and Whiteness

Bonhoeffer and Willie J. Jennings in Dialogue

It is only now in the middle of this book that we arrive at a discussion of the beginning—God's creation of the world. Waiting until this midpoint to discuss God's creation aligns with Bonhoeffer's own discussion of the beginning from *Creation and Fall*. He comments, "We can *know* about the beginning in the true sense only by hearing of the beginning while we ourselves are in the middle."[1] The beginning, Bonhoeffer will suggest, is grasped from the passive event of hearing, a hearing that occurs after words have already been spoken. God has already spoken a beginning, a beginning lost in a fallen world of secondary words that continually resist God's address. Chapter 1 acknowledged God's speaking, and in light of God's invocation chapter 2 recollected our own speaking. Together these chapters represent how we come to the beginning not as a fresh start but as a word already addressed to us,

---

1   *DBWE* 3:30. "The middle" is the terminology Bonhoeffer employs in *Creation and Fall* to talk about the complete rupture of sin after humanity's fall. "The middle" designates how human beings always live within the boundaries of God's beginning and end, even when this beginning and end are resisted.

a word spoken by God in the midst of our resistance to God's speaking. We come to the beginning in recognition that we stand not at the beginning but in the middle.

In this respect the previous chapter on the history of white peoples in the United States provides a preparatory role in more ways than one. First, it supplies us with an awareness of the specific middle in which we find ourselves. Second, it also reveals how we constantly seek to evacuate this middle with our own new beginnings. Whiteness shelters us from "the middle" by giving us the power to continually create an illusory fresh start, originally in the fabrication of becoming white and more recently through the repossession of European ethnicity. These attempts at finding a new beginning characterize precisely what it means to be in what Bonhoeffer calls the "anxiety-causing middle."[2] Trapped in the middle, we look to turn the middle into a beginning.

Rather than seeking to escape this middle, the remainder of this book is devoted to wrestling inside it. This wrestling begins by presenting a dialogue between Bonhoeffer and Willie J. Jennings—specifically, Bonhoeffer's writings on creation and sin and Jennings' accounts of creation and whiteness from *The Christian Imagination*. The intent of this dialogue is not simply to present a systematic expression of ideas but to listen to God's speaking through an interactive exchange.

In listening to Bonhoeffer and Jennings, we discover two similar yet distinct approaches to hearing God speak today. Both seek a connection to creation through God's direct address, but how each theologian describes this address differs. These differing approaches to hearing God's address are evaluated here to further delve into the question posed in this book: how does the triune God speak through the sinful community of the Christian church that, in our context, has been historically marked by whiteness, and how does God speak through this community without capitulating to the Christian church's sin or to whiteness? To even ask this question requires clarification regarding what is meant by "sin" or "sinful." Additionally, this question necessitates a discussion around how "sin" relates to and is distinct from "whiteness." By distinguishing between "sin" and "whiteness," a dialogue between Bonhoeffer and Jennings arrives at congruencies regarding how sin distorts God's good creation on one level and how whiteness obstructs access to God's good creation on another.

2   *DBWE* 3:30.

Creation and Sin/Whiteness

Bonhoeffer does not talk about whiteness in his writings, but he frequently discusses sin. Jennings, on the other hand, does not talk directly about sin in *The Christian Imagination*, but he frequently addresses whiteness. Where Bonhoeffer's discussions of sin and Jennings' discussion of whiteness coalesce is in a conversation about how one gains access to the fallen earth as God's good creation. Bonhoeffer's writings examine how the complete rupture caused by sin bars us from our beginning with God. Jennings' *The Christian Imagination* describes how whiteness severs us from Israel's beginning with God. In respectively addressing sin and whiteness, the question that Bonhoeffer and Jennings raise is not "Where do we begin?" but rather "Where have we already begun?"

Bonhoeffer: Creation and Sin

The beginning point for Bonhoeffer is God's direct address in Jesus Christ, God's living word, God's command that connects all of creaturely life to its Creator. This starting point suggests that a beginning is received within the community of those responding to God's address, and for Bonhoeffer this primarily means the Christian church. The church is where God's beginning is discovered and received in a distinct manner. Bonhoeffer suggests that where we have begun is in the *continuity* of the historical community of Christ into which we are already incorporated through God's *contingent* act of revelation—God's direct speaking. Bonhoeffer presents these themes of *contingency* and *continuity* in his second doctoral work, *Act and Being*. In this early writing, he brings together act and being, contingency and continuity, to explain how the church knows itself, strictly from within sin, to be connected to God's address of a beginning.

Act and Being, in one sense, is a treatise on how human beings can know and speak about God (i.e., theological epistemology). In this work Bonhoeffer explores how those in the church can talk about God when our very knowing and speaking stems from our being in sin. Despite the impenetrability of this question, two-thirds of the way through *Act and Being* Bonhoeffer proposes he has come up with a novel answer. He writes, "On this basis it is possible to speak *theologically* of the essence of human beings, of the knowledge of God that belongs to human beings, and the knowledge of human beings that is God's."[3] In what follows,

3   *DBWE* 2:109 (emphasis added).

an analysis is given concerning Bonhoeffer's "basis" for an ecclesial knowing and speaking. This "basis" will prove instrumental, not only for Bonhoeffer's accounts of sin and creation, but more importantly, for everything that follows in this book.

In the introduction to *Act and Being*, Bonhoeffer describes his innovative approach for considering the church's speaking in terms of a revelation that must "yield an epistemology of its own."[4] He describes this epistemology yielded by revelation as an "ecclesial form of thinking" [*Kirchlichen Denken*] found in the historical church and given in reference to the direct apprehension of Christ in the church's proclamation of Word and sacrament.[5] It is the church itself as a "reality of revelation" and as directly "established by God,"[6] Bonhoeffer claims, that allows for a coordination between God's *contingent* act of revelation and the *continuity* of God's revelation. God's *contingent* act of revelation is given in the direct act of faith (*actus directus*) as a response to God's address, and the *continuity* of God's revelation is given in the church's theological knowing (*actus reflexus*) as an already "being in Christ."[7] Bonhoeffer works out this coordination by suggesting that the church's theological knowing is given "in reference to" the direct act of faith in Christ, and, at the same time, this faith is "suspended" in the historical continuity of the church's knowing constituted by its "being in Christ." Thus, there is no faith apart from the historical community of Christ, and there is no church apart from faith.

Bonhoeffer comes to this formulation in conversation with Karl Barth's early dialectical theology. He concurs with Barth that the contingency of God's directly spoken word leaves God's direct revelation beyond the grasp of direct human reflection.[8] As expressed in Barth's metaphor of the heavenly manna cited by Bonhoeffer, "The heavenly

4   *DBWE* 2:31.

5   *DBWE* 2:31; *DBW* 2:26.

6   The church as a "reality of revelation" in being directly "established by God" is the central claim Bonhoeffer defends in *Sanctorum Communio* and that he builds upon in *Act and Being*. Bonhoeffer describes the church as a "reality of revelation" on a number of occasions in *Sanctorum Communio*. See *DBWE* 1:15, 127, 130, 134, 138, 144. He argues that the church is directly established by God through Christ's vicarious representative action. See *DBWE* 1:145–47. The importance of Bonhoeffer's understanding of Christ's vicarious representative action is discussed further in chapter 4.

7   *DBWE* 2:102–3.

8   See *DBWE* 2:55, 81–87. Many have suggested that the later Barth shifted from this earlier dialectic approach. Charles Marsh, for example, suggests that a shift took place in Barth's thinking with his discovery of Anselm, which led to his axiom "God's being in his act." For Marsh's discussion of this, see Marsh, *Reclaiming Dietrich Bonhoeffer*, 16–18.

manna in the wilderness does not, as we know, let itself be saved up."[9] At the same time, Bonhoeffer worries that this contingency *alone* leaves the church without the ability of knowing and speaking about God, sin, or creation. He criticizes Barth's early understanding of God's revelation as pure act, which Bonhoeffer contends leaves no place for the continuity of the church's theological knowing and speaking.[10] Bonhoeffer writes,

> It would be possible to talk of God, or to know about God, and to have theology as a scholarly discipline only if revelation were not understood as pure act, if there were somehow a being of revelation outside my existential knowledge of it, outside my faith, on which my faith, my thought, my knowledge could "rest."[11]

Bonhoeffer's concern is that Barth's early dialectical theology emphasizes the contingency of God's direct address in such a way that it gives up the church's theological knowing as an already "being in Christ."

In response to this perceived shortcoming, Bonhoeffer coordinates Barth's understanding of the *contingency* of God's revelation as *act* with an understanding of the *continuity* of God's revelation as a *being* in Christ. Bonhoeffer argues that the act of faith is "suspended" in the church's being "in Christ," and, at the same time, the church knows itself as church, Christ's new humanity, only "in reference" to the direct act of faith.[12] On the one hand, the contingent *act* of God's revelation

9   *DBWE* 2:83. For Barth's essay referenced by Bonhoeffer, see Karl Barth, "Fate and Idea in Theology," in *The Way of Theology in Karl Barth: Essay and Comments*, ed. H. Martin Rumscheidt (Eugene: Pickwick, 1986), 25–62.

10   Bonhoeffer's full critique of Barth takes issue with both Barth's definition of God's freedom (*DBWE* 2:81–87) and his treatment of the continuity of the Old and New "I" (*DBWE* 2:99–100). In reference to *Act and Being*, Michael DeJonge asserts, "From Bonhoeffer's point of view, person-theology is superior to Barth's act-theology because it can account for the fullness of Christian life." See DeJonge, *Bonhoeffer's Theological Formation: Berlin, Barth, and Protestant Theology* (Oxford: Oxford University Press, 2012), 77. While DeJonge provides an insightful distinction between Barth and Bonhoeffer, his identification of Bonhoeffer's person-theology requires an account of how Bonhoeffer addresses sin and its bearing on persons in a nuanced manner.

11   *DBWE* 2:95.

12   Bonhoeffer writes, "At issue, rather, are historical human beings who know themselves transposed from the old to the new humanity, who are what they are on account of membership in the new humanity, persons newly created by Christ. All this they 'are' only in referential-act toward Christ. Their being—'in reference to'—Christ is rooted in their being in Christ, in the community of faith, which means that the act is 'suspended' in being just as, conversely, being is not without the act" (*DBWE* 2:120). The struggle that Bonhoeffer is working through here is how to account for human beings in history as both old and new. At bottom, the question is how to deal with sin in the new humanity of Christ.

assists in guarding against interpretations of revelation that are purely ontological, leaving speech about God entrapped within the closed circle of sin (in this regard, Bonhoeffer expresses concern about the *analogia entis*).[13] On the other hand, the continuous *being* of revelation guards against interpretations of revelation that are purely act, leaving the community of faith without material content for reflection, for knowing and speaking (what Bonhoeffer refers to as the *actus reflexus*).[14] It is this distinct union between the act and being of revelation that Bonhoeffer will argue constitutes the faith community's speaking about God and human beings.[15] This is the initial basis on which Bonhoeffer will reason that God can work and speak through a sinful community without condoning sin.

To know in a theological sense is bound up with an ecclesial being that relies on the direct apprehension of Christ. As ecclesial, it is already found in the being of revelation, which Bonhoeffer defines "as the being of the person of Christ in the community of persons of the church."[16] For Bonhoeffer God concretely claims a person through the living word in the communicative event corresponding to the call of word and the response of faith. God's word comes as a contingent event that like the manna in the wilderness cannot be stored for later.[17] The event of God's word means one cannot preach the gospel to oneself, but instead faith finds one already in the church, where Christ is apprehended directly in the church's proclamation of Word and sacrament. Bonhoeffer explains, "Someone offers me the sacrament: you are forgiven . . . And I hear the gospel, join in the prayer, and know myself bound up in the word, sacrament, and prayer of Christ's community of faith."[18] One not

13   See *DBWE* 2:74–76, where Bonhoeffer discusses the *analogia entis* in relation to the Catholic theologian Erich Pryzwara. In this discussion, Bonhoeffer argues that the analogy of being offers a self-reflective continuity between humanity and God that creates an "illusory transcendence" (*DBWE* 2:75).

14   See Bonhoeffer's discussion of the *actus reflexus* in the context of his response to Barth in *DBWE* 2:100. Bonhoeffer clarifies that the direct act of faith only in its intentionality, directed to and found in Christ, "does not enter into reflection" (*DBWE* 2:100).

15   *DBWE* 2:109.

16   *DBWE* 2:125.

17   Bonhoeffer provides a comparison between the Word in the form of God's Living Word and human words in the form of ideas in his *Lectures on Christology*. He explains, "Christ as the Word of God is distinguished and separated from the human logos in that he is the Word in the form of the Living Word to humankind, whereas the human word is word in the form of an idea" (*DBWE* 12:316).

18   *DBWE* 2:120.

only receives Christ as the object of faith in the church's proclamation of Word and sacrament; one also participates with Christ as the subject of faith by joining in the tangible worship of Christ's community of faith.[19] Theological knowledge as an ecclesial reflection, Bonhoeffer maintains, preserves this event of God's contingent revelation "as something that exists in the historical church."[20] The contingency of God's Word as an event is preserved and understood as such through an ecclesial knowing that flows from and toward the event of God's speaking. The church's collective reflections on the direct act of faith, received in its proclamation of Word and sacrament, constitute an ecclesial knowing and speaking.

What this formulation means in practical terms is that theology serves as a function of the church given in reference to and support of the church's proclamation of Word and sacrament. Theology "stands," Bonhoeffer claims, "between past and future preaching" and "is to make the connection between past preaching and the person of Christ, as Christ preaches in, and is preached by, the community of faith."[21] This is the reason why Bonhoeffer will maintain that the task of theology is only possible when done from within the church. Theology must be done from within the church, because the church's proclamation of Word and sacrament places a necessary limit on theological thinking and knowledge, which remains fundamentally systematic in the way it constructs and contributes positive knowledge to the church. "Because theology turns revelation into something that exists," Bonhoeffer explains, "it may be practiced only where the living person of Christ is itself present and can destroy this existing thing or acknowledge it."[22]

The same logic of ecclesial knowledge is at work in Bonhoeffer's understanding of how one comes to know sin and God's creation at the beginning. As with all ecclesial knowledge, knowledge of sin and creation is a knowing given from within the community of faith in reference to the direct act of faith. With regard to sin, Bonhoeffer applies this presupposition of ecclesial knowledge in the final part of *Act and Being* to explain Luther's dictum that "by faith alone we know that we

19 Joshua Kaiser contends that Bonhoeffer resolves the tension between act and being by suggesting that Christ becomes "both the subject and object of faith." See Kaiser, *Becoming Simple and Wise*, 36. For representative texts that support this claim, see *DBWE* 2:92, 112.

20 *DBWE* 2:130.

21 *DBWE* 2:130.

22 *DBWE* 2:131.

are sinners."[23] This statement, Bonhoeffer argues, must be understood as an existential designation of faith that grasps one's deeds of sin as suspended within one's "being in Adam."[24] Faith as an "existential designation" means that faith does not remove the human being's placement from within Adam but recognizes sin from within Adam in direct reference to Christ. As Bonhoeffer puts it, "This is knowledge from revelation, which can never be had apart from it, that is, precisely, in Adam."[25] Only after already being placed in truth does one recognize the untruth of sin. Christ directly breaks into the untruth of the isolation of sin through the contingency of God's address, revealing that the individual person can never be thought of separately from humanity as a whole.[26] Bonhoeffer writes, "Only to faith, in revelation, do we have access to the knowledge that we are sinners in the wholeness of our being, since it is only then, by God's word, that the wholeness of our being can be placed into the truth."[27]

Bonhoeffer applies the same approach of contingency and continuity (act and being) to describe an ecclesial knowledge of God's creation in *Creation and Fall*. His "theological exposition" of the creation narrative presents the words of Genesis as God's *contingent* address that meets human beings afresh in the middle.[28] This is why Bonhoeffer will say, as discussed in the introduction of this chapter, "We can *know* about the beginning in the true sense only by hearing of the beginning while we ourselves are in the middle."[29] It is only from God's direct address to human beings *within* sin that one comes to know about the beginning and end—God's beginning and end is never intuitively grasped but externally gifted. To understand the biblical narrative in this manner is to already find oneself within the *continuity* of Christ's community.[30]

---

23   *DBWE* 2:136. Bonhoeffer's citation of Luther is found in Martin Luther, *Lecture on Romans*, ed. Hilton C. Oswald (St. Louis: Concordia, 1971), 215.

24   *DBWE* 2:136.

25   *DBWE* 2:137.

26   See *DBWE* 2:141. Bonhoeffer repeatedly argues that the direct act of faith is a passive act that cannot be captured in reflection but that finds one incorporated into God's working in the world. Bonhoeffer writes, "Human beings, when they understand themselves in faith, are entirely wrenched away from themselves and directed towards God" (*DBWE* 2:135).

27   *DBWE* 2:137.

28   See *DBWE* 3:29.

29   *DBWE* 3:30 (emphasis original).

30   Bonhoeffer explains this ecclesial approach to the Bible in the introduction to *Creation and Fall*. See *DBWE* 3:21–23.

This leads Bonhoeffer to claim that "the Bible is after all nothing other than the book of the church. It *is* this in its very essence, or it is nothing."[31] The Christian church, in a sense, is where the written word comes to life through the Spirit in the hearing and receiving of the living Word that finds one already in the community of faith. While the words of the Bible are recorded and spoken through human beings in the middle, God speaks through them as the one from the beginning. As Bonhoeffer reasons, "No one can speak of the beginning but the one who was in the beginning."[32] Here Bonhoeffer has in mind the triune God, "the very God, Christ, the Holy Spirit."[33] The triune God speaks to God's people, and through the response of faith in the church's proclamation of Word and sacrament, the community of faith is opened to hear God speak in all times and places, in a fallen creation bound to God through God's own word.

Coming back to the original question, where have we begun? Bonhoeffer suggests we have already begun with God's direct address to the historical community of Christ. It is through God's already given address in the midst of sin, the middle, that the community found in Christ is afforded a unique way of speaking through its dependency on God's direct address. The church does not speak simply from its own knowledge but from a communal knowledge discovered in being Christ's community. This is what allows the church to speak of sin from within sin and of a beginning already given by God. God's contingent address does not evacuate the middle but claims the middle as between God's beginning and end. As will be further discussed in what follows, God tangibly claims the fallen earth in the church's celebration of the sacrament as elements taken from the earth are declared to be Christ's body and blood. This tangible practice connects us to the fallen earth through God's direct and external claim spoken over it.

To be absolutely clear, this section has *not* sought to define sin or God's good creation but to explicate how, for Bonhoeffer, one comes to know sin and God's creation theologically from within the church. It is premature, then, to draw any connections between sin and whiteness or to discuss their compounding impact on God's creation. Instead, Bonhoeffer's understanding of how one comes to an ecclesial knowledge of

---

31   *DBWE* 3:22. Bonhoeffer offers a better statement of this idea in his original introduction to these lectures: "One can never hear it, if one does not at the same time live it—and this involves especially *execritium* [practice]" (*DBWE* 3:23, n. 11).

32   *DBWE* 3:29.

33   *DBWE* 3:29.

sin and creation offers a decisive warning for contemporary theological race discourses. If theological discourses concerning race are to be
theological, they must be given in direct relation to the living person
of Christ, encountered in the church's proclamation of Word and sacrament. Without the grounding and reference point of the historical
church that continually encounters and bows to the living Word, theological discourses on race can cause drastic harm, as seen in Bonhoeffer's own lifetime.[34] This harm is caused when the words of human ideas
are offered as God's living Word, which is to wrongly identify the middle
as God's beginning. Bonhoeffer inserts a cryptic warning of this nature
against the German Christians of his own day in his introduction to the
1933 published version of *Creation and Fall*. After asserting that these
"children of the world" (the Nazi party of the German church) wish
to "claim the church," he states, "They want the new, and they know
only the old."[35] In other words, Bonhoeffer accuses German Christians
of using Christ and Christ's church to fabricate a new beginning that
evacuates the middle, and in this way, "they know *only* the old." The
community of faith, in contrast, knows the old and the new at once, the
new creation in fallen creation. It knows that to know Christ is to know
oneself as condemned, as dead, as already in Adam. At the same time,
it knows of a new life in Christ. These two, death and life, must be held
together as one speaks theologically of whiteness and how whiteness
continually resists God's speaking.

Jennings: Creation and Whiteness

Jennings, like Bonhoeffer, takes as his theological starting point God's
direct address, but for Jennings this address is more decidedly understood as coming through *Israel* and *Israel's* Messiah—Jesus of Nazareth.
Jennings will suggest that where we have already begun is with God's
election of Israel. Gentiles in the Christian church, then, must remember that we hear God's address through being joined with Israel in the
advent of Jesus Christ. This starting point presents warnings regarding how God's address is heard in the historical Christian church, and
specifically for how Bonhoeffer talks about the church in this manner.
Jennings' cautious approach toward the Christian church is reflected in

---

34 For a discussion of the occurrence of racial theology during the time of Hitler's rise
to power, see Susannah Heschel, *The Aryan Jesus: Christian Theologians and the Bible in
Nazi Germany* (Princeton: Princeton University Press, 2008).

35 *DBWE* 3:21–22.

the overarching question that he explores in *The Christian Imagination*: how did a Christianity that is about neighborly love and intimacy allow the construct of race to abide? He comes to this question by suggesting that, rather than following its own deep wisdom and power of joining, historical Western Christianity adhered to a joining that "often meant oppression, violence, and death."[36] At the heart of this distorted form of joining is a Christian imagination that severs God's address to Israel from God's creation of the earth. Whiteness administers this severing by transferring a Christian imagination linked with place (God's creation) to one linked with race (a human creation).

Jennings contends that this transfer from place to race was enacted as European Christians, in the midst of exploring new lands, dislodged the creation story from its historical roots within Israel. The particularity of the creation story, Jennings argues, was universalized through a more flexible supersessionist reading of it. He explains, "In the age of discovery and conquest supersessionist thinking burrowed deeply inside the logic of evangelism and emerged joined to whiteness in a new, more sophisticated, concealed form."[37] First, in interpreting the creation story apart from Israel, Jennings shows how European Christians perceived foreign peoples "without necessary permanence either of place or of identity."[38] Second, in interpreting the creation story apart from Israel's Messiah, Jennings observes how European Christians were able to transfer Christ's authority over all creation to themselves as representatives of Christ.[39] These two subtle alterations to the doctrine of creation, Jennings declares, are the "two bedrock hermeneutical principles" on which the colonial enterprise turns.[40] It is also upon these two subtle theological distortions of the doctrine of creation that a perverted Christian imagination is built—a Christian imagination that has not only allowed the construct of race to abide but also continues to fund and facilitate whiteness today.

The first movement in the creation of race is not so much a creation as it is an utter destruction of creaturely contingency. This destruction materializes through the *displacement* of the creature's intrinsic relation to God's creation. The impetus for this destruction, Jennings asserts, emanated from European Christians who saw themselves as ordained

36 Jennings, *The Christian Imagination*, 9.
37 Jennings, *The Christian Imagination*, 36.
38 Jennings, *The Christian Imagination*, 28.
39 Jennings, *The Christian Imagination*, 36.
40 Jennings, *The Christian Imagination*, 36.

by God to "enact a providential transition."[41] This providential transition led to a mass movement of peoples, opening up new possibilities and imaginations. While this movement was not necessarily harmful, the theological imagination behind it was. Jennings maintains that a supersessionist reading of creation led to new ways of imagining God's creating out of nothing: "European Christians, from the Iberians through the British, saw themselves as agents of positive, if not divine, change, as it were, the markers of creaturely contingency."[42] The new lands and peoples were perceived as vacant and unconditioned, leading to "the destruction of the fine webs that held together memory, language, and place."[43] Foreign peoples were seen as barbarians in need of culture, and lands were perceived as wilderness to be developed into square plots of private property for inhabitable civilization. To make way for this transformation, the land itself had to be stripped of its meaning, and in the process the creature's intrinsic relation to the creation is displaced. Creation is displaced not merely because Europeans were intent on economic development but because the joining to Israel, which leaves Gentiles subject to God's contingent address through another distinct people, was surpassed with a joining facilitated by whiteness. With the creation story declared by Israel's God no longer seen as the beginning place for joining, a new beginning was fabricated through a racial rewriting that utterly reimagined the creation narrative apart from God's distinct people of Israel.

The second movement in the creation of race happens at the same moment as the destruction of place. In this movement, place (God's creation) is reinterpreted through the lens of racial designations (a human creation). Jennings calls this movement *translation*. In the same moment that identification markers like geography and language are displaced, European Christians reimagined the interconnectedness of space through disembodied, reflexive acts organized around white bodies. A new "Christian" translation of space writes itself over place, over God's creation story with Israel. The creation of race, then, is not a suspension of the relation between human bodies and places but a new facilitation of these relations administered around white European bodies. Whiteness enacts its own beginning, again and again. This facilitation of race is illustrated by Jennings through his discussion of Columbus' reflexive

---

41   Jennings, *The Christian Imagination*, 60.
42   Jennings, *The Christian Imagination*, 60.
43   Jennings, *The Christian Imagination*, 58.

organization of the peoples he discovered both in the Americas and in Africa, discussed in the previous chapter. Columbus describes these peoples not through listening to the intricate webs of language, geography, and memory that hold them together, but through a conference of identity bound to his own self-reflections. Rather than joining in the already given place of Israel, the creation of whiteness provided a new hostile space for joining.

Whiteness is formed, and continually reformed, in these two movements: the displacement of the creature from God's creation and a self-reflexive facilitation of a new racial scale indexed to white bodies. Supersessionist thinking funds both of these movements by imagining the doctrine of creation apart from the election of Israel. As Jennings writes, "Indeed, supersessionist thinking is the womb in which whiteness will mature."[44] Whiteness presents a new beginning and, in doing so, it insulates us from God's beginning given through God's direct address to Israel. This false beginning is created when we forget that the creation story is not directly addressed to the Christian church but is discovered through the church's incorporation into Israel through Jesus Christ.

Along with his account of colonialism, Jennings provides a sophisticated analysis of how supersessionist thinking continues to function today within the contemporary theology of two eminent historians of Christian mission, Lamin Sanneh and Andrew Walls.[45] Jennings demonstrates how both of these missiologists succumb to a nuanced version of the supersessionist thinking that originally funded colonialism. Jennings describes Sanneh's vernacular approach to translation as a universalizing of Israel's particularity. Sanneh sees translation as a planting of the gospel into the soil of different cultures, which allows the gospel to grow naturally as a repudiation of cultural imperialism. Jennings responds, "If the practice of translation disrupted colonialist hegemony, it did so by making room for something else, cultural nationalism."[46] By affirming every culture through a universalization of the gospel, Sanneh's understanding of translation sets up different cultures against one another, leaving no place for genuine joining. Along with

44 Jennings, *The Christian Imagination*, 36.

45 Along with the Protestant critique of translation discussed here, Jennings provides a parallel critique of the Catholic approach to virtue ethics. For an account of this critique, see Andrew Draper's chapter "Jennings and Virtue Ethics" in Draper, *A Theology of Race and Place*, 215–70.

46 Jennings, *The Christian Imagination*, 157.

this, it joins with colonialism by imagining itself from the towering heights, inadvertently placing itself as the arbitrator of every culture.

Jennings goes on to observe how Walls takes a slightly different approach to translation. For Walls, "Incarnation is translation."[47] Walls suggests that this means Christians live as pilgrims, always between worlds, expressed through a tentative posture towards one's culture, people, and nation. While more subtly done than by Sanneh, Jennings argues that Walls migrates *from* the particularity of Israel as a people *to* a cultural universal accessible to all peoples. Jennings writes, "Like Sanneh, Walls draws a tight circle around language and culture and nation with the effect that the incarnational reality of God in Christ embodied in translation resolves itself in nation. Christ enters the DNA of a nation by means of its language."[48] Even though Walls offers a tentative posture towards one's own culture, his view of translation still works from the logic of independent cultures unrelated to Israel, which creates a Christian-endorsed nationalism.

It is precisely in Sanneh and Walls' cognizance of the history of colonialism that their understandings of translation allow for a more nuanced form of supersessionism. As Jennings reasons, "Theologically, Sanneh and Walls have imbibed a subtle form of supersessionism that is now lodged deeply inside their historiographic imaginations."[49] This supersessionism is observed in how Sanneh and Walls offer a vernacular understanding of the gospel that disarms "Christian particularity of its central scandal, the election of Israel and through Israel the election of Jesus."[50] By giving up this particularity, the place of joining within Israel is translated into a joining within whiteness.

For Jennings, where we have already begun is with the particularity of Israel as a people directly addressed by God. This is reflected in Jennings' blunt question: "When did we leave Israel's world?"[51] In all of this, Jennings' fundamental point is that, by forfeiting the particularity of Israel, Christians have given up the possibility for joining and intimacy. He writes, "The worlds of Christian language are inside Israel's house. Israel's house is a space where people are joined in worship and where

47   Andrew Walls, *The Missionary Movement in Christian History: Studies in the Transmission of Faith* (Maryknoll: Orbis Books, 1996), 27. Cited in Jennings, *The Christian Imagination*, 158.

48   Jennings, *The Christian Imagination*, 159.

49   Jennings, *The Christian Imagination*, 159.

50   Jennings, *The Christian Imagination*, 160.

51   Jennings, *The Christian Imagination*, 160.

ways of life come into the communion of the common, of eating, sleeping, and living together."[52] The particularity of Israel challenges every culture, and, by challenging every culture, Israel provides the particular space for joining with others and with God's creation.

Bonhoeffer and Jennings: Where Have We Begun?

Bonhoeffer and Jennings provide two different starting points for the question "Where have we begun?" With a focus on *sin*, Bonhoeffer presents God's direct address to the community of faith as that which connects us to God's beginning and end and thus orients us to our being in the middle. We have begun with God's direct address, suspended within the continuity of the historical church as Christ's community on earth. With a focus on *whiteness*, Jennings presents God's direct address in the election of Israel as constituting a place for joining in the contingency of God's creation. We have begun with God's direct address, already given in the election of Israel and Israel's Messiah. These two divergent starting points offer different strengths and weaknesses that are illuminated through bringing Bonhoeffer and Jennings into dialogue with one another.

By situating the starting point within an already established place of joining in the historical church, Bonhoeffer reorients the discussion of sin and whiteness from problems to overcome to a discovery of how God's speaking is already challenging every obstruction that stands in the way of hearing God's Word. This discovering of God's already present working relates to how Bonhoeffer describes the church's knowledge of sin and the church's participation with Christ in preparing the way. Sin (and whiteness) is not something one must overcome to reach joining; instead, the joining that already temporally and concretely takes place in the proclamation of Word and sacrament makes God's people aware of what sin is. Additionally, God's people are incorporated into a preparing of the way that anticipates the surprise of God's speaking. In short, addressing whiteness begins from God's already given place of joining in Christ's body, where faith in God's direct address locates one in the continuity of the historical church.

In contrast, Jennings' discussion of whiteness warns of the danger of beginning with the historical Christian church when the Western Christian church's imagination is funded by an embodied commandeering of Israel's story that is translated into a violent joining within

---

52 Jennings, *The Christian Imagination*, 160.

whiteness. Beginning with Israel as a constraint on the Christian church assists in safeguarding Christians from domesticating God's address into the self-reflective responses of whiteness. Jennings is mindful of how the self-reflective responses of whiteness not only represent a severing from Israel but also incorporate people of color into this severing.[53] People of color are included in the story of whiteness, along with white people, through a conference of exclusionary inclusion—their exclusion is facilitated through the controlled way whiteness specifically includes them. Jennings' return to a beginning within Israel provides a direct challenge to the displacement of Israel that funds the violent joining of whiteness. While this direct challenge is an urgent one, it requires consideration of how God continues to speak in the middle, in our falling away, in our resistance to God's speaking.

As Bonhoeffer reminds us, it is only through the direct act of faith in Christ, occurring in already given community, that we come to know sin and our own resistance to God's address. While the historical church in the West is marked by the violence of whiteness, it is also upheld by God's contingent address that whiteness resists and to which preparing the way must attend. If one problem is not recognizing how whiteness resists God's speaking, the inverse problem is not recognizing that it is God's speaking that initiates our wrestling with the resistance of whiteness in the first place. God's speaking upholds the world in its continual falling away. In this regard, Bonhoeffer is sensitive to how considerations of God's creation must account for God's preservation of that same creation: "To say that God upholds the created world is a judgment that accepts the present moment in its reality as from God."[54] The struggle, then, is not to overcome whiteness but to hear God's judgment against our resistance in whiteness as God's continued care for his creation.

The pressing question that Jennings indirectly raises is whether there is a point where a Christian denomination or congregation excludes itself from God's speaking. This was a serious question that Bonhoeffer faced in his own day as discussed above in reference to his comments

53   Jennings discusses this incorporation of people of color into the story of whiteness as part of the impetus for writing *The Christian Imagination*. See Jennings' introduction to *The Christian Imagination*, 1–8. He also asserts that whiteness as the facilitating reality presents a "form of identity inside of which all other identities could be imagined" (275). In reference to how African Americans are imagined in this space, Jennings explains, "By their being virtually consigned to the lowest rank of race—the black body presented the shame concealed inside whiteness, its bloody journey to power" (275).

54   *DBWE* 3:47.

about the German Christian church. Bonhoeffer's general response to this question is that it is not the Christian church's sin (or whiteness) that excludes it from God's address, but its refusal to acknowledge and repent of its own sin (or whiteness) as recognized in God's already given address. Acknowledging sin and wrong allows the Christian church to be seen as part of history rather than offering a new beginning that remains exempt from history. The German Christians' refusal to acknowledge sin and a history marked by sin is what led Bonhoeffer and others to a collective confession that named the German Christian church an apostate church. Even here, though, Bonhoeffer relies on the specific church councils of Dahlem and Barmen, in reference to the historical church councils, to offer this judgment as given from God.[55] One of Bonhoeffer's greatest concerns was for a fragmentation of the Christian church, as seen in the American context, that makes it difficult for these judgments to be risked as spoken by God and attended to by the community of faith.[56] This is where Jennings' challenge of whiteness carries great weight when there is little that Christian denominations in America have done collectively to make a public confession that acknowledges whiteness and that, through a preparing of the way, attends to how whiteness resists God's address.

Jennings' challenge of whiteness, also, provides a potent warning in relation to Bonhoeffer's theological starting point of the historical church. There are many comments made throughout Bonhoeffer's writings that reflect a tendency to displace Israel with a historical church understood within a Western purview. One example of this has already been cited from *Creation and Fall*, where Bonhoeffer states, "The Bible is after all nothing other than the book of the church. It *is* this in its very essence, or it is nothing."[57] Approaching the Bible and the creation narrative in this manner has both a positive and a negative result. On the positive side, it provides the church's concrete practices as a qualification that challenges cultural misuses of the Bible, as seen

55   In his illegal seminary, Bonhoeffer warned his seminarians of the danger of defecting to the German Christian church that had already been condemned in the confession given at Dahlem and Barmen. For Bonhoeffer on adherence to this confession, see Bonhoeffer's essay "Lecture on the Path of the Young Illegal Theologians" in *DBWE* 15:421–22.

56   Bonhoeffer discusses the fragmentation of the American Church in his essay "Protestantism without Reformation." He writes, "*The denominations in America* are faced from the start with an unimaginable variety of Christian communities. None of them can dare to make the claim to be the one church" (*DBWE* 15:443, emphasis original).

57   *DBWE* 3:22 (emphasis original).

in the German Christians' distorting of the Bible through the exclusion of the Hebrew Scriptures. On the negative side, this statement reflects how Bonhoeffer often inserted the church into the Hebrew Bible, thus removing the fact that the creation narrative belongs distinctly to Israel.

The danger of supersessionism in Bonhoeffer's theological exposition of the creation story is laid bare by Jennings' theological account of colonialism. Rather than reading the creation narrative as a Gentile outsider, Bonhoeffer moves toward extracting the creation story from biblical Israel, opening the door to a vernacular universalization of the gospel that funds a Christian form of nationalism, as observed in Jennings' critique of Sanneh and Wells. Bonhoeffer's interpretation of the creation narrative lacks Jennings' attention (and Carter's as well, discussed in the next chapter) to how the creation story is God's direct address to Israel, forming Israel as a people, spoken into existence by God's word.[58] The creation narrative is circumscribed by the social concreteness of biblical Israel.[59] Bonhoeffer's early reading of the Hebrew Bible seen in *Creation and Fall*, along with other similar interpretations found in his writings, demonstrate a dangerous tendency in his thought to overshadow biblical Israel with the Gentile church.[60]

Together Bonhoeffer's attendance of sin and Jennings' challenge of whiteness garner important considerations for the question of where we have begun. The Christian church and Israel must both be accounted for in discussing this question. Faith that finds one already in the community of Christ connects one not only to the historical Christian church

58   Carter makes this point when he talks about God's call on Abram-Abraham as a creation out of nothing. He writes, "YHWH presents the story of Israel, beginning with the call of Abram-become-Abraham to create ex nihilo a people who before did not exist, as a compendium of the story of creation, which too came into being" (*Race*, 33).

59   Bonhoeffer almost comes to this conclusion when he talks about how those "who wrote the Bible" offer God's words "from the middle not from the beginning" (*DBWE* 3:30). However, he never connects this to Israel, which reflects an inner dialectic in Bonhoeffer's thought that works primarily between creation, sin, and Christ.

60   Bonhoeffer's Bible study on "King David" shows a similar interpretation of the Old Testament that replaces Israel with the church. See Andreas Pangritz, "Who Is Christ, for Us, Today?" in *The Cambridge Companion to Dietrich Bonhoeffer*, ed. John W. de Gruchy (Cambridge: Cambridge University Press, 1999), 145–48. Many have shown how Bonhoeffer's later reading of the Hebrew Bible in *Letters and Papers from Prison* reflects a different approach. The time Bonhoeffer spent in prison reading the Hebrew Bible led him to interpret biblical Israel not as surpassed but as the hermeneutical horizon for understanding how all of creaturely reality is upheld by God's ultimate word given in Jesus Christ. For Bonhoeffer's development in relation to his reading of the Hebrew Bible, see Pangritz, "Who Is Christ, for Us, Today?" 148–51; and Barry Harvey, *Taking Hold of the Real*, 216–18.

but, simultaneously, to the history of Israel, culminating in Israel's Messiah. Jennings' insights remind us that whiteness hinders our access to God's creation through a displacement of Israel. Bonhoeffer's insights remind us that sin distorts the gift of God's creation with the lie of our own continuous beginnings. Both whiteness and sin then, in their own distinct ways, sever us from God's beginning declared to Israel and discovered through Israel in the historical Christian church. If sin and whiteness present two distinguishable obstructions to God's creation, the subsequent question is how to distinguish the two.

Defining Sin and Whiteness

The preceding discussion moves between talking about "sin" and "whiteness" with a certain ease. Theological discussions of race, similarly, often move forward without a clear distinction being drawn between these two terms. While sin relates to whiteness, the two terms are not interchangeable. A theological distinction is needed, because whereas sin (specifically original sin) is a term that connotes universal consequence, whiteness is a term that connotes particular consequences. While Bonhoeffer never discusses whiteness, his discussions of sin in its various forms assist in offering a helpful distinction between sin (in terms of original sin) and whiteness. Comparing Bonhoeffer's account of original sin with his discussion of "the natural" draws out this distinction. Distinguishing between sin and whiteness is pivotal in narrowing the target from a general challenge of sin to a specific challenge of whiteness as that which pointedly hinders us from hearing God's address today.

Bonhoeffer: Original Sin and the Community of Sinners

Bonhoeffer speaks about sin in so many different and nuanced ways and with so many different terms in his corpus that it becomes difficult at times to pin him down on the subject.[61] *Sanctorum Communio* speaks

---

61 For an excellent discussion of Bonhoeffer's understanding of sin in relation to shame, see Christiane Tietz, "The Mysteries of Knowledge, Sin, and Shame," in *Mysteries in the Theology of Dietrich Bonhoeffer: A Copenhagen Bonhoeffer Symposium*, ed. Kirsten Busch Nielsen and Christiane Tietz (Göttingen: Vandenhoeck & Ruprecht, 2007), 27–48. For a general treatment of Bonhoeffer's hamartiology, see Kirsten Busch Nielsen, "Community Turned Inside Out: Dietrich Bonhoeffer's Concept of the Church and of Humanity Reconsidered," in *Being Human, Becoming Human: Dietrich Bonhoeffer and Social Thought*, ed. Jen Zimmermann and Brian Gregor (Eugene: Wipf & Stock, 2010), 91–101.

of sin as "ethical atomism."[62] *Act and Being* speaks of sin in terms of the heart turned in on itself, "*cor curvum in se.*"[63] *Creation and Fall* speaks of sin as a being in "the middle."[64] While each of these glosses on sin has its own slightly nuanced meaning, they all speak to how sin isolates and encloses the human being; that is, they speak to how sin excludes community. This definition of sin seems to contradict Bonhoeffer's assertion that the church is a *community* of *sinners*. How can isolated sinners be in community when sin by definition excludes community? Offering Bonhoeffer's answer to this question from *Sanctorum Communio* helps clarify his definition of what sin is.

In *Sanctorum Communio* Bonhoeffer comes at a definition of sin through a roundabout approach. First, he must explain a form of community existing before the fall, so that, second, he can distinguish how isolated sinners after the fall can be in community.[65] Community before the fall, Bonhoeffer suggests, was generated between human beings from below through the Spirit in direct relation to the triune God. The fall into sin constitutes a complete rupture that disallows community from being generated in this way, that is, from below. Within the conditions of the fall, Bonhoeffer argues that community is not generated from below but from God's external command from above. This fallen form of community he calls the "ethical collective person."[66] Ethics originate not from human perceptions of good and evil but as a response to God's external address. After the fall, God's direct and external word allows the individual not only to see her or his own isolation but, also, to see herself or himself as part of a sinful humanity, as Bonhoeffer illustrates through the example of the prophet Isaiah.[67] The recognition of shared guilt and culpability among isolated individuals, as given

62   *DBWE* 1:33.
63   See *DBWE* 2:46, 58, 80, 89, 137.
64   See *DBWE* 3:85, 87, 89–93, 111–13, 121, 141, 172.
65   The following section provides an abbreviated presentation of Bonhoeffer's solution to the problem of community after the fall. For a detailed discussion of Bonhoeffer's solution to the social-philosophical problem of community, see Michael Mawson, "The Spirit and the Community: Pneumatology and Ecclesiology in Jenson, Hütter and Bonhoeffer," *International Journal of Systematic Theology* 15, no. 4 (2013): 453–68.
66   For Bonhoeffer's full discussion of the "ethical collective person," see *DBWE* 1:118–21.
67   Bonhoeffer references Isaiah 6:5 to make this point: "The experience of ethical solidarity and awareness of oneself as peculator pessimus [the worse sinner] belong together" (*DBWE* 1:116).

directly from God's external judgment, is what Bonhoeffer defines as "the ethical collective person" grouped together under the heading of Adam.[68] Bonhoeffer makes this clear later in *Sanctorum Communio*: "Judgment applies to persons. But this obviously means that it applies not only to individual persons, but also collective persons. This, in turn, entails the notion that the individual is judged not only in isolation, but also as a member of collective persons."[69] While sin separates humankind into isolated individuals, Bonhoeffer suggests that God's direct word, given externally from above, places these isolated individuals into a community of shared culpability and guilt under God's address.[70]

Bonhoeffer will argue that this understanding of the "ethical collective person" applies to all of "humanity-in-Adam" but is only recognized as such by those who by faith are already found within Christ's community, the community of saints. He explains,

> Thus out of utter isolation arises concrete community, for the preaching of God's love speaks of the community into which God *has* entered with each and every person—with all those who in utter solitude know themselves separated from God and other human beings who believe this message.[71]

This, for Bonhoeffer, is how community is established among sinners from within the community of saints. Again, Bonhoeffer's designation of "preaching" locates the church's knowing in immediate reference to the direct act of faith (described above from *Act and Being*), which places one already in the community of saints. In this way the community of sinners gains its external designation as a *community* and as individual *sinners* from within the community of saints addressed by God in faith.

It is upon this understanding of the ethical collective person that Bonhoeffer develops his ecclesial definition of sin as simultaneously individual and collective. He argues that sin is the mutual reinforcement of one's individual sins and one's already being in Adam, without

68   See *DBWE* 1:121.

69   *DBWE* 1:284.

70   In *Ethics* Bonhoeffer's presentation of the four mandates (work, marriage, government, and church) function on this same understanding of the ethical collective person. The mandates are externally given from above as God's command to preserve the fallen world. See *DBWE* 6:68–74.

71   *DBWE* 1:149 (emphasis original).

either being the cause of the other.[72] He writes, "Everything obviously depends upon *finding the act of the whole in the individual act*, without making the one the reason for the other."[73] When Bonhoeffer talks about sin in this way, he is talking specifically about original sin. In his discussion of original sin in *Sanctorum Communio*, Bonhoeffer argues that the *coercion* of sin as collective and the *culpability* of sin as individual must be thought of as inextricably related. This inextricable relation between coercion and culpability, collective and individual, expresses the unfathomable rupture of the fall, which reserves a dependency on God's direct word received by faith. Bonhoeffer maintains that the past attempts of various theologians to theologically define sin (1) merely as collective coercion or (2) merely as individual culpability obscure the unfathomable nature of sin.[74] Both of these one-sided attempts to identify the source of sin wrongly assume that fallen human beings can define sin, when, in fact, sin defines the human being.[75] Original sin defines the human being as both encased in sin and the perpetrator of this encasement. Bonhoeffer starkly presents this view of sin by stating that every sinner is the "first" sinner.[76] Thus, Bonhoeffer's conception of the community of sinners suggests that sin is understood as individual and collective at once, and it is in this way that the community of sinners is understood to be a community as believed from faith. Faith in the external word of God reveals that fallen human solidarity is discovered in the togetherness of each human being's utter isolation.

This theological understanding of sin is important for the church, because it establishes how Bonhoeffer sees the community of sinners within the church as a representative of all humanity in Adam. Sin

72   Bonhoeffer describes the mutual reinforcement of the act and being of sin, as well, in *Act and Being*. See *DBWE* 2:146.

73   *DBWE* 1:115 (emphasis original).

74   In speaking of sin merely as coercion, Bonhoeffer takes issue with Augustine's view of inheritable sin. Bonhoeffer writes, "Augustine evidently thought of the sinful collective act as the basis for every individual act, and Anselm and Thomas basically get no further than this" (*DBWE* 1:115). In speaking of sin merely as culpability, Bonhoeffer argues that Protestant German liberal theologians, seen representatively in Albrecht Ritschl, placed the weight of sin on individual sinful acts, "not sufficiently grounding the universality of sin" (*DBWE* 1:115).

75   Bonhoeffer writes, "The concept of the species should be based upon the concept of culpability, not vice versa" (*DBWE* 1:114).

76   *DBWE* 1:115. Bonhoeffer offers a similar rendition of this statement in his subsequent works. In *Act and Being*, he writes, "In my fall from God, humanity fell" (*DBWE* 2:146). And in *Creation and Fall*, he states, "The guilt is mine alone: I have committed evil in the midst of the original state of creation" (*DBWE* 3:105).

has meaning, theologically speaking, only within the community designated by God's external address. This is why Bonhoeffer claims, "It is precisely at this point," when one begins to theologically discuss the church, "that the meaning of the *peccatorum communio* [communion of sinners] first becomes relevant."[77] Sin is only known from within the believing community, and it is known as a community of sinners—both individual and collective at once.

Bonhoeffer's theological understanding of sin assists theological discourses on race by demonstrating that whiteness should not be equated hastily with sin. Whiteness certainly presents itself with characteristics that are similar to sin in that whiteness has a coercive aspect (the historical and social construct of race) and a culpability aspect (explicit and implicit individual racist acts). Still, sin is distinct in that it remains an unfathomable rupture with universal consequence whereas whiteness is a targeted obstruction with specific consequences. This is not to downgrade the seriousness of whiteness and its horrific history of colonialism, slavery, lynching, mass incarceration, gentrification, and much more. Instead, by distinguishing whiteness theologically from sin, one can attend to how whiteness does not affect all humanity equally, as does sin. Whiteness affords power and privilege to some and weakness and disadvantage to everyone else. To attend theologically to whiteness, one must find a way to speak theologically about how whiteness specifically works as an organized lie that resists the truth of God's address.

Bonhoeffer: The "Natural and Unnatural" and a Theological Definition of Whiteness

In *Creation and Fall*, Bonhoeffer begins to explore sin from new angles, expanding his thinking on the subject from his earlier works, *Sanctorum Communio* and *Act and Being*. The question Bonhoeffer entertains in *Creation and Fall* and then expands upon later in *Ethics* is not simply what sin *is* but how sin relates to and impacts God's good creation. It is in his chapter on the "Natural Life" from *Ethics* that Bonhoeffer offers his most precise theological formulation for how to speak about this interrelation between God's good creation and sin. He writes, "We speak of the natural as distinct from the created, in order to include the fact of the fall into sin. We speak of the natural as distinct from the sinful in order to include the created."[78] The "natural" is Bonhoeffer's theological

---

77   *DBWE* 1:123.

78   *DBWE* 6:173.

term for a sin-bearing creation after the fall. As the title itself suggests, *Creation and Fall* pertains to a theological discussion about the natural, the impact of the fall into sin on God's creation. *Creation and Fall*, in a sense, is a discussion of the "natural" before Bonhoeffer had arrived at this terminology later in his *Ethics*. This makes it helpful to review Bonhoeffer's discussion of the natural and unnatural from *Ethics*. From there Bonhoeffer's account of a "living death" from *Creation and Fall* can be employed to work toward a theological definition of whiteness.

In his chapter on the "Natural Life," Bonhoeffer begins by lamenting how the natural as a category has been eliminated from Protestant thought. For some theologians, he states, the term "was completely lost in the darkness of general sinfulness."[79] For the rest, he writes, the term "took on the brightness of the primal creation."[80] The problem, as Bonhoeffer sees it, is rooted in an inability among Protestants to correctly relate the ultimate and penultimate. Protestants who see creation as "completely lost in the darkness of general sinfulness" wrongly exclude the continuity of God's speaking as upholding fallen creation in terms of the penultimate. Conversely, Protestants who interpret fallen creation in "the brightness" of Eden exclude the contingent surprise of God's ultimate word.

For Bonhoeffer the penultimate relegates a relative space either open to Christ's coming (natural) or closed to Christ's coming (unnatural). Bonhoeffer explains how both the natural and the unnatural are relative: "The natural does not compel the coming of Christ, nor does the unnatural make it impossible, in both cases the real coming is an act of grace."[81] Thus, the "Natural Life" is Bonhoeffer's explanation of how the penultimate leaves open these two relative options in relation to the surprise of God's gracious speaking. The natural preserves the penultimate in anticipation of the surprise of God's ultimate word; the unnatural destroys the penultimate in resistance to the surprise of God's ultimate word.

These relative options are crucial, because they delineate how the natural inherently challenges the unnatural. This intrinsic challenge embedded in God's creation is what Bonhoeffer points out was lacking in Protestant thought leading up to the Second World War. Bonhoeffer explains, "The only antithesis to the natural was no longer the unnatural, but the word of God."[82] This opens the danger of misapplying God's ulti-

79   *DBWE* 6:171.
80   *DBWE* 6:171.
81   *DBWE* 6:173.
82   *DBWE* 6:172.

mate word against God's good creation burdened by sin. Christ's incarnation refuses this direct application of God's word. As Bonhoeffer charges, "Christ has entered natural life. Only by Christ's becoming human does natural life become the penultimate that is directed toward the ultimate."[83]

With this understanding of the natural in place, Bonhoeffer bluntly asks, "How is the natural recognized?"[84] Bonhoeffer's first answer to this question is that the natural is recognized through God's direct word in Jesus Christ. [85] His more nuanced answer to this question follows from this direct response. He argues that the natural is embedded in fallen creation with a thereness that can only be received, never appropriated. The natural has already been set and decided in such a way that individuals, communities, and institutions receive their respective share in it, without any of these entities being able to define or claim the natural.[86] To declare oneself as the arbitrator of the natural, he warns, is to act "against the natural that already exists."[87] This leads Bonhoeffer to reason that the "unnatural is something that requires organization," whereas "the natural cannot be organized but is just there."[88] The natural's unorganized persistence provides a relative optimism about creaturely history within the limits of the fallen world.[89] The unnatural (e.g., whiteness) may have its day, but over the many days and nights of history, the unnatural faces the inevitable demise of running up against the natural that already exists. As seen in Jennings' discussion of whiteness, the unnatural vies for the passing power to create and organize. Countering the unnatural, the natural rests in a creaturely existence constituted by the triune God, the Creator and Preserver of creation.

From this understanding of the natural and unnatural, *Creation and Fall* may be read as a treatment of similar themes in relation to sin and creation.[90] Rather than a direct discussion of sin, *Creation and Fall* is a meditation on sin's pervasive and exhaustive impact on all of God's good creation. As Bonhoeffer comments, "The extent of the fall is such

83   *DBWE* 6:174.

84   *DBWE* 6:174.

85   Bonhoeffer calls this the formal side of the natural, that which "can only be recognized by looking at Jesus Christ" (*DBWE* 6:174).

86   See *DBWE* 6:175.

87   *DBWE* 6:175–76.

88   *DBWE* 6:177.

89   See *DBWE* 6:177.

90   As justification for this reading, it may be noted that *Creation and Fall* refers directly to sin only twice, once in reference to original sin and once in reference to how the conscience may use sin as an excuse to evade God. See *DBWE* 3:124–25, 128–29.

that it affects the whole created world."[91] This distinction between sin itself and sin's impact on creation is significant, because it gives Bonhoeffer the theological grounding to talk about the social concreteness of a creation darkened by sin. Hence, Bonhoeffer discusses how sin isolates human beings not only from God and from one another but also from the creation itself.

The way sin isolates human beings from creation is observed in Bonhoeffer's metaphor of "twilight" [*Zwielicht*].[92] The creation has been darkened by the knowledge of good and evil, leaving God's creation opaque and shrouded in contradiction from a fallen human perspective. Bonhoeffer describes this contradiction of good and evil as interwoven into the human being's thinking, being, and existence.[93] In *Creation and Fall*, Bonhoeffer names this grounding in contradiction a living death: "*To be dead means to-have-to-live.*"[94] Humanity lives from a continual rejection of God, who preserves creation and humanity in this continual rejection.

In terms of Bonhoeffer's later language, a living death is a constant rebellion against God's gracious preservation of the natural. A living death, therefore, is the unnatural. Bonhoeffer depicts the embodied acts of a living death as deadening reflexes that tangibly refuse God's care. God's care is repudiated through humanity's rejection of the immanent boundaries of creaturely existence. This understanding of an animated death, for Bonhoeffer, is derived from the life and vivacity that God establishes through the act of divine speech that resurrects Jesus Christ, and that raises all of creation to live with the risen Christ: "It is God's command which creates that which lives out of what is dead—it is God's being able to raise up children to Abraham out of these stones, and calling Christ to rise up from the dead earth."[95] The embodied life that God as Creator and Preserver bestows on God's fallen creatures through resurrection occurs within the deadening existence that transpires after the fall.

The creation narrative, as Bonhoeffer presents it, elaborates the transition *from* a creaturely life that worships God through free, tangible responses to God's care *to* a living death that refuses God's care habitually. Creaturely life is to worship God precisely in the contingency

91   *DBWE* 3:120.
92   *DBWE* 3:104.
93   *DBWE* 3:92.
94   *DBWE* 3:91 (emphasis original).
95   *DBWE* 3:57.

of one's material existence in historical time. This creaturely life is displaced by a deadening renunciation of God's speaking that subsumes one within the contingency of material existence and seeks to eternalize time. Christ comes bodily into this living death to resurrect the dead by restoring a bodily responsiveness through the Spirit. As the first human's worship of God was a tangible worship given in relation to other bodies and the earth,[96] Bonhoeffer contends that, in the sacrament, a tangible worship of God is reconstituted in such a way that fallen humans are now freed by the Spirit to live in relation to other bodies and the earth, but this time in the context of sinful conditions. This means that one receives one's existence from Christ as one relates to the sheer *thereness* of other bodies in the wholeness of persons, in sin, whiteness, and all. It is through Christ that one relates to other human bodies by the Spirit, and it is through this relation to other human bodies that one's bond to the earth is restored.[97]

Bonhoeffer suggests that humanity's embodied refusal of God's care is exemplified in the crucifixion of Jesus Christ. However, in this bodily destruction of Christ Bonhoeffer perceives an opening to a new responsiveness given bodily to human beings in the church's tangible worship:

> That is why where the original body in its created being has been destroyed, God enters it anew in Jesus Christ, and then, where this body too is broken, enters the forms of the sacrament of the body and blood. The body and blood of the Lord's Supper are the new realities of creation promised to fallen Adam. Because Adam is created as body, Adam is also redeemed as body [and God comes to Adam as body], in Jesus Christ and the sacrament.[98]

The sacrament is an embodied receipt of divine care that relates a person to the earth and to other bodies. In this event through the Spirit, Bonhoeffer states, "in their bodily existence human beings find their brothers and sisters and find the earth."[99] God's free act of love in Christ bodily restores a Spirit-driven responsiveness that locates Christ's community in creaturely history and place.

96 Bonhoeffer discusses this in terms of the gracious limit of the tree of good and evil and the limit of another human body given in Adam and Eve's mutual relation to one another. See *DBWE* 3:117–18.

97 Bonhoeffer explains, "Without God, without their brothers and sisters, human beings lose the earth" (*DBWE* 3:67).

98 *DBWE* 3:79.

99 *DBWE* 3:79.

Bonhoeffer's embodied account of a living death assists in elu-
cidating whiteness as unnatural, as an organized destruction of the
penultimate that remains closed to Christ's coming—the surprise
of God's gracious speaking. Moreover, Bonhoeffer's description of a
living death offers purchase on theologically naming the implicit violence of whiteness as a deadening reflex that tangibly refuses God's
care by rebelling against the immanent boundaries of creaturely
existence in history. Whiteness is expressed insidiously through the
countless deadening responses, reactions, gestures, and denials based
on instincts of good and evil racially defined, as seen in the history of
white people in the United States discussed in the previous chapter.
Whiteness is an embodied movement that arises out of the immediacy of one's daily, situated encounters with other bodies, as seen in
Yancy's account of "the elevator effect." This movement is deadening
because it is not open and responsive to God's tangible working in history through peoples and places, and in this way whiteness remains
closed to Christ's coming.

Bringing Jennings Back into the Dialogue

As with Bonhoeffer's description of the unnatural, Jennings' theological
description of whiteness attends to a specific resistance of God's care and
preservation of the fallen creation. Jennings' discussion of whiteness does
not pertain to the condition of sin that besets us all but a distinctly organized racial hierarchy that is closed to Christ's coming. It is important to
note that Jennings never makes a direct connection between whiteness
and sin, but nor does he carefully distinguish the two terms.[100] Without a
clear distinction, there is the implicit risk in Jennings' theological analysis

---

100 Jennings comes close to drawing a distinction between original sin and whiteness in
his discussion of Jesus' temptation. See Jennings, *The Christian Imagination*, 260–61. Even
here, however, the aim is to show how Jesus' distinct temptation relates to Israel rather than
Adam. By way of comparison, Bonhoeffer's *Bible Study on Temptation* draws a sharp contrast between Christ's temptation and Adam's. See Bonhoeffer, "Bible Study on Temptation,
June 20–25, 1938," in *DBWE* 15:386–415. Bonhoeffer writes, "Everything else that happened in terms of human temptations must be understood in relation to these two stories
of temptation. We are either tempted *in Adam*, or we are tempted *in Christ*" (*DBWE* 15:390,
emphasis original). Bonhoeffer's and Jennings' distinctive accounts of the temptation of
Jesus illustrate, on the one hand, how Bonhoeffer is more attentive to the unfathomable
rupture of sin than Jennings and, on the other hand, how Bonhoeffer is less attentive to Israel than Jennings. Bonhoeffer asserts the stark contrast between Adam and Christ; Jennings
traces how the thread between Christ and Israel extends to all nations.

of race that an understanding of sin as a complete break may be confused with whiteness as a specifically targeted resistance to God's care.

This risk is heightened with Jennings' careful tracing of how whiteness is enacted on a global stage. Through considering the global reach of European colonialism, whiteness is rightly portrayed as an international phenomenon into which all the peoples of the world are inducted and inculcated. The global scope of whiteness that Jennings presents, though, should not be confused with the universal rupture of original sin. To do so would inflate the specificity of whiteness from a distinct resistance of God's care into a complete rupture of separation from God. While whiteness may have a global scope, it does not define all human beings with the same culpability or under the same coerciveness, as does original sin. The danger of elevating whiteness to the complete break of original sin is bound up with the inverse risk of reducing original sin to the particular resistance of whiteness. The suggestion made here is not that Jennings offers one of these problematic conclusions but that his discussion of whiteness does not adequately safeguard against either.

The distinction Bonhoeffer draws between the unnatural and sin illuminates how whiteness requires a different response than the universal break of sin. The organized resistance of whiteness, unlike sin, is not directly addressed by God's ultimate word but, instead, is addressed through preparing the way for God's ultimate word. This distinction between (original) sin and the unnatural allows Bonhoeffer to understand the Christian church as both resistant to God's call and incorporated with the whole world into a preparing for God's address. Insofar as whiteness is to be understood as unnatural, Jennings' theological critique of whiteness should be understood as a penultimate challenge given in reference to and in preparation of God's ultimate judgment on and forgiveness of sin. This makes Jennings' challenge of whiteness no less urgent or significant. If anything, Jennings' challenge becomes all the more acute when whiteness is considered as a continual resistance to God's word to Israel, compounding over days, years, decades, and centuries. When whiteness is grasped with this urgency, each moment represents the opportunity to join with Israel's God in a preparation already underway.

Joining and Community

Joining is a central motif in Jennings' *The Christian Imagination* that becomes especially prominent and ubiquitous in the book's final chapter. Jennings opens this chapter by stating, "Although the history of Christianity in the colonial West shows the difficulty of people imagining space and peoples together, Christianity itself offers hope of their *joining*."[101] Joining, for Jennings, is not simply about joining different peoples but about a particular imagining of the interconnectedness between peoples and places. This form of joining is not something new but a joining in motion from the very beginning, within the intimacy of Israel's conversation with their God. Christianity itself, Jennings suggests, offers the hope of this kind of joining in that its true origins reside not in the colonial West but in Israel—not simply in Israel as a people or in Israel as a place, but in the imaginative space created in God's address to Israel that connects Israel as a people to God's creation for the sake of the world. This joining between places and peoples offered in Israel runs downstream to Christianity itself in that Israel's Messiah constitutes a joining into which Gentile Christians are included as outside recipients. In sum, the joining that Jennings describes works on two interdependent levels—a joining *in* Israel and a joining of Gentiles *with* Israel.

In a similar yet distinct fashion to Jennings' concept of joining, community plays a distinguishing role in Bonhoeffer's writings. Bonhoeffer's concept of community is a complex one, first worked out in *Sanctorum Communio* and later discussed in *Life Together*. Throughout his writings, Bonhoeffer uses the term "community" [*Gemeinde*] in a way that is specifically ecclesial and yet that remains attendant to broader sociological and historical concepts of community.[102] Referring to the church as a community reflects how Bonhoeffer accounts for the empirical, already existing church as concurrently a fully human community and a reality of God's revelation. In other words, Bonhoeffer seeks to deal with the existing church as it is on the ground, as a human community like any

101 Jennings, *The Christian Imagination*, 250 (emphasis added).
102 This ecclesial specificity is highlighted by the translators and editors of *DBWE* 1 when they translate Bonhoeffer's well-known axiom "*Christus als Gemeinde existierend*" as "Christ existing as church-community." See *DBWE* 1:16. At the same time, Bonhoeffer's aim in *Sanctorum Communio* is to detail how theology can draw upon social theory in a way that does not compromise distinctively theological claims about the church. For an examination of how Bonhoeffer uniquely speaks of the church in this way, see Mawson, *Christ Existing as Community*.

other, and to understand this distinct community as God's present form on earth in the living person of Jesus Christ.

Jennings' specific use of joining and Bonhoeffer's ecclesial use of community present two distinctive challenges to whiteness. These distinct challenges are explored here not as mutually exclusive but as mutually supportive. Jennings' proposal of joining confronts whiteness with the continuity of Israel to reveal the vast distances the Christian church in the colonial West has traveled from its foreign home in the vulnerable joining of Israel. Bonhoeffer's ecclesial concept of community assists in confronting whiteness with the fragmented continuity of the Christian church to reveal the lengths to which Jesus Christ has gone in order to extend Israel's home to a Christian church buried underneath the colonial soil of the West. While their concepts of joining and community may travel in divergent directions, the hope is that Jennings and Bonhoeffer collectively imagine a space that meets in the middle.

Jennings: Israel as the Place of Joining

In the final chapter of *The Christian Imagination*, Jennings offers his constructive proposal of Israel as the place of joining. He suggests that the hermeneutical horizon of Israel not only exposes the missteps of a distorted Christian imagination facilitated by whiteness but also offers its own imagining of space.[103] Israel does not merely help one imagine space; Jennings goes beyond this by arguing that Israel also represents the concrete possibility of "a rerootedness, continuity, and life-giving newness."[104] In the same way whiteness creates a new space in the same moment that it creates race, Israel and Israel's Messiah provide a space for concrete joining in a renewed Christian imagination. Jennings invites his Christian readers to join in Israel's movement with their God to reimagine space.

The first step in this joining with Israel, Jennings states, "is remembering Gentile existence."[105] This step requires that Gentiles remember that they are found outside the story of Israel. Jennings states, "Reading

103 When Jennings speaks of Israel in this way, he suggests that his designation "Israel" includes "biblical Israel" and "living Israel," as well as having in "view Israel as an ethnic, cultural, even racial reality" (*The Christian Imagination*, 251). Theologically understood, Jennings explicates that there is only living Israel and biblical Israel. Ethnic Israel is a reflexive designation of whiteness that must be overcome with the theological significance of Israel.

104 Jennings, *The Christian Imagination*, 251.

105 Jennings, *The Christian Imagination*, 252.

Israel's story is intended to be disruptive, especially for Gentile existence."[106] This disruption is seen in that there is no explanation for Israel's conquest of Canaan other than God's direct word.[107] This is not a
repeatable act, Jennings explains, but an act of divine speech that confronts Gentiles without explanation, only intensifying the reality that
Israel's story is not the story of the Gentiles. The history of biblical Israel
shows that God's word stands between Israel and the land, even while
land and word are bound together as constitutive of Israel's life. This
intimate relationship between Israel and Israel's God is what Gentiles
are invited into through recognizing our own distance from this intimacy. By recognizing "that we are not addressed in the conversation
of biblical Israel with its God," Jennings argues, Gentiles are admitted
into Israel's story.[108] Gentiles gain entrance into Israel's story by hearing
about this story as outsiders, by listening in on the story already being
told within Israel.

The plot of Israel's story thickens with the advent of Israel's Messiah.
This thickening of the plot only further requires that Gentiles remember
their positioning outside of Israel's story. Jennings explains that Gentiles must remember that Jesus, as the elect one of Israel, "is the slen-
der thread that holds Gentiles inside Israel as authentic not exclusive
inheritors of its legacies."[109] Israel's Messiah both challenges Gentiles to
again remember Gentile existence and, simultaneously, challenges Israel
from within Israel's own covenantal story. Jennings illustrates this double challenge through the story of Jesus' encounter with the Canaanite woman. In contrast to Volf's interpretation of a broadening of Jesus'
mission discussed earlier,[110] Jennings argues that this pericope intensifies the reality that Gentiles remain external to Israel's story. This is
seen in Jesus' prohibition that his gifts are for Israel and not for (Gentile)
dogs. To remove the offense of Jesus' words is to eliminate the scandal
of Israel's particularity. Jennings writes, "The Canaanite woman stands
in for all Gentiles who would presume on the grace of God. Yet, more
important, she marks the path forward."[111] The path forward is seen in

106 Jennings, *The Christian Imagination*, 255.

107 Jennings writes, "Divine word certainly precedes land" (*The Christian Imagination*,
252).

108 Jennings, *The Christian Imagination*, 252.

109 Jennings, *The Christian Imagination*, 272.

110 See the discussion of Volf's interpretation of this passage from *Exclusion and Embrace* in chapter 1.

111 Jennings, *The Christian Imagination*, 262.

how the Canaanite woman takes on her lips the words of Israel when she cries out, "Have mercy on me, Lord, Son of David" (Matt 15:21).[112] As a Gentile outsider, the Canaanite woman finds herself inside Israel's story through being drawn into it by Israel's Messiah.

While Jesus' prohibition to the Canaanite woman situates him firmly within Israel, Jesus' acceptance of the Canaanite woman locates Gentiles inside of Israel's story as well, revealing the very meaning of Israel's story with God. Jennings explains, "He is one with their story, but he has become the new storyteller."[113] Jesus works within Israel's story to remove any false allegiance to which Israel can bow; they must bow only to their God, who is given to them in Jesus of Nazareth. The challenge that Jesus *is*, Jennings contends, confronts the false allegiances both of the Gentiles and of Israel, carrying them both "into the scandal of choosing him and thereby choosing a new reality of kinship."[114] Jennings remarks that before one can join with the particularity of who Jesus is, one's own allegiances of kinship must be scandalized by his exclusive particularity. This does not negate one's desires for one's own people but reorders one's desire around Jesus' own body. Jennings writes, "Jesus places his body between the many and their desires."[115] So while Israel's election confronts Gentiles with a remembrance of Gentile existence, the election of Israel's Messiah forms a particular space and imagination within Israel, where the rest of the world is joined with Israel and Israel's God.

The continuity that Jennings presents is a continuity found in the rhythms of being in step with God's movement with Israel, culminating in Israel's Messiah. Christian Gentiles have no claim on this movement but are incorporated into it by Jesus Christ. Jennings distinguishes this concept of continuity from a Catholic approach, described as "a historical construct that posits the Jesus movement as simply a reform movement in Judaism" or a Protestant approach detailed as following "a vernacularization thesis that isolates the gospel message into its essential components."[116] These two approaches correlate to Jennings' critiques

112 Jennings does not note that this cry comes before Jesus' prohibition. See *The Christian Imagination*, 262. This further emphasizes Jennings' point that even when Gentiles offer the words of Israel, they do so as outside inheritors of Israel's story.

113 Jennings, *The Christian Imagination*, 263.

114 Jennings, *The Christian Imagination*, 265.

115 Jennings, *The Christian Imagination*, 265. The language of desire reoccurs in his commentary on Acts. See Willie James Jennings, *Acts* (Louisville: Westminster John Knox Press, 2017), 10–12, 102–8.

116 Jennings, *The Christian Imagination*, 265.

of the Roman Catholic Church (represented by Alasdair MacIntyre) and the Protestant Church (as seen in Jennings' critique of Sanneh and Walls).[117] In place of these two approaches, Jennings writes, "I suggest an advent of a new form of communion with the possibility of a new kind of cultural intimacy between peoples that might yield a new cultural politic."[118] Jennings presents this "advent of a new form of communion" through his discussion of the book of Acts.[119]

There are three particular events in the book of Acts that Jennings discusses: Pentecost in Acts 2, Peter's encounter with Cornelius in Acts 10, and the Jerusalem Council in Acts 15. His narration of each of these chapters highlights the necessity for an embodied joining between Israel and the Gentiles. In discussing Pentecost, Jennings argues that if this event is incorrectly reduced to merely an audible event as it has often been interpreted, then "Jesus may be translated in every tongue" without any need for joining.[120] This reductionist interpretation of Pentecost makes Jesus abstract and removes Israel as the concrete place of joining. Jennings offers his own interpretation: "Here the disciples dramatize not simply the miracle of hearing and the claim of the God of Israel on all peoples, but, more significantly, they dramatize the joining of bodies and lives in the worship of the God who was witnessed by Jesus."[121] Jennings argues that Pentecost is the story of the Creator reclaiming the world through communion within Israel's story.

Jennings continues a similar narration with the story of Peter and Cornelius from Acts 10. Here again the point, for Jennings, pertains to an embodied joining, but this time specifically between Israel (Peter) and the Gentiles (Cornelius and his family). Jennings proclaims, "If a world caught in the unrelenting exchange system of violence was to be

117 For Jennings' critique of Alasdair MacIntyre as a tradition shaped by Jose de Acosta, see Jennings, *The Christian Imagination*, 68–69, 71, 86. Jennings' comments are primarily aimed at MacIntyre's *After Virtue: A Study in Moral Theory* (Notre Dame: University of Notre Dame Press, 1981). For an analysis of this critique, see Draper, *A Theology of Race and Place*, 215–70.

118 Jennings, *The Christian Imagination*, 265.

119 In his commentary on Acts, Jennings presents a similar idea but with more clarity when he argues that the events Luke records in Acts are not immutable principles of ecclesial structures but Luke's tracing of how God's people are trying to keep pace with God's irrevocable movement. He writes, "This irrevocability in Acts sometimes gets confused with immutability so that Acts gets interpreted as the historical foundation of the church's life" (Jennings, *Acts*, 3).

120 Jennings, *The Christian Imagination*, 266.

121 Jennings, *The Christian Imagination*, 266.

overcome, then here was the very means God would use to overcome violence."[122] This second Pentecost constitutes the boundary-shattering love between stranger and enemy found in a particular place inaugurated by Jesus and announced by the Spirit. Israel's story with God is the story of embodied joining in which Gentiles are now included. This Spirit-driven joining demonstrated in Acts 2 and Acts 10 faces a setback in the Jerusalem Council.[123]

Jennings argues that rather than perceiving God's working among the Gentiles as a joining constituted within Israel's story, the Jerusalem Council "could at best only imagine parallel theological universes in which the Gentiles imitated Israel's *contra mundi* posture as the fundamental signature of their newfound faith in the God of Israel through Jesus Christ."[124] Jennings suggests that instead of actually joining with the Gentiles, the Jerusalem Council set up parallel channels that relinquished Israel as the particular place of joining. He writes, "This meant they did not imagine the reformulation of ways of life (Jew and Gentile) established in the spatial reality created by Jesus himself."[125] In other words, the Jerusalem Council could not imagine the space of joining and, thus, never made the joining of Jews and Gentiles a reality. Jennings is quick to point out that this response of the Jerusalem Council should not be interpreted as sinful but, instead, testifies to "the tremendous challenge toward intimacy created by the presence of the Spirit of God."[126] This resistance to the Spirit of God, Jennings suggests, created a fissure that only grew with time. He comments that "the tragedy here is cumulative."[127] This cumulative tragedy leads Jennings to the conclusion that the Gentile church from the very outset was informed by a segregationalist mentality. He comments,

> If the struggle toward cultural intimacy was not faced by the church as inherent to the gospel itself, despite the constant work of the Spirit to turn Israel and Gentile peoples toward one another, then over time the only other option was the emergence of a Christian segregationalist mentality. The best Christian theology has been

122 Jennings, *The Christian Imagination*, 269.

123 Again, Jennings adds more depth and clarity to his short accounts of these passages in his new commentary on Acts. See Jennings, *Acts*, 29–33, 102–14.

124 Jennings, *The Christian Imagination*, 270.

125 Jennings, *The Christian Imagination*, 272.

126 Jennings, *The Christian Imagination*, 270.

127 Jennings, *The Christian Imagination*, 271.

able to suggest this side of the epochs of conquest and the Shoah is a return to the original social imaginary of the earliest church groping to articulate separate yet faithful existence, a theological Jim Crow existence for Jews and Christians.[128]

Jennings' scandalous suggestion, then, is that Gentile Christians and present-day Jews must collectively imagine and live into a reality that even the earliest followers of Jesus fell short of fully realizing.

What Jennings proposes is a renewed imagination discovered in the concrete joining of present-day Jews and Gentile Christians. This joining must go beyond interreligious dialogue, Jennings argues, because much of the interreligious dialogue taking place between Jews and Gentile Christians continues to capitulate to the modernistic problematic, where the "black body" presents the truth of racial existence and "the racialized Jewish body" presents its lie.[129] One place where Jennings seems to see the act of joining within the particularity of Israel to actually have taken place is in the exchange between Jews and Black Gentile Christians during the Civil Rights Movement.[130] However, he laments that this fruitful exchange was cut short at the end of the Civil Rights Movement, which "was the most powerful counterattack on both racism and anti-Semitism" and, simultaneously, "the most absolute surrender to the theological vision of the racial imagination."[131]

Despite all these setbacks, Jennings holds out the hope that a joining within the particularity of Israel is "not first a possibility" but a "reality unrealized," which still "may become a profoundly visible place."[132] He writes that "the space of communion is always ready to appear where the people of God reach down to join the land and reach out to join those around them."[133] To the very end, Jennings stays consistent to the scandal of Israel's election and, through Israel, to the election of Jesus Christ. The boldness of his proposal will be lost on most, as he acknowledges,[134] because of its sheer expansiveness and the daring risk it involves. Once

128 Jennings, *The Christian Imagination*, 271.

129 Jennings, *The Christian Imagination*, 275.

130 See Jennings' account of this in his section titled "Jew, Black, and Interracial" in *The Christian Imagination*, 275–86.

131 Jennings, *The Christian Imagination*, 279.

132 Jennings, *The Christian Imagination*, 286.

133 Jennings, *The Christian Imagination*, 286.

134 Jennings writes in his conclusion, "For some, my account of Jesus-space and communion will seem idealistic, a denial of Christian failure and the realities I rightly pointed toward in the previous chapters. If my account of space looks like an idealist account, it is

one enters the world that Jennings describes as inaugurated by Israel's Messiah, there is no going back.

Bonhoeffer and Jennings: The Mediation of Jesus Christ

Jennings' *The Christian Imagination* is not simply about the *imagination* but about a *bodily joining* that imagines the world rightly, as within God's story with Israel. The legacies of supersessionism and whiteness rewrite God's story through a bodily joining violently mediated around white bodies. Jennings decisively breaks from this distorted form of joining, going back to Israel's story to discover a joining given by Israel's God. The particular body of Jesus Christ is found within Israel, and from within Israel, Jesus' body is positioned between Israel and the rest of the world. This is to suggest that Jesus' body mediates joining in a particular manner. Jesus' mediation provides a bodily joining of peoples and their ways of life not abstractly, but through God's particular pursuit of Israel and through Israel to the rest of the world.

While the thrust of Jennings' proposal is aimed toward the wonder of a bodily joining within Israel, his interpretation of Christ's mediation focuses on the language of desire. He writes, "Jesus, in forming a new Israel in the midst of Israel, positioned himself as the new source of desire."[135] In his account of Jesus' temptation, Jennings proposes that the desire of every nation and group to be secured and to belong is not ultimately thwarted by Jesus but fulfilled in a reorientation of desire toward Jesus' body.[136] The desire to be bodily joined in Jesus' body faced immediate resistance in the Jerusalem Council. The Jerusalem Council reflects the failure to enter into a bodily joining around the body of Jesus. The question here is how Jennings' understanding of a mediation of desires relates to a meditation of bodies. The difficulty lies in holding these two together.

Jennings is aware of this difficulty as he discusses the "social and cultural instability engendered by involvement with Jesus."[137] A desire for Jesus' body creates a confrontation with our deeply ingrained alliances and allegiances configured historically by whiteness. As discussed previously, an example of this confrontation is given in Yancy's

---

precisely because it is an account held in stark contrast to the utter inversion of the Israel/Gentile relation" (Jennings, *The Christian Imagination*, 288).

135 Jennings, *The Christian Imagination*, 264.

136 Jennings, *The Christian Imagination*, 260–61.

137 Jennings, *The Christian Imagination*, 264.

recounting of "the elevator effect." The white woman Yancy approaches in the elevator may have a desire to join with him and even with Jesus' body in Israel, but she still automatically clutches her purse. How do we account for Christ's bodily mediation in these quotidian encounters that may allow for a mediation of desires but seem to rupture Jennings' proposal of a bodily joining in Israel?

Whereas Jennings positions Jesus' body between Israel and the rest of the world as a mediation of desire, Bonhoeffer places Jesus' body between sinful persons in the existing church's celebration of the sacrament.[138] Bonhoeffer argues that the sacrament is the place where God reaches down to the fallen earth so that "in their bodily nature human beings are related to the earth and to other bodies."[139] The Lord's Supper is where a community of fallen human beings discover what the creation *is* as one takes the bread and wine from another and finds oneself joined to the earth and other bodies. In this way Bonhoeffer provides a concrete place in the Lord's Supper where the living person of Christ mediates the joining of bodies and directly confronts our bodily resistance to this joining. In the celebration of the Lord's Supper, one is confronted by the broken and humiliated body of Christ, causing a visceral response that opens one to an embodied reorientation to others and the earth. Jennings is correct to highlight the scandal of gathering around Christ's body as "the bread that must be eaten."[140] Still, his discussion of consuming Christ's body does not situate Christ concretely between bodies but "between the many and their desires."[141] The suggestion offered here is that the bodily practices of whiteness necessitate the embodied challenge of the church's liturgical life.

Lifting up the Lord's Supper as an embodied enactment of joining within the existing community of the church furthers Jennings' constructive proposal by offering a concrete practice that confronts the resistance of whiteness in the Western Christian Church as it stands.

138 This distinction between Jennings and Bonhoeffer follows the historical divide between Reformed and Lutheran views of Christ's real presence in the Lord's Supper. For Bonhoeffer's discussion of this divide, see his *Lectures on Christology* in *DBWE* 12:320–23. Bonhoeffer parts ways with both the Reformed tradition and his own Lutheran heritage by arguing that both traditions wrongly ask "how" Christ is present rather than, "Who is the Christ who is present in the sacrament?" (*DBWE* 12:322). A further discussion of Christ's presence in the sacrament is reserved for chapter 5 in relation to Bonhoeffer's ecclesiology.

139 *DBWE* 3:79.

140 Jennings, *The Christian Imagination*, 264.

141 Jennings, *The Christian Imagination*, 265. Jennings speaks of communion in the same way in his commentary on the book of Acts. See Jennings, *Acts*, 10.

At the same time, in correspondence with Jennings' warning to Gentile Christians, including Bonhoeffer, there is a need to understand this embodied joining as occurring within Israel. One must go beyond Bonhoeffer in remembering the Lord's Supper as a practice held by Jesus' Jewish disciples in continuity with Israel's celebration of the Passover.[142] God's word that stands between Israel and the land includes God-given rituals that orient Israel to the land, one another, and the rest of the world. In the Passover Israel is given a tangible response to God's care through the earth that opens Israel to the giving of the Torah and Israel's commission of divine violence.[143] The Passover shares with the Lord's Supper the contingency of a God-given practice *within history*, joining Israel and the Christian church to God's creation.[144] It is through these temporal and tangible practices given by God that God's people, living Israel and Gentile Christians, are first opened to a new perception of peoples and places. God's speaking in this distinct manner opens God's people to respond to God's speaking in all place and times.

Jennings' insights on remembering Gentile existence and a joining in Israel protects the Lord's Supper from the abuses and distortions of whiteness that sever these practices from Israel's story. In considering the Lord's Supper from Bonhoeffer's perspective of community, one must attend to both God's part in it and the sociological dimension of the church in it (as will be examined in chapter 5). The sociological dimension of the church leaves the Lord's Supper susceptible to human distortions, as introduced by whiteness, requiring a continual preparing of the way for God's direct word to be heard in the church's proclamation of Word and sacrament. This tension between the church as a fully human community and as a reality of God's revelation informs Bonhoeffer's insights about God's claiming of the earth and bodies through

142 While Bonhoeffer does not explicitly make this connection, Luther develops it by referencing the Passover in relation to the Lord's Supper. See Martin Luther, "Psalm 111," in *Luther's Works*, American ed., 55 vols., ed. Jaroslav Pelikan and Helmut T. Lehmann (Philadelphia: Muehlenberg and Fortress, and St. Louis: Concordia, 1955–1986), 13:371–73.

143 Jennings' interpretation of Israel's conquest of Canaan theoretically closes the possibility of divine violence beyond Israel's history. This raises the question of how to make sense of boundary cases in theological ethics, such as Bonhoeffer's involvement in the assassination of Hitler or in John Brown's raid on Harpers Ferry. For a thoughtful approach to the problem of divine violence and the repercussions it has for the limits of ethics, see Smith, *Weird John Brown*.

144 A discussion of how the Passover and the Lord's Supper relate to one another falls outside of the scope of this project. As a result, the relation between Passover and the Lord's Supper remains an open discussion that requires further research.

the practice of the Lord's Supper, here and now. The Lord's Supper is not for a perfect community but constitutes how God joins peoples in the midst of our bodily resistance to being joined by God. It is in this middle space, in the gathering of a sinful community, where Jennings' concept of joining meets the existing church to challenge whiteness in its doxological practices of hearing God's invocation today.

Bonhoeffer and Jennings: Joining and the Christian Church

In *Act and Being*, Bonhoeffer voices similar concerns to those expressed by Jennings about how Catholics and Protestants have domesticated the surprise of God's revelation in different ways.[145] Bonhoeffer seeks to repair these distortions in Catholicism and Protestantism by bringing the two together. He pairs the *continuity* of the historical church generally emphasized by Catholics with the *contingency* of God's word broadly emphasized by Protestants. Direct faith in God's contingent address finds one already in the continuity of the historical church.

Jennings' concern regarding the domestication of God's address by Catholics and Protestants derives from a wholly different set of motivations. Jennings is concerned with how Catholics and Protestants both live within a theological narrative severed from Israel's story, a supersessionism that comes to maturity in whiteness. This means Jennings' intent, unlike Bonhoeffer's, is not necessarily to repair Catholicism and Protestantism with one another but to reimagine both within the original narrative—God's story with Israel. The book of Acts has utmost importance for Jennings because it describes both how Israel as the place of joining was lost and how rejoining in God's story with Israel may be realized today.

Jennings' concern is not to show how Catholics and Protestants are to reform themselves within their own traditions but to reimagine their traditions through joining with Israel. Jennings goes to the root of the problem, which he locates in Acts 15. He insists that the problem is not primarily about Christian ecumenism but about why we have to have the conversation about ecumenism in the first place. Why do we talk insistently about the differences between our Christian traditions

145 Bonhoeffer addresses three incorrect ways of approaching divine revelation: revelation in terms of being in doctrine, revelation as experience of consciousness, and revelation as an institution. Within these corrections, he critiques Catholics for casting the church's being as an institution and Protestants for basing the church's being on verbal inspiration. See Bonhoeffer, *DBWE* 2:103–7.

with little regard for the original schism between Gentile Christians and Israel? In all of Bonhoeffer's ecumenical work, there is little indication that a question of this magnitude was on his radar.[146] Jennings' work guides the Christian church into a memory of Gentile existence that has been so buried in history that we often no longer know what questions to ask. The resistance of whiteness is a resistance we are still learning how to theologically name.

Bonhoeffer's writings on the Christian church deal with a slightly different set of challenges. Generally, Bonhoeffer's writings on the church deal with how Western Christianity has turned the church and Christian doctrine into a self-creation. This aligns in part with Jennings' concerns but comes at the problem from another angle. Whereas Jennings seeks continuity with Israel's story, Bonhoeffer seeks continuity in history through Christ's presence on earth as community. The Christian church, for Bonhoeffer, cannot be self-created when it is a community in which we already find ourselves after hearing God's call. This presupposition of an already-given community comes with a cost. It must attend to the historical inequities already given in this existing community. Herein lies the crux of the issue with a Christian church marked by whiteness today. God's call finds people of color (and also women) included in an existing community that distinctly excludes them.

Jennings discusses his own struggles with this incorporation into a historical Christian community through recounting his mother's encounter with local white missionaries in their garden and his preaching as a student at Calvin College.[147] As well as communicating the violence of finding himself in a community that excluded him as a Black man, these stories express Jennings' memory of being found in already existing Christian community. Jennings' challenge in *The Christian Imagination* is to reimagine this already existing Christian community as rooted in Israel. Bonhoeffer's challenge, instead, is to show how God's speaking continually confronts this already existing community with a vulnerable joining that we continually resist.

This brings us back to the differences between Jennings' motif of joining and Bonhoeffer's ecclesial concept of community. Jennings contrasts two divergent forms of joining, the violent joining of whiteness

---

146 For a discussion of Bonhoeffer's ecumenical work, see Keith Clements, "Ecumenical Witness for Peace," in *The Cambridge Companion to Dietrich Bonhoeffer*, ed. John W. de Gruchy (Cambridge: Cambridge University Press, 1999), 154–89.

147 See Jennings, *The Christian Imagination*, 3–7.

and the vulnerable joining of Israel. This contrast offers two mutually exclusive forms of joining. Thus, it seems that Jennings presents a joining that one day was at Pentecost and one day might be again. The historical continuity of joining with Israel is a reality always there but never fully actualized. Joining with Israel, at least for now, remains a "reality *unrealized*."[148] As Jennings writes, "The space of communion is *always ready to appear* where the people of God reach down to join the land and reach out to join those around them."[149] The concreteness of Jennings' proposal, an actual joining between Gentiles and Jews, should not be lost, but it must be undergirded by an already given place of joining if it is to deal fully with the historical Christian church of the West in which we find ourselves.

Rather than contrasting two mutually exclusive forms of joining, Bonhoeffer's ecclesial concept of community addresses a tension presently given within the historical church as both a fully human and sinful community and a reality of God's revelation. This tension is held through a faith that locates one already in Christ's community in history. It is from this placement in Christ's community that sin is not only known as sin but also is fundamentally challenged—first, through participation with Christ in the church's tangible worship and, second, through a preparation with Christ for the surprise of God's direct address. Bonhoeffer's ecclesial concept of community, thus, suggests a present and anticipative challenge to whiteness through careful attendance of how the triune God speaks in the midst of a community of sinners. Bonhoeffer maintains that the community of sinners (i.e. the church) is confronted by its own joining already established in fallen creation through the broken body of Jesus Christ, who "enters the forms of the sacrament of the body and blood."[150] The place of joining, for Bonhoeffer, is not a place "always ready to appear" but a historical community already there. It is *from within* this historical community that a direct challenge to whiteness is given as a preparation for the hearing of God's direct address.

In sum, Bonhoeffer and Jennings are both concerned with how the Christian church obstructs the surprise of hearing God's address today. The difference between the two is that each challenges a distinct obstruction—sin in Bonhoeffer's case and whiteness in Jennings'. Rather than competing ideas, the insights that Bonhoeffer and Jennings

---

148 Jennings, *The Christian Imagination*, 286 (emphasis added).
149 Jennings, *The Christian Imagination*, 286 (emphasis added).
150 *DBWE* 3:79.

offer the Christian church serve to sharpen one another. Bonhoeffer details how Christ's community is a community already joined in history by God's direct address, and how those found in this community are incorporated into a preparing of the way that challenges our continued resistance to this joining. Jennings accounts for how the church in the colonial West, both Catholic and Protestant, has resisted the embodied joining between Jews and Gentiles, specifically through whiteness. Jennings sharpens Bonhoeffer's reliance on God's joining of a historical community by connecting this community back to its origins in Israel. Bonhoeffer sharpens Jennings' imagination of a joined space within Israel by connecting this space with the surprise of God's direct address, discovered in the already occurring practices of the Christian church's worship. Together Bonhoeffer and Jennings further contemporary theological discussion of race by guiding us into receiving God's care through a good creation distorted by sin and obscured by whiteness.

Conclusion

Bonhoeffer and Jennings each offer theological proposals that utterly reimagine the very venture of theology itself. Theological knowing and speaking, according to Bonhoeffer, is only possible in direct reference to the apprehension of Jesus Christ given in the church's proclamation of Word and sacrament. And the whole enterprise of Western Christian theology, often unknowingly, according to Jennings, finds itself within the tight confines of a racial modality that decouples Israel and the doctrine of creation. These sweeping claims reflect how Bonhoeffer reimagines theology with a keen awareness of sin and how Jennings reimagines theology with a keen awareness of whiteness.

In bringing these critical approaches to theology together, it was suggested that Jennings presents an important penultimate critique of whiteness when interpreted within Bonhoeffer's framework of the ultimate and penultimate. Addressing whiteness is a preparing of the way. Bonhoeffer provides this framework of an ecclesial preparing of the way by describing how the church's ecclesial knowing is always given in reference to the direct act of faith, which already finds one in the historical church. It is only within the community being addressed by God that Christ's community knows itself as a community of sinners. In this way Bonhoeffer's presentation of an ecclesial knowledge of sin offers the historical Christian church nowhere to stand outside of sin in the context of the fallen creation. For this reason the next chapter turns to discuss how Bonhoeffer's Christology attends to how Christ meets humanity in the midst of the fallen world and how this encounter includes the church's response of preparing the way for Christ's coming.

4

Christology and Whiteness

Bonhoeffer and J. Kameron Carter in Dialogue

In his *Lectures on Christology*, Bonhoeffer makes the fascinating claim that the central problem for all Christology is not God's becoming *human* but the God-human's *humiliation*. The central problem for all Christology is that Jesus Christ comes to fallen creation incognito, in the humiliation of being numbered with sinners, "in the likeness of sinful flesh" (Rom 8:3).[1] Jesus Christ, Bonhoeffer explains, "comes among sinners as the one without sin, but also as a sinner among sinners."[2] It is this focal point on how Jesus Christ is revealed in the visible humiliation of sinful flesh that makes Bonhoeffer's Christology uniquely apt for addressing the central question of this study: how does the triune

---

1   Bonhoeffer refers to Romans 8:3, that God sends "his own Son in the likeness of sinful flesh," to discuss the hiddenness of Christ's coming at a number of key junctures in his corpus. For specific examples see Bonhoeffer's discussion of this verse in *Discipleship*, where he writes, "The flesh borne by Christ was sinful flesh" (*DBWE* 4:214); and his discussion of Christ's humiliation in his *Lectures on Christology*, where he explains, "In Christ's being humiliated, we are talking about neither the divinity nor humanity, but rather the ὁμοίωμα σαρκὸς [likeness of sinful flesh]" (*DBWE* 12:356).

2   *DBWE* 12:356.

God speak through a historical church marked by sin, and undeniably shaped by whiteness, without succumbing to sin or its outworking effects in terms of whiteness? Whereas the last chapter attended to how Bonhoeffer understands the creation as fallen, this chapter turns to examine how Bonhoeffer's Christology addresses a fallen creation precisely in its fallenness. Bonhoeffer's careful attention to how Jesus Christ is revealed in the fallen creation directs us to consider how God continues to speak today in a historical church enclosed in sin yet bound to the One without sin.

While Bonhoeffer's Christology focuses on Jesus' coming in the likeness of *sinful* flesh, J. Kameron Carter develops a Christology in *Race: A Theological Account* that concentrates on Jesus' *Jewish* flesh.[3] What brings Bonhoeffer and Carter together is their mutual focus on how God is revealed concretely in history through the person of Jesus Christ. Bonhoeffer's christological writings focus on how God is revealed in *sinful history* through the *wonder* of Jesus Christ's coming in the visible *humiliation* of *sinful* flesh. Comparatively, Carter's Christology attends to how God is revealed in Israel's *covenantal history* as culminating in the *miscegenation* of Jesus' *Jewish* flesh. In what follows, these respective foci are developed and placed in dialogue with one another to illuminate their promise and limitations for advancing contemporary theological discussions of race.

The Shape of Christological Reflection

As the epicenter of theological thinking, Christology constitutes the nexus point where all the various theological doctrines (creation, sin, Israel, church) meet, overlap, and interlock. Christology is not a standalone doctrine but one that shapes and depends on other theological loci.[4] This interlocking character of theological doctrines was explored in the previous chapter, when Bonhoeffer's accounts of creation and sin

---

3   While Carter's thought has certainly developed since the publication of *Race* more than a decade ago, the following chapter seeks to engage Carter strictly in relation to this seminal work and its careful attendance to Israel. Carter's groundbreaking approach in *Race* is often mentioned in passing, but few have offered a sustained interaction with it. One exception to this is Andrew Draper's *Theology of Race and Place.*

4   The approach to systematic theology presented here is not so much concerned with presenting a system of thought but with raising an awareness of the interlinking character of thinking itself. For a discussion of this form of systematic theology in terms of "systematicity," see Williams, *The Architecture of Theology.*

were shown to gain their shape and content in relation to the Christian community's direct encounter with Jesus Christ through faith. Sin is only known in the concrete community's encounter with Jesus Christ, and in this encounter, sin is known as individual and collective at once.[5] In the same manner, the shape of one's Christology depends on an awareness of what interlocking theological doctrines are developed in congruence with it.

Bonhoeffer's and Carter's Christologies are distinct in that each theologian attends to different theological loci in relation to the revelation of Jesus Christ. This distinction will be drawn out by considering the divergent theological constellations that respectively inform their Christologies. Generally, Bonhoeffer's Christology works within the tension of a creation corrupted by sin that is reconciled in Jesus Christ. For Bonhoeffer the reconciliation of Christ given concretely in the historical church does not surpass sin but, instead, must account for God's declaration of human beings as both created and sinful. In contrast, by and large, Carter's Christology traffics between creation, Israel, and Christ. For Carter, the whole of creation is recapitulated in Israel's history and is brought to completion in Jesus' Jewish flesh. Whereas Bonhoeffer's Christology is shaped by his attention to *sin*, Carter's Christology is shaped by his concentration on *Israel*. These differing shapes of Christology offer significant points of contention as one considers them in relation to modernity's racial imagination.

The Shape of Bonhoeffer's Christology: Creation, Sin, and Christ

Bonhoeffer presents a Christology that corresponds to and handles the Christian church's existence in sin. The church is established through Christ's acting on the sinful world's behalf. This means, for Bonhoeffer, that the revelation of Jesus Christ's person does not come in the form of prelapsarian Adam (sinless humanity) but in the form of fallen Adam in the hiddenness of sin. Because Jesus Christ is revealed in the hidden form of visible humiliation, his person is only accessible through the direct act of faith given in the Christian church's encounter with the living Christ. The Christian church, in this way, is incorporated into Christ's visible humiliation as it participates with Christ in bearing the guilt of sinful humanity. Here, the rupture of the fall remains as Jesus Christ establishes a new form of community, precisely, within the fallen

5   See the discussion of Bonhoeffer's understanding of sin as individual and collective in chapter 3.

creation. Three representative examples of how Bonhoeffer develops this christological topography are offered from *Sanctorum Communio*, *Creation and Fall*, and his final chapter of *Discipleship*.

Although *Sanctorum Communio* focuses explicitly on the church, Bonhoeffer's conception of Christ's vicarious representative action [*Stellvertretung*] offers the hinge on which the whole book turns.[6] It is through this theological concept, seen throughout his later works,[7] that Bonhoeffer is able to explain how Christ establishes a historical community in the midst of the fallen world, by standing both over this community and within it. What is key is how Bonhoeffer describes Christ's vicarious representative action as establishing a new social existence within the parameters defined by the fall. Observing his use of this concept from *Sanctorum Communio* demonstrates how Bonhoeffer understands Jesus Christ in relation to creation and sin as from within the church.

In *Sanctorum Communio* Bonhoeffer makes an essential distinction between Adam's vicarious representation and the vicarious representative action of Christ. Adam's vicarious representation is relative in that Adam does not intentionally act on humanity's behalf, but instead enacts a representation of how humanity shares solidarity in the isolation of each individual's sin. This differs from Christ's vicarious representative action in that Christ does for humanity what it cannot do for itself. Bonhoeffer explains, "Everyone becomes guilty by their own strength and fault, because they themselves are Adam; each person, however, is reconciled apart from their own strength and merit, because they themselves are not Christ."[8] This distinction allows Bonhoeffer to safeguard the singular Lordship of Christ over the community of faith. Yet, at the same time, it offers Christ's vicarious representative action as

---

6   A standard criticism of *Sanctorum Communio* is that Bonhoeffer does not sufficiently distinguish Christ from the existing church. For a discussion of this critique and a refutation of it on the basis of Christ's vicarious representative action, see chapter 6, "Christ, Spirit, and Church," in Michael Mawson's *Christ Existing as Community*, 121–49.

7   For later examples of Bonhoeffer's treatment of Christ's "vicarious representative action," see *DBWE* 4:90; 5:55; 6:257–89; 11:296–99. In commenting on *Sanctorum Communio* in relation to Bonhoeffer's later works, Joachim von Soosten states, "One of the recurrent theological leitmotifs dominating Bonhoeffer's work after his doctoral dissertation was the concept of vicarious representative action [*Stellvertretung*]. It is this concept that provided him with the theological foundation for connecting Christology, ecclesiology, and ethics" (Joachim von Soosten, "Editor's Afterword to the German Edition," in *DBWE* 1:302).

8   *DBWE* 1:146.

the very being of community in the midst of sin.[9] Christ reveals the isolation of humanity-in-Adam and, in the same instance, breaks through
this isolation of sin by standing in humanity's place as the second Adam.
As Bonhoeffer eloquently states it,

> The cord between God and human beings that was cut by the first
> Adam is tied anew by God, by revealing God's own love in Christ,
> by no longer approaching us in demand and summons, purely as
> You, but instead by *giving God's own self as an I, opening God's
> own heart.*[10]

Through the giving of "God's own self as an I," Bonhoeffer stipulates
how Christ breaks through the isolation of sin by taking fallen Adam's
place to establish a new creation, opened to communing, in the midst
of a fallen world. This standing in for fallen Adam does not remove
Christ's Lordship but affirms it; Christ takes Adam's place apart from
and in opposition to Adam's own striving. In this manner, Bonhoeffer
suggests that Christ's vicarious representative action means Christ's
relation to the church is not only "communal" but also "governing."[11]
It is by holding these two aspects of Christ together that Bonhoeffer is
able to conceive of Christ as the very being of community without losing
sight of the complexities of sin. Jesus Christ's vicarious representative
action reveals humanity as fallen and establishes the church in the same
instance. As Bonhoeffer explains, "The reality of sin and the communio peccatorum [community of sinners] remain even in God's church-
community."[12] Jesus Christ establishes the church within a fallen world
that is known as fallen precisely through Christ's bearing of sin.

How Christ creates a new community in the midst of the fallen creation is elaborated upon further in *Creation and Fall*. As in *Sanctorum
Communio*, in *Creation and Fall*, Bonhoeffer seeks to explain how God
works on behalf of the fallen world and within it through Jesus Christ.
He does this by presenting Christ as the new limit and center [*Grenze
und Mitte*] placed in the midst of the fallen world.[13] This limit and center

9   See *DBWE* 1:147.
10   *DBWE* 1:145 (emphasis original).
11   *DBWE* 1:147.
12   *DBWE* 1:124.
13   Bonhoeffer's usage of the term "*Grenze*" refers both to a creaturely limit or bound-
edness that describes the finitude of human's creatureliness, and also to God's gracious prohibition that gives human beings a tangible way of living as God's creatures. See *DBWE*
3:85–86.

must be resituated after humanity's fall, Bonhoeffer argues, because "Adam now stands in another place."[14] Whereas the limit of God's command (not to eat from the tree) once guided Adam from the center of his existence, Bonhoeffer explains that after the fall God's command serves as a limit, assailing "Adam from outside."[15] God's limit is now a restraining and ordering that preserves the fallen world in preparation for Christ's coming. Bonhoeffer expounds on this by arguing that God's action "does not break the new laws that now apply to the earth and humankind after the fall; it participates in them."[16] Ultimately, God participates in the fallen world by placing a new limit and center precisely in the new place Adam now stands. "In the center of the world," Bonhoeffer comments, "from the wood of the cross, the fountain of life springs up."[17] Christ places a new center, a wellspring of life, in the midst of the fallen world through the limit of the cross. Now, in the midst of the fallen world, fallen Adam has been given a limit that can, once again, guide Adam from the center of his existence.

In *Creation and Fall*, Bonhoeffer connects this new limit and center to the embodied life of the church in his brief comments on the Lord's Supper.[18] He argues that in the Lord's Supper God claims a piece of the fallen world to restore the limit and center lost at the fall. Just as the two trees in the center of the garden constituted God's limit as the center of Adam and Eve's bodily existence, the Lord's Supper constitutes a limit found at the center of human beings' bodily existence within the conditions of the fall. As discussed in the previous chapter, Bonhoeffer argues that the Lord's Supper is exactly where "in their bodily existence human beings find their brothers and sisters and find the earth."[19] The living Christ tangibly restores a limit in the midst of the fallen world in a manner that accounts for human beings' material existence as impacted by sin. This limit restores the creaturely boundaries surpassed by fallen Adam by distinctly placing human beings in relation to other sinful human beings and the fallen earth. Christ stands over the church as its tangible limit (governing)

14   *DBWE* 3:139.

15   *DBWE* 3:144.

16   *DBWE* 3:139. This point is important for Bonhoeffer because it shows "that God accepts human beings for what they are, as fallen creatures" (*DBWE* 3:139).

17   *DBWE* 3:146.

18   *DBWE* 3:79.

19   *DBWE* 3:79.

and, as the church's limit, Christ constitutes the very life of the church in the midst of the fallen world (communal).

In the final chapter of *Discipleship*, Bonhoeffer presents similar ideas in terms of Jesus Christ's form [*Gestalt*] in fallen creation. This chapter is particularly pertinent to the present discussion, because in it Bonhoeffer discusses how Christ's form is given not to a perfect world but to the fallen world of Adam. The title of the chapter, "The Image of Christ," speaks to a distinction that Bonhoeffer makes between the image of *Christ* and the image of *God*. Whereas the image of *God* pertains to pre-fallen human beings, the image of *Christ* pertains to how God's very image is now pressed into the contours of the fallen creation. In Jesus Christ, Bonhoeffer declares, "God's own image has come into our midst in the form of our lost human life, in the likeness of sinful flesh."[20] Christ takes form in the midst of fallen creation specifically in the form of the church. The church is Christ's image, Bonhoeffer contends, and "through the church so too are all its members the image of Christ."[21]

As a result, Bonhoeffer suggests that the church's visible form reflects how Christ's image manifests itself through Christ's visible humiliation in the fallen creation. He writes, "It is by Christians' being publicly disgraced, having to suffer and being put to death for the sake of Christ, that Christ himself attains visible form within his community."[22] This humiliation, still, is not to be relied on as a visible confirmation of Christ's working in the world. For in this humiliation, Christ is hidden to the world and to his disciples.[23] Bonhoeffer explains, "I no longer cast even a single glance on my own life, on the new image I bear. For in the same moment that I would desire to see it, I would lose it."[24] Faith looks to Christ as the primordial form and fullness of God's image embedded within the fallen world. The Christian bears this image only by looking to Christ, which infers looking beyond one's own reflection of this image. In this way Christ's humiliated form is embedded in the fallen world through the church's being bound up with the image of the incarnate, crucified, and risen Christ.

20 *DBWE* 4:284.
21 *DBWE* 4:287.
22 *DBWE* 4:286.
23 Jennifer McBride draws from this point to support her thesis that Bonhoeffer's public theology suggests a "witness to Christ in a nontriumphal manner" (*The Church for the World*, 6).
24 *DBWE* 4:286–87.

Bonhoeffer's Christology is instructive in how it attends to the conditioning of the fall in relation to Jesus Christ. The theological constellation that Bonhoeffer's Christology illuminates is not merely between Adam and Christ but between *fallen* Adam and Christ. This small shift reorients the community of faith *from* a search for quick answers to the pressing problem of whiteness *to* a listening that attends to how Jesus Christ is already presently challenging and countering every form of whiteness that resists his coming. Christ's working in the midst of a sinful world does not justify the church's propagation of and participation in whiteness but implicates the church in Christ's *already* given struggle against enclosures that obstruct his coming. Thus, Christ confronts the church's complicity in whiteness not simply as an idea that provides couched responses but with his very presence that involves the church in walking with him up the hill of Golgotha.

The Shape of Carter's Christology: Creation, Israel, and Christ

While Bonhoeffer expounds on the relationship between Christology and sin, J. Kameron Carter's *Race: A Theological Account* explores the relationship between Christology and whiteness. Carter launches this investigation on the basis that Christology offers the discursive site for "negotiating the meaning of material existence."[25] The central contention of his book is that modernity's racial imagination negotiates a political system of whiteness founded upon a supersessionism that extracts Jesus Christ from his Jewish roots. In response to this, Carter seeks to develop a Christology that recovers Jesus' Jewish, covenantal flesh.

Carter offers this recovery of Jesus' Jewish flesh through a complex argument presented over three voluminous sections. At the center of Carter's argument is his Christology, developed from three early church fathers: Irenaeus of Lyons, Gregory of Nyssa, and Maximus the Confessor.[26] By presenting these church fathers in the prelude, interlude, and postlude of the book, the structure of *Race* resembles a musical composition, with Carter's Christology forming the cantus firmus of its polyphonic arrangement. This christological cantus firmus serves as a

25   Carter explains that central to the argument of his book as a whole is approaching Christology as a discursive site (*Race*, 12).

26   Andrew Draper suggests that Carter focuses on three Eastern thinkers to subvert the commonly used voices of Augustine and Aquinas. Draper offers his own interpretation of the reasoning behind this choice: "Carter finds Eastern theological anthropology to suggest a more dynamic conception of being than that of the Latin West" (*A Theology of Race and Place*, 38).

pre-existing melody supporting the three main sections of Carter's theological proposal.[27] The already given Jewish flesh of Jesus of Nazareth is the pre-existing melody that all of creation joins in singing to YHWH.

While Carter's interactions with Irenaeus, Gregory, and Maximus each draw strong connections between creation, Israel, and Christ, it is in his discussion of Irenaeus that these connections are the most pronounced. For this reason, the following section presents Carter's explorations of Irenaeus, leaving his interactions with Gregory and Maximus for later.

Carter proposes that Irenaeus works out a Christology "that makes the *Jewish, covenantal* flesh of the redeemer *Jesus of Nazareth* the locus from which to understand all *created reality* in relationship to YHWH, its Triune Creator."[28] This statement highlights the theological connections between creation (created reality), Israel (Jewish, covenantal flesh), and Christ (Jesus of Nazareth) that Carter seeks to capture from Irenaeus' concept of recapitulation. These connections between creation, Israel, and Christ fund Carter's direct challenge of whiteness, as seen in how he frames his discussion of Irenaeus.

Carter asserts that Irenaeus' concrete understanding of how Christ became flesh (John 1:14) counters the incorporeal thinking of Gnosticism in Irenaeus' own day, a disembodied form of thought that continues on today in modernity's racial imagination. When Jesus is severed from his Jewish roots, Carter states, "theology as discourse becomes distorted into a Gnostic or Gnostic like discourse of death."[29] This discourse of death takes place in modernity through the pseudo-theological program of whiteness that adapts and applies Israel's covenantal history to the politics of the nation-state

---

27   Carter focuses on the particularity of Jesus' Jewish flesh to offer a discursive site that exposes and counters the theological distortions of supersessionism undergirding modernity's racial imagination and its outworking political system of the nation-state (Part I: Dramatizing Race). He suggests, further, that this Christology provides a better response to whiteness then those presently given within the field of African American religious studies, which he argues continue to capitulate to the supersessionism of modernity's racial imagination (Part II: Engaging Race). Last, Carter contends that Jesus' Jewish particularity outlines a constructive theological program for countering the politics of whiteness as seen in an Afro-Christian existence that struggles with and against whiteness by living into the covenantal reality of Jesus' Jewish flesh (Part III: Redirecting Race).

28   Carter, *Race*, 14 (emphasis added).

29   Carter, *Race*, 34.

(as seen in the myth about blood purity in Nazi Germany).[30] Through the nation-state, whiteness becomes a pseudo-theological dispersion of power bestowed on those classified within the borders of whiteness. Difference is negotiated and maintained within this framework through a violence that defends the "purity" of a nation. In contrast to the modern racial reasoning of the nation-state, Jesus' Jewish flesh, seen in Irenaeus' concept of recapitulation, constitutes the particular place where differences are brought together. People are not gathered into different nation-states but into the one covenantal reality already given in Jesus' Jewish flesh. One receives one's being from the particularity of Jesus' Jewish flesh as the discursive site already provided for negotiating material reality.

In opposition to modernity's racial reasoning, Carter argues that, for Irenaeus, Jesus' Jewish flesh constitutes the locus in which the recapitulation of the whole creation transpires. This suggests that the recapitulation of the whole world passes through the birthing canal of God's covenantal people of Israel, concentrated in Jesus' Jewish flesh. Carter summarizes this argument by suggesting that Irenaeus' understanding of recapitulation works within three concentric relationships running between (1) creation, (2) Israel, and (3) Christ.[31]

Carter describes the *first* concentric relationship as moving diachronically from creation to Israel, and then from Israel to Christ's life, death, and resurrection. In this concentric relationship, creation serves as the primary optic through which the subsequent moments in the narrative unfold in the story of Israel and Christ. The *second* concentric relationship is synchronic, with its focal point on Israel. As synchronic it disrupts a simple, linear reading of history. Carter explains that "creation as proton and Christ as eschaton are read through the mediating term of Israel and the story of this covenantal people with YHWH."[32] The story of Abraham and Israel offers input both for the story of creation and for Christ. In regards to creation, God's calling of Abram functions as a creation of a people out of nothing—a compendium of

---

30   See Carter's discussion of this in chapter 2, "The Great Drama of Religion," in *Race*, 79–124.

31   Carter's understanding of concentric relationships is similar to the idea of systematicity presented in this project. The careful manner in which Carter describes the optionality of different focal points for Irenaeus helpfully demonstrates how the ordering of theological loci informs the shape of one's theology.

32   Carter, *Race*, 34.

God's creation of the world ex nihilo.[33] Similarly, in regards to Christ, the Virgin Mary suggests how Israel functions as a mediating term between creation and Christ in that Mary offers a reversal of Eve's disobedience.[34] The *third* and final way of understanding the concentric relationship between creation, Israel, and Christ is also synchronic, but this time moving from the end in Christ. Carter comments, "In this regard, the eschaton is not merely last (as in diachrony). It is first. It is proton also."[35] Carter reports that Irenaeus grants theological priority to this third concentric relationship. This priority is given based on Irenaeus' belief that Christ as the Word of God was already at work in the beginning and throughout Israel's history.

Based on this description of Irenaeus' motif of recapitulation, Carter argues that Christ's humanity is an "*inter*humanity" and a new "*intra*humanity."[36] He suggests that the Jewish Jesus is "always already *inter*sected by the covenant with YHWH and in being *inter*sected it is always *intra*racial (and not merely multiracial)."[37] Carter's suggestion is that Jesus' Jewish flesh does not only allow different people to come together in a shared space (multiracial) but constitutes an actual exchange or mixing between persons (*intra*racial) through the Holy Spirit.[38] Jesus' Jewish flesh demands this intermixing of humanity, Carter contends, because the particularity of Jesus' Jewish flesh is the single body in which all differences inhere.[39]

In Carter's analysis of Irenaeus, the concentric circles of creation, Israel, and Christ overlap and mutually inform one another, giving Carter's Christology a distinct shape. Based on this distinct Christology, Carter presents an understanding of Jesus' Jewish flesh that directly challenges the modern theological trappings of whiteness. Whereas whiteness draws borders, Jesus' Jewish flesh recapitulates all of creation into an intermixing that challenges the falsely fabricated borders of whiteness.

33   Carter writes, "YHWH presents the story of Israel, beginning with the call of Abram-become-Abraham to create *ex nihilo* a people who before did not exist, as a compendium of the story of creation, which too came into being" (*Race*, 33).

34   See Carter, *Race*, 31–32.

35   Carter, *Race*, 34.

36   Carter, *Race*, 30 (emphasis original).

37   Carter, *Race*, 30 (emphasis original).

38   Carter does not mention the Holy Spirit in this context but gestures toward it when he claims, "Jesus' existence, which is covenantally Jewish, is therefore Pentecostal" (*Race*, 30).

39   Carter, *Race*, 30.

Bonhoeffer and Carter: The Shape of Christology

In both Bonhoeffer's and Carter's Christologies, there are important connections made between all of creation and Jesus Christ. Where the shape of their Christologies differ is in how each interprets what is meant by all of creation. For Bonhoeffer all of creation must account for the rupture of the fall as known from within the church's encounter with the living Christ, who is revealed in the likeness of sinful flesh. For Carter all of creation is referenced more generally in terms of a material existence that is negotiated within the concrete Jewish flesh of Jesus. Whereas Bonhoeffer accentuates the relationship between *fallen* Adam and Christ, Carter focuses on the recapitulation of creation (Adam) through Israel, culminating in Jesus Christ. Bringing these two divergent christological approaches together in dialogue assists in showing how they collaboratively push back on one another.

Part of the reason for the different shapes of Bonhoeffer's and Carter's Christologies is bound up with the distinct problem each theologian seeks to address. Carter's specific concern is whiteness, while Bonhoeffer's is sin more generally. These distinctive concerns are seen respectively in how Bonhoeffer deals with the conditions of the fall placed on Jesus Christ and in how Carter directly addresses whiteness with the particularity of Jesus' Jewish flesh. While Carter will talk about the first and second Adam, he does so without direct reference to sin. For example, when Carter discusses Irenaeus' concept of recapitulation, he details how Jesus faced all the challenges of living in a corporeal body but does not specifically address how this relates to the conditions of sin brought on by the fall.[40] Carter's lack of attention to how Jesus Christ is revealed in the midst of the fallen creation allows for a positive description of Jesus' Jewish flesh that serves as a direct challenge of whiteness. The potential consequences of Carter's direct christological challenge of whiteness will be explored as this chapter continues to unfold. The main point here is to highlight how Carter's Christology attends to a different christological landscape than that of Bonhoeffer's.

The specific christological landscape that Carter presents reveals pertinent limitations in Bonhoeffer's Christology. In particular, Carter's focus on Israel as a mediating term between Adam and Christ raises

---

40   See Carter's discussion of how Irenaeus talks about Jesus Christ as tied to all humanity through Israel in *Race*, 31–35. This discussion addresses how Jesus hungers, is wearied, cries, and the like, but it does not specifically address the specific problem of how Christ is revealed in the likeness of sinful flesh.

immediate attention on Bonhoeffer's potential supersessionism. Bonhoeffer's supersessionism and his comments about the Jews have been a vexing topic of discussion among Bonhoeffer scholars.[41] While many have held up Bonhoeffer as an example for post-Holocaust theology,[42] Stephen Haynes convincingly dismisses such sentiments. Haynes argues that Bonhoeffer's christological reading of Scripture is the very basis for his supersessionism. He remarks that Bonhoeffer's "bold christological assertions" make it difficult for him "to hear Jews testify to anything other than the rejection of a messiah who is their only hope of salvation and only access to truth."[43] What is needed, Haynes suggests, is a more "modest" Christology that defers Christ's identity to the eschatological horizon and allows the Old Testament to speak for itself.[44] In sum, Haynes' argument is that Bonhoeffer's supersessionism was fundamentally integrated into his theology in relation to his christological reading of Scripture.

Not only is Haynes' critique of Bonhoeffer's supersessionism directed toward Bonhoeffer, but it represents a critique of many of the early church fathers who also read the Old Testament through similar christological lenses. This connection between Bonhoeffer and the church fathers, which Haynes acknowledges,[45] makes Carter's reading of the church fathers an interesting counterpoint to Haynes' critique. As shown in his discussion of Irenaeus, Carter suggests that the church fathers counter a supersessionist reading of the Old Testament by interpreting Israel and Israel's Messiah as mutually informative. Reasoning in this way, Carter indirectly supports Bonhoeffer's general approach to the Old Testament, requiring one to look elsewhere for the source of Bonhoeffer's supersessionism. In contrast to Haynes' critique of Bonhoeffer, Carter's Christology insinuates that Bonhoeffer's supersessionism does not take his christological reading of the Old Testament far enough.

---

41   For a survey of this discussion, see Haynes, *The Bonhoeffer Legacy*, 29–41.

42   Haynes offers a treatment of the various Christian theologians who have championed Bonhoeffer as a guide for post-Holocaust theology, including Eberhard Bethge, William Jay Peck, Robert E. Willis, Edwin Robertson, Christine-Ruth Müller, Alejandro Zorzin, and Geoffrey Kelly; see Haynes, *The Bonhoeffer Legacy*, 29–41.

43   Haynes, *The Bonhoeffer Legacy*, 97.

44   Haynes, *The Bonhoeffer Legacy*, 97–98.

45   Haynes openly acknowledges a resonance between Bonhoeffer's Christocentric reading of the Old Testament and that of many of the early church fathers. See Haynes, *The Bonhoeffer Legacy*, 23.

The problem with Bonhoeffer's christological reading of the Old Testament is that it disregards Carter's emphasis on Israel as a mediating term between all of creation and Jesus Christ. Whereas Bonhoeffer draws important connections between creation, sin, and Christ, Carter adds to this "the mediating term of Israel" placed between creation and Christ.[46] The subtle dangers of Bonhoeffer's supersessionism are seen in how he seeks to tie Israel's history exclusively to the Western world in his essay "Heritage and Decay" from *Ethics*.[47] In this essay Bonhoeffer famously argues that driving out "the Jew" from "the West" is to drive out "Christ with them, for Jesus Christ was a Jew."[48] While this appears to be an affirmation of the Jews and has often been read in this way,[49] Bonhoeffer's broader argument uses the Jews to affirm "the West" as a privileged historical entity. Bonhoeffer writes, "Jesus Christ has made the West into a historical unit. The decisive turning points in history are of Western dimensions."[50] Bonhoeffer goes on to claim that Christ has held the West together despite its wars, whereas wars of extermination and annihilation are "still possible in the Asian region."[51]

By exclusively connecting Israel's Messiah to the Occident, Bonhoeffer embraces a myopic vision that subsumes Israel into the West. This exclusive connection between Israel and the West neglects Israel's relationship to those outside of the West and bluntly falls as a blatant disdain of those on the "underside of modernity."[52] Josiah Young observes this disdain in Bonhoeffer's final writings about the "world come of age." As discussed in chapter 1, Young points out how some of Bonhoeffer's last writings on "the world come of age" place Europe at the center, inherently slighting those from the East and from the African continent.[53] Based on this, Young wonders whether "Bonhoeffer was attracted

46 Carter, *Race*, 34.

47 See *DBWE* 6:105–10.

48 *DBWE* 6:105.

49 See, for example, Harvey, *Taking Hold of the Real*, 217–18; and Pangritz, "Who Is Christ, for Us, Today?" 145.

50 *DBWE* 6:109.

51 *DBWE* 6:109.

52 In *Race* Carter borrows this phrase from Enrique Dussel. See Dussel, *The Underside of Modernity: Apel, Ricoeur, Rorty, Taylor, and the Philosophy of Liberation*, trans. Eduardo Mendieta (Atlantic Highlands: Humanities, 1996).

53 Young, *No Difference in the Fare*, 3–4. Bonhoeffer focuses on the Roman Church and the Reformation in his discussion of Israel in "Heritage and Decay." See *DBWE* 6:106–21.

to blacks only insofar as they bore the impress of the West."[54] This speculation is supported by the fact that Bonhoeffer never explored the Africanness of Black people in the United States as Carter does in his examinations of African American religious studies and of New World Afro-Christian faith.[55] In all of this, Bonhoeffer's prioritization of the West reflects his continued inability to read Israel positively as a mediating term between all of creation and Christ.

Whereas Stephen Haynes locates Bonhoeffer's supersessionism in his christological reading of Scripture, Carter's theology of Israel upholds Bonhoeffer's christological reading of Scripture and, instead, repairs Bonhoeffer's theology by filling in a gap that his theology broadly skips over. That is, while Bonhoeffer draws connections between fallen Adam and Christ, he does not speak of Israel as a mediating term, as done by Carter. Thus, Carter's Christology of Jesus' Jewish flesh helpfully refuses Bonhoeffer's reductionist reading of Israel and the configurations of whiteness that go along with this bargain.

The Limits of Christological Reflection

The previous section detailed how Bonhoeffer's Christology acquires a distinct shape in reference to sin, while Carter's Christology is unfolded in reference to God's covenantal history with Israel. This section examines what is at stake in these two different approaches to Christology, especially in relation to how each Christology provides a distinct challenge of whiteness. Whereas Bonhoeffer's Christology sets limits on human thinking, Carter's is more focused on defining a reality that directly challenges whiteness. These differences are rooted in how Bonhoeffer draws attention to the *hiddenness* of the living Christ revealed in the givenness of a *sinful community* versus how Carter attends to the *covenantal* reality of Jesus' Jewish flesh revealed in the givenness of *Israel's history* with YHWH. As a result, Bonhoeffer's Christology presents limits that offer an indirect challenge of whiteness, whereas Carter's Christology moves toward a much more direct challenge of whiteness. While

---

This demonstrates how Bonhoeffer failed to explore the ways that Eastern Christianity influenced the African continent and beyond.

54   Young, *No Difference in the Fare*, 5.

55   See especially Carter's interactions with Albert Raboteau and Charles Long, chapters 3 and 5 in *Race*. Carter argues that Afro-Christianity offers a creative mixture between the African ritual life and Christian rituals discovered in the New World. See Carter, *Race*, 133–34.

at first glance it may seem more appropriate and helpful to directly challenge whiteness with the reality of Jesus' Jewish flesh, as done by Carter,
Bonhoeffer's Christology raises some questions about the expediency of
such an approach. To understand the questions Bonhoeffer's Christology raises for Carter's direct challenge of whiteness, we must first take a
closer look at how Bonhoeffer understands the reality of Jesus Christ as
given within fallen history.

Bonhoeffer: Jesus Christ in a Fallen World

For Bonhoeffer the *reality* of the living Christ comes before and after
Christology as a reflective form of thinking. One must always remember
this when making christological claims. Accordingly, the aim of Christology, for Bonhoeffer, is to reflect upon the living reality of Jesus Christ,
concretely encountered in the community of faith, without reducing this
reality to an idea.[56] Jesus Christ is present to the sinful community of
the church, and Christology's task is to reflect upon this already existing
reality in dependence on the church's faith.[57]

Bonhoeffer's focus on the living reality of Jesus Christ is observed
throughout his *Lectures on Christology*. He begins these lectures by discussing the limits of reflective knowledge and the need for silence before
the wonder of God's speaking through Jesus Christ: "To speak of Christ
is to be silent, and to be silent about Christ is to speak."[58] Even knowledge
of Christ, Bonhoeffer argues, remains subject to the enclosed thinking
of humanity's being in fallen Adam.[59] For this reason human reflection alone is inadequate for the task of Christology. Christology begins
not with human reflection but with the church's tangible encounter of

56   Ernst Feil expresses this point by suggesting that Bonhoeffer's theology moves out-
ward "from the mystery of a faith that is beyond complete rational comprehension, and to
that center his reflection seeks to return." See Feil, *The Theology of Dietrich Bonhoeffer*, 5.
The argument in this section slightly alters Feil's statement by suggesting that faith proceeds
not from mystery but from the reality of Jesus Christ encountered in the church's proclamation of Word and sacrament. While Bonhoeffer at times will use the language of mystery, he
more often employs the language of reality with reference to the wonder of Christ's promeity, which helps capture the concreteness of Bonhoeffer's Christology.

57   As Andreas Pangritz explains this point, Bonhoeffer "seeks to preserve the social
concreteness of Christology in relation to the Christian community" (Pangritz, "Who Is
Christ, for Us, Today?" 142).

58   *DBWE* 12:300.

59   Bonhoeffer discusses how attempts to reasonably grasp Christ's person lead to a domestication of Christ. The living Christ remains beyond mere estimations, because Christ
confronts the church again and again in his person. See *DBWE* 12:306–7.

Christ's person. It begins, Bonhoeffer claims, with the people of God falling "on its knees in silence before the inexpressible."⁶⁰ This means that christological inquiry rests on the direct and repeated encounter of Jesus Christ in the church's proclamation of Word and sacrament. As Bonhoeffer states later in his lectures, "Only because proclamation and the sacraments are carried out in the church can we inquire about Christ."⁶¹ Christ is more than a doctrine or an idea, because Christ's real person confronts and comforts the church in the events of the church's proclamation of Word and sacrament.

This description of the living reality of Jesus Christ relies on two guiding motifs in Bonhoeffer's Christology: *hiddenness* and *promeity*. In *Lectures on Christology*, Bonhoeffer summarizes these two motifs in one succinct statement: "The hidden form in which Christ is *present* is, for us, the church's proclamation."⁶² Hiddenness and promeity go together in that Jesus Christ is *hidden* in his being there *for us* (i.e. sinful human beings) in the church's proclamation. Accordingly, Bonhoeffer insists that both motifs depend on the church's faith. Christ's humiliation represents a visible hiddenness seen through the eyes of faith, which observe the living Christ, precisely, as God's being there for us.⁶³ In this way faith finds the church bound up with Jesus Christ's hidden form in sinful history.

In terms of the hiddenness of Christ, Bonhoeffer highlights the dual assertion from Scripture that Christ comes in the "likeness of sinful flesh" (Rom 8:3) "yet without sin" (Heb 4:15). "This is the issue," Bonhoeffer explains, "that the Son entered into the flesh, that he wants to do his work within the ambiguity of history, incognito."⁶⁴ Jesus Christ's incognito status means that the basic problem that troubles Christology is not the gap between God and *humanity* but the gap between the God-human (presupposed in Jesus Christ) and *sin*.⁶⁵ In correspondence with this shift of the christological problem, Bonhoeffer suggests that is not Christ's becoming *human* that hides his divinity but Christ's *humiliation*

---

60   *DBWE* 12:300.

61   *DBWE* 12:310.

62   *DBWE* 12:313.

63   For Bonhoeffer's discussion of Christ's promeity, see his *Lectures on Christology* in *DBWE* 12:310–15. In this discussion, Bonhoeffer writes, "It is not only useless to meditate on a Christ in-himself but godless, precisely because Christ is not there in-himself, but rather there for you" (*DBWE* 12:314).

64   *DBWE* 12:309.

65   See *DBWE* 12:313.

in his coming in the likeness of sinful flesh that hides his person as the God-human. Bonhoeffer explains, "A careful distinction must surely be made between the *humanity* of Christ and the *humiliation* of Christ."[66] The stumbling block that requires faith is located not in God's becoming human but in Christ's humiliation in bearing the likeness of sinful flesh.

While Jesus Christ is hidden in the likeness of sinful flesh, faith asserts that Christ is simultaneously the One without sin.[67] Rather than seeking to explain these paradoxical claims, Bonhoeffer suggests that the community of faith must dare "to make and to endure all the most scandalous assertions about this God-human who has been humiliated."[68] The scandal of these two scriptural assertions must be endured, because the whole Christ, humiliated and exalted, is present to the church by faith.[69] Faith implicates the church in the scandal of Christ's humiliation by insisting that Christ's bearing of guilt is bound up with his triumph over sin. Christ still bears the scars of his crucifixion and remains humiliated in the church. Christ's humiliated form is given in the church's proclamation, but through this humiliation, sin is overcome as the church is implicated in Christ's bearing of humanity's guilt. As Bonhoeffer concludes, "With the humiliated Christ, his church must also be humiliated."[70]

As for the *promeity* of Christ, Bonhoeffer emphasizes how the living Word is directly present to fallen human beings in Christ's humiliated form. Sin veils Christ's being for us in history, both in the humiliation of his earthly ministry and in his present humiliated form in the church's proclamation. Drawing the historical Jesus and the present Christ together, Bonhoeffer suggests that the celebration of the Lord's Supper is "not the becoming-human of Christ but rather the ultimate humiliation of the God-human."[71] The living Christ is visibly humiliated in the sacrament, just as Jesus of Nazareth is visibly humiliated on the cross.

Additionally, because Christ is present to the church in the form of Word and sacrament, the church-community itself constitutes the stumbling block of Christ's humiliated presence in fallen creation.

66   *DBWE* 12:314 (emphasis added).

67   Bonhoeffer writes, "The statement about Jesus being without sin in his actions is not a judgment within a moral system but rather a recognition, through eyes of faith, of the One who does these things, the One who is without sin for all eternity" (*DBWE* 12:357).

68   *DBWE* 12:357.

69   *DBWE* 12:358.

70   *DBWE* 12:360.

71   *DBWE* 12:319.

Christ's being is this community as sinful and righteous, Bonhoeffer argues, which like his being as Word is "a being in the form of the stumbling block."[72] Christ works in the midst of the fallen world through a sinful community and, in this way, his humiliated form as the stumbling block is revealed as a *being for* the world.

Christology preserves the living reality of Jesus Christ through attending to Christ's given humiliation in his historical life and his present humiliation in the church's proclamation. The hiddenness of Christ's humiliation preserves the wonder of Christ's coming. This is why Christ's coming to sinful humanity always entails the surprise of God's gracious address through faith. As Josiah Young summarizes this point in reflecting on Bonhoeffer's theology, "A true gift has no rhyme or reason. Freely given, it always takes us by surprise."[73] Christology is a reflection on this surprise through a faith that directly encounters the one who walked the earth, was crucified, and yet lives, who was rejected and yet loves. Christology's primary task is to uphold and preserve the wonder and surprise of Christ's humiliated coming through ecclesial reflection.[74]

Bonhoeffer's *Lectures on Christology* are primarily dedicated to this task—keeping the surprise of Christ's advent just that, a surprise.[75] Bonhoeffer's explanation of this task is given in a Christmas letter from 1939 written to his Fickenwalde seminarians:

> "God revealed in the flesh," the God-human Jesus Christ, that is the holy mystery, which theology was instituted to preserve and protect. What foolishness, as if it were the task of theology to decode God's mystery, pulling it down to the commonplace, miracle-less words of wisdom based on human experience and reason! Whereas this alone is its charge—to keep the miracle of God a miracle, to comprehend, defend, and exalt the mystery of God, precisely as mystery. The early church meant the very same thing when it concerned itself with the mystery of the Trinity and the person of Jesus Christ with tireless fervor.[76]

---

72 *DBWE* 12:323.

73 Young, *No Difference in the Fare*, 7.

74 See *DBWE* 2:130.

75 This is seen in that only the last brief section of Bonhoeffer's *Lectures on Christology* is devoted to "Positive Christology," and even in this section Bonhoeffer remains focused on how the reality of Christ's person is veiled by sin. See *DBWE* 12:353–60.

76 *DBWE* 15:528–29.

In this letter Bonhoeffer suggests that the task of theology from the councils of the early church until today is to preserve the wonder of Christ's advent. The church's dogma is given not as an oppressive rule but as a necessary limit that points to the impenetrable reality of Christ's ultimate coming to a fallen world. By drawing this limit, theology is a political act that challenges misuses of Christian doctrine that overstep the boundaries of the reality of Christ encountered in the church.

From this perspective, Bonhoeffer's reading of the Church councils, offered in his 1933 *Lectures on Christology*, represents a political challenge against efforts being leveled at the time to construct an "Aryan Jesus."[77] In these lectures Bonhoeffer challenges a conception of an "Aryan Jesus" not by presenting a Jewish Jesus but by upholding the limits set by the councils on human definitions of Jesus Christ altogether.[78] He highlights these limits on human reflection in his treatment of the Council of Chalcedon. The early church's intent with this council, Bonhoeffer contends, was to provide conceptual boundaries that preserve the wonder of encountering the living Christ in the community of faith. As a result, Chalcedon adheres to these boundaries through its conflicting conceptual claims. Bonhoeffer explains, "The Chalcedonian formula itself reveals the limitations of its own concepts . . . [it] is an objective, living assertion about Christ that goes beyond all conceptual forms."[79] Bonhoeffer mirrors this approach in his dual assertions that Christ comes in the likeness of sinful flesh yet without sin. This twofold assertion upholds the living reality of Christ as beyond all conceptual forms yet visibly present in sinful history through the faith of the existing church.

By speaking of the councils in this manner, Andreas Pangritz suggests, Bonhoeffer's *Lectures on Christology* do more than merely defend Christian tradition against those like his teacher Adolf von Harnack, who questioned the councils.[80] Bonhoeffer's apologetic preservation of

---

77 For a discussion of racial theology during the time of Hitler's rise to power, see Susannah Heschel's *The Aryan Jesus*.

78 In contrast to Bonhoeffer's approach, Carter relies specifically on the Jewishness of Jesus to provide a political challenge of racial conceptions of Jesus.

79 *DBWE* 12:343.

80 Adolf von Harnack critiques the councils by arguing that early Christians used dogma to set up a rule of faith. He writes, "They set it up as a standard of truth in matters of faith and made its acceptance the condition of membership in the Church." See Adolf von Harnack, *Outlines of the History of Dogma*, trans. Edwin Knox Mitchell (New York: Funk & Wagnalls, 1893), 86.

the Christian tradition had and has political implications. As Pangritz explains, "At this time when the 'German Christians' (the *Deutsche Christen* or the Nazi party of the church) attempted to construct an 'Aryan' Christ, such a merely apologetic conception of Christology would have indirect political implications."[81] Bonhoeffer's Christology is political in its refusal to reduce Christ to an idea, Aryan or otherwise. Such a Christology has implications for contemporary theological race discourse.

In many cases current theological discussions about race have become a rhetorical battle over who gets to define Jesus.[82] Bonhoeffer's Christology assists in advancing these discussions by suggesting that Christ is not, firstly, an idea up for debate, but a living person concretely encountered in the community of faith's worship. Christ is not an idea but a living person that confronts and comforts God's people, again and again, within the midst of the fallen creation. It is in this way that Christ's very being as the church guards against the danger of domesticating his person within the closed circle of fallen human thinking. This suggests that even well-meaning attempts to construct a Christ that refutes racist inclinations may capitulate to reducing Christ to an idea if detached from the living Christ encountered in the community of faith. As Josiah Young so beautifully expresses this point, "Without the *irrefutable* presence of the Christ in the midst of history, like a force field invulnerable to transience and corruption, every anti-racist Christology is a waning candle in the dark."[83] The only genuine antiracist Christology is one that closely attends to the limitations of every human conception of Jesus Christ.

Bonhoeffer's sensitivity to these limitations is what makes his Christology advantageous for theological discourses on race. His Christology provides an *indirect* challenge of whiteness by leaving human conceptions of Christ subject to the living Christ encountered in the church. Such a Christology suggests that Christ is at work in the midst of a historical church marked by whiteness through Christ's own challenge of the church's limited conceptions of his person. Christ's challenge, at the same time, invites the church into a life of faith that participates in Christ's bearing of racial wounds to bring healing to a racialized church and world.

81   Pangritz, "Who Is Christ, for Us, Today?" 136.

82   For example, see the thirteen essays presented in George Yancy, ed., *Christology and Whiteness: What Would Jesus Do?* (New York: Routledge, 2012).

83   Josiah U. Young III, "Who Belongs to Christ?," in Yancy, *Christology and Whiteness*, 129 (emphasis original).

Carter: Jesus Christ in a Racialized World

In contrast to the indirect challenge of whiteness provided by Bonhoeffer's Christology, Carter's Christology presents a much more direct challenge of whiteness. For Carter, the reality of Jesus' Jewish flesh constitutes an intermixing that directly challenges the exclusionary forces of whiteness. Whereas "whiteness exports itself but never receives itself," Carter explains that Jesus' Jewish flesh enacts an "intrahuman exchange," where one receives one's being from another in the vulnerability of divine love.[84] All the particularities of creation adhere in the reality of Jesus' Jewish flesh as the culmination of Israel's covenantal history with YHWH. Carter summarizes this Christology with his musical metaphor of Jesus' Jewish flesh as the tune "that the symphony of creation, the many, plays."[85] Each particularity articulates a distinct intonation, Carter proclaims, that resonates with every other particularity to form a harmony within the amphitheater of Jesus' Jewish flesh. Through this metaphor, Carter suggests that all peoples have already been united in the reality of Jesus' covenantal flesh, and that when one receives oneself from Christ in this way, an exit from the imaginary confines of whiteness transpires.

Carter's musical metaphor reaches its climax in his discussion of Maximus the Confessor. It is from Maximus that Carter suggests a distinct way of understanding the assertions of the Council of Chalcedon as from within Israel's covenantal history with YHWH. Based on Chalcedon, Carter argues that Maximus brings together the one and the many in the hypostatic union of Jesus Christ's person (*hypostasis*). Carter employs the language of the *communicatio idiomatum* (communication of properties) to suggest that Christ's person constitutes both a vertical exchange of properties between the divine and human natures and a horizontal exchange between human persons. As Carter puts it, "The *communicatio idiomatum* happens all the way down."[86] The exchange of properties must be accounted for on both the vertical and horizontal levels, because both are necessary for "a full articulation of what has occurred in Christ's flesh," as Maximus conceives of it.[87] Based on this exchange of properties, Carter describes his proposal as an entering

---

84   Carter, *Race*, 352.
85   Carter, *Race*, 248.
86   Carter, *Race*, 353.
87   Carter, *Race*, 352.

"into the miscegenized or mulattic existence of divinization (*theôsis*)."[88] Jesus' Jewish flesh offers a new modality, a new way of being, that is expressed through a mixing of persons in the vulnerable receiving of one's very being from another.

This specific modality of Jesus' Jewish flesh is one that Carter observes as a participatory reality, into which Maximus enters through his inhabiting of the scriptural witness. Carter comments that Maximus' theology is formed in participation with the biblical witness of God's overcoming of tyranny through the specific people of Israel, culminating in Israel's Messiah. Thus, Abraham is marked by an openness to receive his identity from God, and in this openness, Abraham opens himself up to the nations. This is how Maximus speaks of Abraham as a precursor to Christ that resembles the modality of Jesus' Jewish flesh as incorporating all peoples into an "intrahuman exchange." Carter argues that Maximus understands Christ "from inside Israel's covenant story," who "in bringing Israel's story to crescendo reintegrates the differences of creation into their intended one-many structure."[89] This reintegration of difference is connected to the Christian church, most poignantly in Maximus' account of Pentecost. In the Pentecostal reality of the church, different peoples are brought together through a reordering and reimagining of language and identity.[90] Carter relies on Maximus' theological inhabiting of Scripture to support his overarching thesis: one must exit whiteness to enter a new ecstatic and eschatological being in Jesus' Jewish flesh. There is no "separate but equal" to be found in the Confessor's Christology, Carter declares, but instead the constitution of identities found in "being-in-another" enacted through Jesus' Jewish, covenantal flesh.

---

88   Carter makes this statement in the concluding part of his chapter on Gregory. See Carter, *Race*, 192. For Carter's references to divinization in relation to Maximus, see Carter, *Race*, 348–49, 350, 367.

89   Carter, *Race*, 354. Carter does not claim that Maximus develops a Christian theology of Israel, but that Maximus presupposes an account of Israel in formulating a Christology suited for his own time. Like Gregory of Nyssa, the Confessor reads Scripture against the grain from within Israel's story (seen in his reflections on Abraham, Moses, and Elijah). See *Race*, 355–66.

90   See Carter, *Race*, 364–65. Carter's discussion of Pentecost is similar to Jennings' in that he understands this event as a miscegenation of persons in the given history of Israel. The difference between Carter and Jennings is that Carter does not go on to address the Jerusalem Council (Acts 15) and the possibility of fragmentation in the early church, as Jennings does.

The upshot of Carter's Christology is observed in his pivotal chapter that discusses the late James H. Cone's Black Liberation Theology.[91] Carter relies on his interpretation of Chalcedonian Christology, drawn from Maximus, to demonstrate how Cone's Black Liberation Theology remains caught within the supersessionist claims of whiteness. The problem with Cone's theology is that it suffers from a dialectical I-Thou structure inherited from Karl Barth and Paul Tillich.[92] Carter contends that this I-Thou structure is too impoverished by a binary separateness to explain how Black theology itself gestures toward a "miscegenation," in that it requires white people to enter the horizons of Black existence.[93] More broadly, Carter explains that this strictly dialectic structure is supersessionist, because it refuses the "positivity of the world" in which God works through the covenantal people of Israel.[94] Cone's Black Theology, in a sense, inherently recognizes the need for a "miscegenation" but places this "miscegenation" in the wrong location—in blackness rather than in the already given reality of Jesus' Jewish flesh. In this way Cone's Black Theology capitulates to the supersessionist thinking of whiteness.

Rather than working from binaries, Carter maintains that Chalcedon testifies to a communal being found in Jesus' Jewish flesh. Carter goes on to define this communal being as given in Israel as a mulatto people and as constituted by the reality that "Jesus himself as the Israel of God is Mulatto."[95] Jesus is mulatto in that Jesus' Jewish body incorporates all peoples into an "intrahuman exchange." It is precisely in Jesus' Jewish body that all difference adheres, challenging whiteness (and the blackness that whiteness creates) in its usurpation of the particularity of

---

91   See chapter 4, "Theologizing Race: James H. Cone, Liberation, and the Theological Meaning of Blackness," in Carter, *Race*, 157–94.

92   See Carter, *Race*, 189–91.

93   Carter, *Race*, 190.

94   Carter, *Race*, 190. One of Carter's central goals is to challenge a dialectic structure that emphasizes the otherness of God with the dynamic theological anthropology he draws out from Eastern theology. This dynamic theological anthropology is what Carter appreciates in the later works of Albert J. Raboteau. See Raboteau, *A Fire in the Bones: Reflections on African-American Religious History* (Boston: Beacon Press, 1995). In particular, Carter appreciates how Raboteau's later works recast his engagement with history in iconic rather than dialectical terms. See Carter, *Race*, 152.

95   Carter, *Race*, 192. Elsewhere Carter suggests that in the context of modern racial reasoning, "Christ's existence, being both divine and human, is mulattic or 'interracial'" (*Race*, 447, n. 26). The significance of referring to Jesus as a "mulatto" will be discussed further in interaction with Brian Bantum in the next chapter.

Israel. Thus, Carter suggests that a Jewish, covenantal identity given in Jesus Christ directly challenges one's imagined racial identity through a miscegenation that blurs the lines of binary distinctions.

Bonhoeffer and Carter: The Limits of Christology

Bonhoeffer and Carter present two distinguishable interpretations of the Council of Chalcedon. It is in these divergent interpretations of Chalcedon that we come to the heart of how Bonhoeffer's and Carter's Christologies each offer a unique challenge of whiteness. In Bonhoeffer's account of Chalcedon, the council's dogmatic claims are presented as a practice of christological reflection that preserve the living reality of Jesus Christ in the historical, and even sinful, community of faith. Here, limits are placed on Christology in a manner that indirectly challenges whiteness. In Carter's account of Chalcedon, the council reflects an inhabiting of Israel's covenantal reality as a "intrahuman exchange" constituted by Jesus' Jewish flesh. In this manner Carter presents a distinct Christology that directly challenges whiteness. Bonhoeffer draws limits in relation to the *hiddenness* of Jesus Christ; Carter presents a focal point on the *revealedness* of Jesus' *Jewish* flesh. The major concern that arises from this comparison is that Carter's direct Christological challenge of whiteness oversteps a careful boundary upheld throughout Bonhoeffer's christological reflections.

Similar to Carter's questioning of a binary dialectic, early in Bonhoeffer's theological career he questioned Karl Barth's early dialectical theology.[96] In Bonhoeffer's case, though, the problem pertains to a specific binary dialectic that is framed between God and humanity rather than a dialectic that recognizes the inner fragmentation of sinful history.[97] As seen in his *Lectures on Christology*, the dialectic in which Bonhoeffer works is not between God and humanity but between the God-human and sin.

---

96 For a discussion of how Bonhoeffer distinguishes himself from Barth's dialectical theology, see Mawson, *Christ Existing as Community*, 23–35. Mawson contends that in *Sanctorum Communio* Bonhoeffer positions his own approach between Ernst Troeltsch's historicism and Barth's dialectical theology with a "turn" to the church.

97 In *Sanctorum Communio* Bonhoeffer discusses the importance of accounting for the inner fragmentation of sinful history when one considers the concepts of person and community. He explains that these concepts "are understood only within an intrinsically broken history, as conveyed in the concepts of primal state, sin, and reconciliation" (*DBWE* 1:62). This represents a distinct dialectic in Bonhoeffer's thought that should be distinguished from the dialectical thought offered in Karl Barth's early writings.

Carter's discussion of Cone's Black Liberation Theology, instead, leaves the christological problem between God and humanity. Jesus' Jewish flesh joins human and divine, constituting an "intrahuman exchange," which Carter describes in terms of divinization. In seeking to close the gap between God and humanity, Carter only accentuates this gap by highlighting it as the primary christological problem. Placing the christological problem between God and humanity shifts the conversation away from the inner fragmentation caused by the rupture of sin and toward Carter's direct christological claim that all of life coheres in the particularity of Jesus' Jewish flesh.

Furthermore, in placing the christological problem between God and humanity, Carter risks overstepping the boundary of the inner fragmentation of sin, acknowledged from within the church. In contrast to Carter, Bonhoeffer is more attentive to how the reality of the living Christ is hidden in the ambiguity of a sinful world and to how this ambiguity leaves Christ unavailable for direct human reflection. This allows Bonhoeffer to argue that Jesus Christ is given in the midst of sinful history in a manner that leaves him accessible only by faith. The living Christ makes contact with sinful humanity and thereby places an external boundary on human thinking.[98] Bonhoeffer explains, "[Christ] stands there because I cannot, that is, he stands at the boundary of my existence and nevertheless in my place."[99]

Carter moves toward overstepping this boundary in his interpretation of Chalcedon. While Carter makes the profound suggestion that Chalcedon must be interpreted within Israel's covenantal history, he does not provide similar attention to how Chalcedon is to be understood within sinful history. With the focus on Israel, Carter interprets Chalcedon in term of a human conception of Jesus' Jewish flesh. If the limits on human thinking are not accounted for in Carter's Christology, then his conception of Jesus' Jewish flesh runs the risk of setting up its own ideological borders, which is the very thing that Carter claims whiteness does.

With a sensitivity toward the ultimate break caused by the fall, Bonhoeffer reads Chalcedon as placing a limit on every human conception of Christ. In this manner Bonhoeffer's treatment of Chalcedon safeguards

---

98 Bonhoeffer explains this in *Act and Being* when he writes, "There is a boundary only for a concrete human being in his or her entirety, and this boundary is called *Christ*" (*DBWE* 2:46).

99 *DBWE* 12:324.

the reality of the living Christ and helps explain how Christ is given in the midst of sinful history. This does not suggest that Carter's conception of Christ is erroneous, for it was shown to assist Bonhoeffer's Christology. Instead, the suggestion is that Carter's conception of Jesus' Jewish flesh is a human conception that remains subject to and founded upon an encounter with the living Christ in the community of faith. Whereas Carter's understanding of Jesus' Jewish flesh results in presenting Christ as a covenantal identity that directly challenges racial identities, Bonhoeffer is more cautious to point out that any definition of Christ risks becoming a controlling idea that capitulates to sinful exclusions. Unlike Carter's positive presentation of Jesus' Jewish flesh, Bonhoeffer's positive Christology, seen in the final section of *Lectures on Christology*,[100] leaves the ambiguity of sin in place, necessitating an encounter with Christ opened by the gift of faith. It is not God's becoming *human*, but the *humiliation* of the God-human, Jesus Christ, that constitutes the stumbling block encountered in the sacrament.[101] By reserving this ultimate place for Christ given in the midst of sinful history, Bonhoeffer assists in showing how Christ is not simply an idea available for racial exploitation but, instead, how all our conceptions of Christ are meant to lead us to an actual encounter with the living Christ. In this sense Carter's discussion of Jesus' Jewish flesh provides a necessary and profound insight that prepares God's people for the surprise of God's gracious address.

To be clear, there are times when Carter gestures toward the relation between Christology and Christ's person concretely encountered in the community of faith's worship. For example, he suggests that Afro-Christians "lived into Israel's covenantal dispositions through the liturgical or churchly mediations, such as prayer, of Jesus of Nazareth."[102] And he states that persons of African descent who identified with the people of Israel avoided "the modernist problem of supersessionism" because this identification was "mediated through worship of the Jew, Jesus of Nazareth."[103] Even here, however, the worship of a Jewish Jesus is cast as a mediating idea, in that Carter offers no explanation of how this worship itself informs one's conception of Christ and how it may remain beyond direct human reflection in fallen creation.

---

100 *DBWE* 12:353–60.

101 Bonhoeffer claims, "His being sacrament is his being humiliated in the present" (*DBWE* 12:322).

102 Carter, *Race*, 147.

103 Carter, *Race*, 148–49.

While Carter's proposal of covenantal identity offers a direct challenge to racial identities, it makes this challenge in a manner that fails to
carefully safeguard the ultimate place Bonhoeffer gives to the reality of
the living Christ. As a result, Carter's direct challenge of whiteness risks
idealizing Jesus Christ in a way that removes attention to the complexities of how God works through Jesus Christ in the midst of a sinful community. In short, Carter's conception of Christ does not help one answer
the question posed by this book: how does God work through a historical
church entrenched in whiteness without condoning the church's racial
waywardness? This suggests that there is a repair to Carter's Christology that is necessary, a repair that harnesses his christological challenge
of whiteness with Bonhoeffer's emphasis on the social concreteness of a
Christology given in relation to the community of faith's worship.

Preparing the Way as a Direct Challenge of Whiteness

Thus far the discussion has addressed the *shape* and *limits* of Christology
in relation to a theological challenge of whiteness. In the first section,
Bonhoeffer's Christology was shown to lack careful attention to Israel
as a mediating term that *shapes* christological reflection. In the second
section, it was shown how Carter's Christology sets up a direct challenge
of whiteness that risks overstepping the *limit* placed on human reflection by the rupture of sin. This final section explores how Bonhoeffer's
theological ethics assist in providing a direct challenge of whiteness at
the more concrete level of daily life. Whereas Carter proposes an "exiting" of whiteness that allows for a "miscegenation" in Jesus' Jewish flesh,
Bonhoeffer's ethics suggest that a direct challenge of whiteness is not
found through imaginatively exiting whiteness but in struggling against
whiteness through concretely preparing the way for Christ's advent in
history. The challenge of whiteness here is understood on a penultimate
level that preserves Christ's coming as ultimate.

Bonhoeffer: Responsibility and Freedom

In his chapter "History and Good" from *Ethics*, Bonhoeffer outlines how
the responsible life attends to the occurrence of "the good" in the midst
of historical reality.[104] Bonhoeffer's basic premise in this chapter is that

---

104 Bonhoeffer discusses the responsible life in his two attempts to address "History and
Good." See *DBWE* 6:220–39, 257–88. His second attempt at writing "History and Good" is
primarily treated in this section as it offers Bonhoeffer's more comprehensive presentation
of the concept of the responsible life.

ethical action does not happen in a vacuum, but that it takes place within a history already in motion and between persons bound to one another and to God. An abstract ethic ignores this historical and relational messiness, allowing the formation of principles that guarantee one's personal goodness.[105] In contrast, the reality of Christ constitutes the responsiveness of the responsible life through the *responsibility* Jesus Christ takes for the fallen world in the *freedom* of risking his life to bear the guilt of sinful humanity.[106]

The responsible life,[107] Bonhoeffer contends, is oriented around two christological principles: Christ's *vicarious representative action* and Christ's *accordance with reality*. With regard to Christ's *vicarious representative action*, Bonhoeffer claims that human beings act within the midst of contingent relationships that shape their actions, for better or worse. Jesus Christ himself constitutes this relational reality by making all of life directed toward vicarious representative action. Bonhoeffer explains, "Jesus was not the individual who sought to achieve some personal perfection, but only lived as the one who in himself has taken on and bears the selves of all human beings."[108] Vicarious representative action speaks to how a mother acts on behalf of her family in her working, providing, and suffering. "Every attempt to live as if [s]he were alone," Bonhoeffer claims, "is a denial of the fact that [s]he is actually responsible."[109] The responsible life is not one that seeks purity in the fiction of isolation but sees one's life as bound up with Christ and, through Christ, sees one's own life as bound to others. With whiteness in view, this suggests that rather than imagining a fictious space beyond whiteness, those in the church must bear with one another in a struggle

105 See "History and Good [I]," *DBWE* 6:220; "History and Good [II]," *DBWE* 6:248.

106 This involvement of one's whole life is suggested by Bonhoeffer's definition of responsibility [*Verantwortung*] as a response to the event of Christ's coming at the risk of one's own life. He writes, "At the risk of my life, I give an account and thus take responsibility for what has happened through Jesus Christ" (*DBWE* 6:255).

107 Bonhoeffer's usage of the word "responsibility" [*Verantwortung*] may strike some as deviating from Scripture. Bonhoeffer acknowledges that the term is rarely found in the Bible and argues that the risk of using this term is warranted because ethics and theology "cannot simply repeat biblical terminology" (*DBWE* 6:256). Bonhoeffer also suggests that "biblical terminology cannot be used without danger either" (*DBWE* 6:257).

108 *DBWE* 6:258.

109 *DBWE* 6:258. The gender designation in this citation is changed to illuminate the manner in which women are often assumed as having an intrinsic responsibility for their families while men are given the choice to either take this responsibility or not. Bonhoeffer's supersessionism is not the only danger in his theology, to be sure. Bonhoeffer's handling of gender represents another area where his theology is lacking and in need of further development.

to acknowledge how whiteness informs our relationships in ways that resist Christ's vicarious representative action. Whiteness is directly challenged in acknowledging and addressing it as a resistance found within Christ's binding us together.

Along with the relational reality constituted by Christ's vicarious representative action, Bonhoeffer suggests that Christ situates all responsible action within history in *accordance with reality*. This means, for Bonhoeffer, that a given situation is not a blank slate on which to act, but that the situation is incorporated into "the formation of the act itself."[110] Historical and situational circumstances offer input on one's actions because Christ upholds history as the "Real One."[111] History matters because the real Christ is found concretely within history and not as an abstract idea that works above history.

Bonhoeffer's understanding of Christ's *accordance with reality* suggests that our history of racial inequity must be given serious consideration because it defines and informs our actions, whether we recognize it or not. While everyone is implicated in the modern world's racial history, Bonhoeffer's ethics suggest that there is no one-size-fits-all principle for taking responsible action in accordance with this history. One's response to whiteness is limited by one's particular position in history. This means, in a penultimate sense, that those who have benefited from racial configurations of whiteness are commissioned with a responsibility different from those who have been disadvantaged by whiteness. Attending to the historical specificity of whiteness allows for the inequities configured by whiteness to be directly challenged in preparation for the surprise of Christ's coming.

Because responsible action accounts for a messy history and intertwined relationships, Bonhoeffer suggests that responsible action is always *freely* given, from a strictly human perspective, in that it acts in the absence of universal principles. Responsible action is *free* action in that it works from the limits of creaturely freedom placed on one by another person. Bonhoeffer explains,

> The actions norm is not a universal principle, but the concrete neighbor as given to me by God. The choice is made no longer between a clearly recognized good and a clearly recognized evil; instead, it is

110 *DBWE* 6:261.
111 *DBWE* 6:263.

risked in faith while being aware that good and evil are hidden in
the concrete historical situation.[112]

A human being must make decisions from his or her limited understanding of the world and from the particularity of his or her situation.
This means responsible action is never perfect, but as Bonhoeffer has
already made clear, perfection or a fictitious purity is not the goal of
responsible action; preparing the way for Christ is.

The ethic that Bonhoeffer presents is not one of principles but one
of responsiveness. An ethic of responsiveness guards one's actions
from violating another person, because Christ allows one to encounter
others, even in sin, as responsible.[113] One does not know of one's own
responsibility without the limit of another responsible person.[114] Thus,
each person is given a unique responsibility or "vocation" for addressing
whiteness that acknowledges and refuses to infringe on other responsible persons.[115] One's specific responsibility in addressing whiteness
is discovered not from a *principle* but through a *response* to the concrete neighbor given to one by God. This suggests that people of different racial designations acquire their particular responsibility through
encountering one another as distinctly responsible.

Such an encounter requires a bearing of guilt that corresponds to
Christ's becoming guilty through acting within the historical existence
of human beings.[116] Bonhoeffer argues that Christ's concern for human
beings as they are (i.e., in sin) leads Christ to share in the guilt of human
beings. In God's freedom, Christ is free for sinful human beings. Thus,
Christ bears humanity's guilt to overcome sin. Bonhoeffer comments,
"As the sinless one, Jesus takes the guilt of his brothers and sisters upon

112 *DBWE* 6:221.

113 Bonhoeffer comments, "What distinguishes responsibility from violation is this very
fact of recognizing other people as responsible persons, indeed making them aware of their
own responsibility" (*DBWE* 6:269).

114 See *DBWE* 6:269.

115 Bonhoeffer's treatment of responsibility and freedom becomes even more concrete
in his discussion of vocation, which due to the limits of space could not be explored here.
See *DBWE* 6:289–97.

116 See *DBWE* 6:275. One will notice that Bonhoeffer, in this later writing, refers exclusively to Christ's bearing of guilt rather than Christ's coming in the likeness of sinful humanity, as seen in his *Lectures on Christology*. Guilt indicates how Christ receives the brunt
of sin's effect while safeguarding the assertion that Christ was without sin. For a helpful
discussion of Bonhoeffer's later thinking in relation to one's bearing of guilt, see Matthew
Puffer, "Bonhoeffer's Ethics of Election: Discerning a Late Revision," *International Journal
of Systematic Theology* 14 (2012): 255–76.

himself, and in carrying the burden of this guilt he proves himself as the sinless one."[117] Only Christ can bear guilt in this way, because only Christ is without sin. At the same time, Bonhoeffer proposes that sinful human beings participate with Christ in bearing guilt, in an indirect and relative sense, when they act responsibly, as Christ did in being implicated in humanity's guilt, by acting on another human being's behalf.[118]

While Bonhoeffer's discussion of the bearing of guilt concludes by preserving a distinct space for divine violence in boundary cases,[119] the broader point, which is pertinent for the present argument, is that all responsible action incurs guilt. Bonhoeffer explains that when one's actions "spring from the selfless love for the real human brother or sister—it cannot seek to withdraw from the community of human guilt."[120] With regard to whiteness, one who seeks to live responsibly must acknowledge how he or she is particularly bound to a history that implicates one in the guilt incurred by racial wounding. As seen in Yancy's example of "the elevator effect,"[121] racial wounding is not a thing of the past but a presently enacted response that occurs as we approach one another. Thus to address race is to enter into a painful space where one's concern for others must outweigh one's own claims of personal righteousness. Seeking to place one's personal innocence above one's responsibility for other human beings, as Bonhoeffer indicates, makes one "even more egregiously guilty" by divorcing oneself from the redeeming surprise of Jesus Christ.[122]

Bonhoeffer's understanding of responsibility and freedom suggests that the irrefutable presence of Jesus Christ in history incorporates us into bearing the historical burden of whiteness from each of our particular places in history. His Christology advises that the venture of addressing whiteness should not precede on Christian principles or a Christology that ensures one will remain unmarred, but must be seen instead as a venture of faith that thrusts one into the lives of others to prepare the

---

117 *DBWE* 6:275.

118 See *DBWE* 6:275, 279.

119 See *DBWE* 6:273. Bonhoeffer no doubt had the distinct situation of Germany under Adolf Hitler in mind when he discussed the bearing of guilt as reserving a space for divine violence. For a similar approach to divine violence presented in the context of America's racial history, see Ted Smith's *Weird John Brown*.

120 *DBWE* 6:275.

121 Yancy's description of "the elevator effect" was presented in the introduction of this study to show how whiteness is constantly informing our daily interactions.

122 *DBWE* 6:276.

way for Christ in the fallen world. It is not through a christological principle but through a daily responsiveness to Christ in accordance with
history and the contingency of other human beings that whiteness is
directly challenged. Thus, Bonhoeffer's ethic of responsiveness reserves
a penultimate space where whiteness as a relative obstruction to Christ's
coming is directly opposed through the contrasting action of preparing
the way for Christ's pending arrival.

Carter: Exiting Whiteness

Rather than a preparing of the way in the midst of whiteness, Carter's
Christology calls for a complete break with whiteness. Carter's Christology demands this complete break because he presents the ontology of
Jesus' Jewish flesh (miscegenation) in direct contrast to an ontology of
whiteness (exclusion). These two all-encompassing ways of being in the
world are presented as mutually exclusive. Thus, to enter the reality of
Jesus' Jewish flesh, for Carter, inherently requires an exiting from whiteness. As one is drawn into the covenantal reality that Jesus embodies,
whiteness loses its grip and power. These contrasting ontologies of Jesus'
Jewish flesh and of whiteness are most starkly drawn out in Carter's
treatment of Gregory of Nyssa.

   In his account of Gregory's Christology, Carter examines the theological underpinnings that informed Gregory's staunch opposition of
slavery in distinction to many of his contemporaries.[123] Gregory's opposition to slavery, for Carter, is attributed to two theological motifs. The
first motif concerns how Gregory read Scripture against the grain of
society in a way that receives one's being *ecstatically* from Christ. This
approach to Scripture challenged the social norms of slavery through
exchanging the identity given to one by social orders with an identity
received from Christ. The second motif concerns how Gregory proposed
that the inflections of all human difference are summed up and reinte-
grated *eschatologically* in Christ as the fullness of God's image.[124] This
eschatological inflection challenges slavery by upholding the necessity of
human freedom for each person's participation in the fullness of God's
image given in Christ. These two together, an *ecstatic* and *eschatological*

---

123 Carter argues this support of slavery runs "from Aristotle to Cicero and from Augustine in the Christian West to his contemporary, the golden-mouthed preacher himself, John
Chrysostom in the Christian East" (*Race*, 231).

124 Carter, *Race,* 247.

being in Jesus Christ, constitute a simultaneous exiting of whiteness and entering into Jesus' Jewish flesh.

In Gregory's reading of Scripture against the grain of social norms, Carter contends that one exits a socially defined identity as one enters into the ecstatic being of Jesus Christ. Carter explains that Gregory's reading of Scripture presents one's whole being as drawn into the "unfathomable mystery of the eternal Christ."[125] As one engages in ascetic contemplation, one's desires are shaped and reshaped by one's union to Christ. This signals, for Carter, a leaving behind of one's ties to the worldly order of things to discover a new ecstatic identity given to one by Christ. Carter observes this movement from society's ordering of desires into Christ's ordering of desires in the story of Abram-Abraham. Abram "leaves behind the identity that Ur assigned to him as Abram," Carter writes, and in doing so he receives a new identity as Abraham in relationship to YHWH.[126] Reasoning from Abraham's life, Carter argues that Israel's covenantal identity is not to be thought of in racial or static terms, but as an identity that is always in motion and under the control of YHWH.[127] Christian identity, then, is to leave "behind one mode of identity" (specifically racially given identities) so as to ecstatically join with Israel in "entering into another."[128]

Carter clarifies that this exiting and entering does not remove one's historical place in the world but redefines it in relation to the eschatological being of Christ. Carter notes how Gregory presents Christ as the one "prototypical form" that is given "spatiotemporal and geohistorical depth" through the multifaceted diversity of persons who inflect the image of God eschatologically.[129] One's identity is eschatological in that it is found in the fullness of Christ, which always exceeds the individual. Carter again illustrates this point with Abram-Abraham by suggesting that Abraham's identity always lies before him in the covenantal promise of God.[130] This suggests that Gregory's christological vision of the image of God must be seen in relation to Israel, Carter contends,

---

125 Carter, *Race*, 234. Carter works from Gregory of Nyssa's "Homilies on Ecclesiastes," in *Gregory of Nyssa, Homilies on Ecclesiastes: An English Version with Supporting Studies*, ed. Stuart G. Hall (New York: de Gruyter, 1993), 31–144.

126 Carter, *Race*, 251.

127 Carter, *Race*, 250–51.

128 Carter, *Race*, 234.

129 Carter, *Race*, 246.

130 Carter explains of Israel, "They are the people whose identity, in being a covenantal and thus a nonracial identity, is always eschatologically in front of them" (*Race*, 251).

"for it is from the history of this people's covenantal interactions with God and thus from God's history that God takes up the history of the world."[131] Whereas racial identity reinscribes, Jesus' Jewish flesh constitutes a remaking as one receives one's being eschatologically from Israel's God. Thus Gregory's charge, channeled through Carter, is "exit the power structure of whiteness and of the blackness (and other modalities of race) whiteness created, recognizing that all persons are unique and irreplaceable inflections or articulations . . . of Christ the covenantal Jew."[132] Jesus' Jewish flesh calls us ever deeper into God's being to offer a unique inflection of God's image, which necessitates that we leave behind the racial designations placed on us by the world.

The radicality of Carter's Christology is that it works from the premise that the particularity of Jesus' Jewish flesh has already drawn different persons together in Christ's communal being. This suggests that a challenge of whiteness comes intrinsically out of Christ's very person, who is given within the history of Israel. In addition to Gregory, this challenge of whiteness was seen in Irenaeus' account of recapitulation and Maximus' account of divinization. From all three early church fathers, Carter observes a direct challenge of whiteness offered through entering into the ecstatic and eschatological being given in Jesus' Jewish flesh.

What should be noted is how Carter's challenge of whiteness functions as a direct ontological challenge. Ontology counters ontology: "He, as Christ-Israel, is the one into whom human beings are to venture in exiting whiteness."[133] An ultimate covenantal identity is leveled directly against a racial identity. It is from this ontological challenge that an ethical response to whiteness is necessitated as an exiting from whiteness.

Bonhoeffer and Carter: Preparing the Way

Bonhoeffer's proposal of preparing the way and Carter's call to exit whiteness present two different ethical approaches for addressing whiteness. The decisive difference is found in how Bonhoeffer's proposal of preparing the way offers a challenge of whiteness within a penultimate register, whereas Carter's call to exit whiteness positions an ultimate claim about Jesus' Jewish flesh directly against whiteness. Carter provides a powerful eschatological challenge of whiteness, but the daunting

131 Carter, *Race*, 250.
132 Carter, *Race*, 250.
133 Carter, *Race*, 241.

question is how to connect this eschatological challenge to the historical situatedness of our everyday lives. Bonhoeffer's ecclesial proposal of preparing the way assists in drawing this connection through his motif of the ultimate and penultimate.

Bonhoeffer's and Carter's divergent ethical approaches are first observed in the distinct manner they each understand Scripture and history. Carter seeks to read the scriptural witness against the grain of given social orders. In this manner Carter's overall project runs in the direction of replacing existing political systems with his own theological program.[134] Inhabiting Scripture is to enter a counter-ontology that directly challenges whiteness. Bonhoeffer provides a slightly different approach to Scripture and history. Instead of reading Scripture against the grain of social orders, Bonhoeffer's Christology suggests that reality itself as a whole is found within the scriptural witness. The scriptural witness does not counter the world but reveals the world as it is. Scripture reveals how the world resists God's gracious care that preserves the world for the coming of Christ. Whereas Carter talks about *entering* and *inhabiting* Scripture, Bonhoeffer talks of a direct *encounter* with Christ through Scripture in the church's proclamation of Word and sacrament.[135] To encounter Christ in the church's proclamation of Word and sacrament connects the ultimate with the temporal reality of our everyday lives, with the empirical situation of our local congregations shaped by whiteness. This connection between the ultimate and penultimate is less pronounced in Carter's reading of Scripture and history. Carter's ethical proposal focuses on breaking out of the historical patterns of racialized existence. In contrast,

134 This in part is a trait of Carter's proposal inherited from his continued reliance on John Milbank. While Carter alters Milbank's overall proposal, he shares Milbank's sentiment that the secular sphere is created by a distortion of Christianity resulting in an ontology of violence. See John Milbank, *Theology and Social Theory: Beyond Secular Reason* (Oxford: Blackwell, 1992), 1–3. To challenge this ontology of violence, Milbank offers a counter-ontology just as Carter offers a counter-ontology in terms of a miscegenation constituted by Jesus' Jewish flesh. See Carter, *Race*, 348. Tom Greggs offers an alternative approach to secularism in his engagement of Barth and Bonhoeffer in *Theology against Religion*. Greggs suggests that the problem is not secularism (contra Milbank and Carter) but religion, specifically an understanding of religion that privatizes engagement of the secular. See Greggs, *Theology against Religion: Constructive Dialogues with Bonhoeffer and Barth* (London: T&T Clark, 2011), 1–4.

135 For a treatment of how Bonhoeffer reads Scripture, see Brian Brock, *Singing the Ethos of God: On the Place of Christian Ethics in Scripture* (Grand Rapids: Eerdmans, 2007), 70–94.

Bonhoeffer's reading of Scripture and history offers an ethic of responsiveness that attends to God's activity within a racialized church and world to prepare the way for Christ's coming.

Bonhoeffer's ethic requires a constant responsiveness that attends to situational realities and given relationships, and that seeks to discern how Christ is presently at work in the fallen world. Contrastively, Carter's call to exit whiteness shrinks the space for examining how Christ works in the midst of fallen history. This penultimate space is displaced by Carter's direct application of covenantal identity against racial identities. As Carter explicitly states, "To enter into Christ is to enter into YHWH's covenant, and this entry entails leaving behind through feats of ascetical struggle racialized identity."[136] This sharp dichotomy calls one to leave behind racialized identity, a racialized identity linked to history. Carter's assertion rightly challenges the damaging effects of racialized identity but seems shortsighted in the way it decouples human beings from the history that shapes them. There is no leaving behind of history, nor is there the possibility of a total break from racialized identity from Bonhoeffer's perspective of the responsible life. History itself is incorporated into the risk of acting responsibly to prepare the way for Christ's coming.

The difference between Bonhoeffer's and Carter's ethical approaches are seen further through comparing Bonhoeffer's conception of the responsible life with Carter's understanding of divinization, in terms of an entering into "miscegenized or mulattic existence."[137] To be clear, when Carter speaks of exiting the racial world, he does not suggest a physical leaving behind but a new way of reading and reperforming the world from within "YHWH's covenant with Israel."[138] Carter describes this as a *habitus* that "remakes" rather than "reinscribes" identity.[139] One reinterprets oneself, Carter argues, as one is divinized in being conformed to God through one's existence in Jesus' Jewish flesh.[140] Bonhoeffer's approach is similar but more attentive to sin in that he accounts for God's preservation of fallen creation in terms of how God "does not break the new laws that

136 Carter, *Race*, 366.

137 Carter, *Race*, 192.

138 Carter, *Race*, 323.

139 Carter, *Race*, 235.

140 This is how Carter talks about the Afro-Christian existence witnessed to by Briton Hammon, Frederick Douglass, and Jarena Lee. See chapters 6, 7, and 8 in *Race*.

now apply to the earth and humankind after the fall" but "participates in them."[141] Whereas Carter speaks of Jesus' Jewish flesh as providing a new template for living beyond racial existence, Bonhoeffer
details how Christ's coming to a sinful world means that reality and
history itself are incorporated into the way one responds to Christ in
the world.[142] The import of Bonhoeffer's approach is found in how it
does not seek to rise above or rewrite history but traffics in the reality of history as upheld by the living Christ.

Notwithstanding their differences, Bonhoeffer's discussion
of Christ's vicarious representative action shares similarities with
Carter's understanding of divinization in terms of "an intrahuman
exchange of realities."[143] Bonhoeffer parallels Carter's charge against
whiteness when he argues that Christ frees one from seeking purity
in the fiction of isolation. Rather than working from the isolation of
whiteness, one's actions spring from already being bound to Christ
and, through Christ, being bound to other human beings. In speaking about being bound to others in his ethic of the responsible life,
however, Bonhoeffer is more vigilant than Carter to offer a christological framework sensitive to sin. Carter's proposal drives forward
the idea that Christ's being constitutes an exchange between human
beings with very little attention to how sin complicates and prob-
lematizes this exchange. For Bonhoeffer these complications of sin
are handled within the framework of Christ as the "limit" and the
"center" of human existence after the fall. In terms of the *limit*, one
does not know of one's own responsibility without encountering the
distinctiveness of another responsible person as given by Christ.[144]
This limit safeguards from the dangers of paternalism and the insidious resiliency of whiteness to subsume all. In terms of the *center*,
one is transformed through bearing with others in association with

141 *DBWE* 3:139.

142 This was discussed above in relation to Bonhoeffer's suggestion that Christ situates
all responsible action within history in accordance with reality. For Bonhoeffer's presentation of this concept, see *DBWE* 6:261–63.

143 Carter, *Race*, 352. For an excellent discussion of the debate surrounding whether
Bonhoeffer is in agreement or disagreement with the patristic formula of *theosis* (divinization), see Kaiser, *Becoming Simple and Wise*, 103–4. After discussing the different views,
Kaiser concludes that both sides of the issue miss Bonhoeffer's primary purpose, which
is "to counter what he perceives as the widespread contempt for humanity or misguided
idolization of humanity pervading German society" (*Becoming Simple and Wise*, 103).

144 See *DBWE* 6:269.

Christ's bearing of guilt. Here we are changed through our lives intersecting with one another and by receiving ourselves from one another in the particularity of Jesus' Jewish flesh, as Carter so masterfully substantiates. It is by holding these two, limit and center, together that Christ mediates "an intrahuman exchange of realities" in the midst of sinful history.

Without providing a similar attendance of sin, Carter's proposal of an "intraracial" existence leaves open the threat of supplanting other human beings. This makes Bonhoeffer's attention to creaturely limits an important complement to Carter's proposal. Carter's proposal helpfully signals how all persons are called to live into an existence he observes in early Afro-Christians, who challenged modernity's racial reasoning by interpreting the world from within Israel's covenantal history.[145] But this call must come with a warning that Bonhoeffer provides in his ethic of the responsible life. Bonhoeffer's warning is that one's call to share in this existence must not confuse one's own particular responsibility with the responsibility of another distinct person, and most of all, it must not rob Jesus of his vicarious representative action in uniquely bearing the guilt of the whole world yet being without sin. Thus, by providing an intrinsic limit through Christ's bearing of guilt, Bonhoeffer assists in relating Carter's ultimate claim of covenantal identity to a penultimate outworking in creaturely time, attended to by each follower of Christ.

Conclusion

Bonhoeffer's and Carter's Christologies each provide distinct insights for addressing the modern problem of whiteness. The significance of Carter's proposal was shown in the way it reclaims Israel's covenantal history as mediating God's given revelation culminating in a Jewish Messiah. Whiteness functions on a decentering of Israel, even observed in Bonhoeffer's Christology, that can subtly or explicitly allow one to claim one's own self-election. Theologies of race must always remain attentive to the constant danger and unconscious ways that Jesus is racially exploited to ensure one's own purity to the detriment of others. This danger is subverted through being joined

---

145 This summarizes Carter's constructive proposal offered through his reading of Briton Hammon, Frederick Douglass, and Jarena Lee.

with one another through Jesus' Jewish flesh as the tune that the symphony of creation plays.

The significance of Bonhoeffer's Christology was shown in the way it subjects all conceptions of Christ to a living encounter with the reality of Christ in the community of faith. The community of faith encounters Jesus Christ precisely in his coming to fallen creation in the humiliation of the likeness of sinful flesh. This means that a challenge of whiteness is not directly derived from an ultimate christological claim but is lived out in reference to the ultimate claim encountered in the humiliation of the living Christ. Christ's call frees one to negotiate an already given history in preparation of Israel's messiah, who has already come to a fallen world and who is coming. This preparation must include looking for ways to incorporate the reality of Israel's covenant history and a conception of Jesus' Jewish flesh into the Christian church's liturgical practices. Presenting better representations of Jesus' Jewish flesh, though, must not be misunderstood as ensuring Christ's coming or the Christian church's purity. Instead, it represents a penultimate act of challenging whiteness to clear the way for Christ in the fallen world. Christ is already given in Israel's covenant history and in the midst of a sinful world. Thus, there is no racial obstruction that can stand in Christ's way, as hard as we (white Christians) may try.

Despite their differences, Bonhoeffer's and Carter's Christologies share a strong resonance. This resonance is observed through bringing their distinct musical metaphors into concert with one another. Carter's musical metaphor offers Jesus' Jewish flesh as the amphitheater in which all the different intonations of human particularity sing out in unison. Bonhoeffer's musical metaphor is given in his description of the polyphonic life that refuses to be "pushed back into a single dimension, but is kept multidimensional, polyphonic."[146] The polyphonic life, Bonhoeffer suggests, puts one into the many dimensions of life, all taking place in the same moment. Carter's musical metaphor speaks of the ultimate; Bonhoeffer's musical metaphor addresses the relation between the ultimante and the penultimate. Carter writes, "He is the tune—a jazz or blues tune

---

146 *DBWE* 8:405. In the conclusion of this letter to Bethge, Bonhoeffer suggests that the polyphonic life offers a "preparation for" faith and makes it possible for them to celebrate Pentecost while in the midst of war.

of suffering divine things—that the symphony of creation, the many, plays."[147] Bonhoeffer writes,

> God, the Eternal, wants to be loved with our whole heart, not to the detriment of earthly love or to diminish it, but as a cantus firmus to which the other voices of life resound in counterpoint . . . Where the cantus firmus is clear and distinct, a counterpoint can develop as mightily as it wants.[148]

What both musical metaphors share is Jesus Christ as the cantus firmus.

---

147 Carter, *Race*, 248.
148 *DBWE* 8:394.

5

Ecclesiology and Whiteness

Bonhoeffer and Brian Bantum in Comparison

In many respects the question with which this book wrestles is a pastoral one. How may we honestly account for the manner in which whiteness socially and historically shapes the Christian church, as highlighted by Jennings and Carter, while retaining the historical continuity of God's working and speaking into and through this same community? The crux of this question concerns addressing both how the triune God speaks *through* the historical church, offering historical continuity, and how God speaks *to* this community from above, preventing a capitulation to whiteness. Bonhoeffer's understanding of the church and its sacramental life helpfully attends to this dual concern of how the triune God speaks *to* and *through* the historical church. In addressing this dual concern, Bonhoeffer's ecclesiology provides not only unique insights for theological discourses on race but also the potential of reframing the conversation—namely, a move from a discussion of how the Christian church may overcome whiteness to a discussion of how the triune God has been and is presently at work in the Christian church and world to overcome whiteness.

The explicit turn to ecclesiology offered here illuminates an implicit critique placed on Jennings and Carter in the previous two chapters. Simply stated, the worry is that Jennings' and Carter's proposals lack a robust ecclesiology that attends to the continuity of the triune God's speaking to and through the historical church. This misgiving is not so much with what Jennings and Carter say but with what they leave unsaid and unexplored. Brian Bantum's *Redeeming Mulatto* is significant in how it shares many of the theological intuitions of Jennings and Carter but traces these sensibilities specifically onto the locus of the church.[1] Bantum goes beyond the writings of Jennings and Carter in that he seeks to address the embodied practices of whiteness with the embodied practices of the Christian church's tangible worship. It is this distinct approach that makes Bantum a suitable interlocutor for considering ecclesiology and whiteness in this final chapter.

Rather than setting up a reparative dialogue, as done in the last two chapters, the aim here is to explore the nuanced differences between Bonhoeffer's and Bantum's conceptions of the church and how their distinct understandings of the church provide divergent approaches for addressing whiteness in and through the Christian church. Offering this comparison allows for a final examination of how Bonhoeffer's thought may uniquely assist us in considering how the triune God speaks to and through a Christian church shaped by the language game of whiteness without succumbing to the destructive speech patterns of whiteness.

The Christological and Pneumatological Contours of Ecclesiology

The question "What is church?" lies at the heart of both Bonhoeffer's writings and Bantum's *Redeeming Mulatto*. The concrete community of the church is central, for Bonhoeffer and Bantum, because it is this particular community that constitutes the living presence of Jesus Christ in the world through the Holy Spirit. To know Christ is to participate in Christ's body, that is, the church. As Bonhoeffer starkly puts it, "There is no relation to Christ in which the relation to the church is not

---

1   As this chapter will show, Bantum's *Redeeming Mulatto* takes on many more of the characteristics of Carter's project than of Jennings'. In particular, Bantum's project resonates with Carter's reading of Chalcedon when he suggests that Chalcedon presents an "ontological claim that is best interpreted within a notion of mulattic hybridity" (*Redeeming Mulatto*, 101).

necessarily established as well.''[2] Similarly, Bantum claims that in our confession "we not only speak of [Christ], but we enter into his body and become something new.''[3] This connection between Christ and church leads Bonhoeffer and Bantum into detailed considerations of how the Holy Spirit plays a significant and distinct role in the life of the church. The church is united to Christ through the *Holy Spirit*. Bonhoeffer discusses this in terms of how the historical church is realized by Jesus Christ and actualized by Holy Spirit.[4] Bantum discusses this in terms of how the church is united to Christ's mulattic body (born of flesh and Spirit) through being born of the Holy Spirit. The similarities in how Bonhoeffer and Bantum understand the church in close relation to Jesus Christ and the Holy Spirit provide an interesting point of comparison.

While Bonhoeffer and Bantum both draw attention to the christological and pneumatological contours of the church, they each present slightly different conceptions of Christ and the Holy Spirit. These distinct conceptions attribute different forms to the church, which are considered in what follows. Whereas Bonhoeffer offers an ecclesiology that discerns God's *irruption* into the fallen creation through the historical continuity of the church, Bantum offers an ecclesiology that designates God's *disruption* of a racialized world through the performative life of the church. The question that is examined in the following discussion is how to reconcile one's conception of Christ and the Spirit with a belief in the historical continuity of the church. For if whiteness is to be fundamentally addressed, one must account for how the triune God does not capitulate to whiteness at any point in history.

Bonhoeffer: What Is Church?

Bonhoeffer's understanding of the church has loomed in the background of almost every discussion up to this point. In chapter 3 it was observed how encountering Jesus Christ in the church is the presupposed starting point for Bonhoeffer's theology in general and his understanding of creation in particular. In chapter 4 it was further explained how, for Bonhoeffer, Jesus Christ stands both over the church as a limit on human thinking and within the church as constituting its very being in the fallen creation. In what follows, these

2   *DBWE* 1:127.
3   Bantum, *Redeeming Mulatto*, 10.
4   Bonhoeffer discusses how the church is established in and through Christ and is actualized through the Holy Spirit in *DBWE* 1:145–61.

various threads of Bonhoeffer's thinking on the church are brought together to offer his response to the underlying question of this study: how does God speak to and through a sinful church in history without condoning sin? Bonhoeffer's response to this question is relied upon to explore how the triune God remains at work in a historical church embedded within the language game of whiteness.

In exploring Bonhoeffer's response to how God works through a sinful church, it is important that we recognize his understanding of what is meant by "church."[5] For Bonhoeffer the church-community [Gemeinde] is not an ideal, spotless community but an empirical community in the fallen world defined by Christ's real presence.[6] As Bonhoeffer describes the church in *Ethics*, it is "that piece of humanity where Christ *really* has taken form."[7] Jesus Christ "*has taken* form" (past tense) not in a perfected community but in the historical community that encounters Christ in its proclamation of Word and sacrament. The church, then, according to Bonhoeffer, is both a historical entity and a reality of God's revelation. Bonhoeffer emphasizes this twofold nature of the church in his 1933 essay, "What Is Church?":

> It is an institution that is not a good model of organization, not very influential, not very impressive, in need of improvement in the extreme. However, church is a ministry from God, a ministry of proclamation, the message of the living God. From it come

5   The term "church" is used throughout this chapter to refer broadly to that portion of God's people that have commonly been referred to as the Christian church (primarily constituted by Eastern Orthodox, Roman Catholic, and Protestant churches). God's people include both Israel (past and present) and the Christian church (past and present) without any bifurcation between the two, but with a careful distinction made between the two nonetheless. The portion of Scripture most often used to bifurcate God's people (Old and New Israel) is Romans 9–11. On the unity of God's people in this passage, see Tommy Givens, *We the People: Israel and the Catholicity of Jesus* (Minneapolis: Fortress, 2014), 345–412. Givens argues the Jews opposing the gospel in this passage are still part of God's elect people represented by Paul's faithfulness to them (the whole is represented by the remnant). The covenant should not be understood in ethnic terms but in terms of God's faithfulness to Israel represented by the few who respond to God as representative of the whole.

6   Bonhoeffer's term "*Gemeinde*" used in reference to the church [*Kirche*] is difficult to translate into English. Bonhoeffer uses this term to stipulate how it is not a church organization called church that defines Christ, but Christ that defines the community in which Christ is found. He explains, "It is not as if Christ could be abstracted from the church; rather, it is none other than Christ who 'is' the church. Christ does not represent it; only what is not present can be represented" (*DBWE* 1:157).

7   *DBWE* 6:97 (emphasis added).

commission and commandment; in it arise eternal ties; in it heaven and hell clash; in it judgment on earth takes place. Because the church is the living Christ and his judgment. The preached and preaching Christ, proclaimer and proclamation, ministry and word. Church is the awakening of the world through a miracle, through the presence of the life-creating God calling from death into life.[8]

The church enacts a clash between heaven and hell because it is where, in all of its mundaneness and imperfections, Jesus Christ is encountered through the Holy Spirit. The church's proclamation, "the preached and preaching Christ," enfolds this distinct community into how the triune God speaks within the fallen creation at all times and in all places. And it is precisely in this way that the church is the living Christ, not as an ideal community but as a concrete community that responds to God's speaking to and within the fallen creation.

Bonhoeffer fleshes out how the church is a concrete community that encounters God's speaking to and within the fallen creation in his discussion of the objective spirit from *Sanctorum Communio*. The objective spirit pertains to how Bonhoeffer describes the christological and pneumatological contours of the church in the fallen world. Christ's vicarious representative action establishes an objective spirit from below (lost at the fall) that the Holy Spirit actualizes in history from above. Commenting on the objective spirit established by Christ, Bonhoeffer states, "It has an active will of its own that orders and guides the wills of the members who constitute it and participate in it, and that takes shape in specific forms, thereby providing visible evidence that it has a life of its own."[9] The objective spirit gains its shape from each individual will, but also stands over the empirical community as having its own content and form that shapes each individual.[10] This mutual informing and forming of the church's objective spirit allows Bonhoeffer to suggest how Christ governs a sinful church, even while

8   *DBWE* 12:263.

9   *DBWE* 1:209.

10   *DBWE* 1:99. Along these lines, Charles West claims the objective spirit only becomes real in individual embodiment, allowing for a mutual interdependence between persons. He describes this as "the give-and-take of interpersonal relations among free people who know their mutual dependence, who do not submerge their identities in any human group or principle, but who discern and build together, in conflict and in reconciliation, the law and structure of responsible community." See Charles C. West, "Ground under Our Feet," in *New Studies in Bonhoeffer's Ethics*, ed. William J. Peck (Lewiston: Edwin Mellen Press, 1987), 235–73.

working in it and through it. Bonhoeffer writes, "Christ is at work in the form of the objective spirit in spite of all the sinfulness, historical contingency and fallibility of the church."[11]

Bonhoeffer goes on to describe how God speaks to and through the church as the Holy Spirit actualizes the church's objective spirit in history. Throughout his discussion of the empirical church in *Sanctorum Communio*, Bonhoeffer takes great care to distinguish the Holy Spirit and the church's objective spirit.[12] He makes this distinction by insisting that the Holy Spirit works from above, while Christ's vicarious representative action establishes how the church's objective spirit is formed from below.[13] The ever-changing and imperfect objective spirit of the human community is bound to its own generation, whereas the eternally one and perfect Holy Spirit is *free* to bear the objective spirit to make the church-community the place of God's revelation. The Holy Spirit bears the objective spirit by gathering and sustaining the social activity of the church-community in the midst of all its sinfulness and imperfections.[14] For Bonhoeffer the inclusion of sinfulness in the objective spirit makes it impossible to equate the church's objective spirit with the Holy Spirit.[15] Instead, the Holy Spirit works through the objective spirit to form the church's social life while giving it a level of autonomy that is sensitive to the reality of sin in the Christian community. It is the Holy Spirit's continual bearing from *above* of an objective spirit shaped from *below* that forms the church as a witness to Christ in its concrete, social life without succumbing to the church's sinfulness.

Bonhoeffer suggests that the Holy Spirit bears the forms of the church's life by standing behind and within the church's objective spirit as "the guarantor of the efficacy of these forms; these forms are

11   *DBWE* 1:215.

12   Bonhoeffer's main concern here is the work of Hegel, who he feels "simply identifies the Holy Spirit with the corporate spirit of the church" (*DBWE* 1:198).

13   See *DBWE* 1:215–16.

14   Bonhoeffer makes a careful distinction between sin and imperfection: "The sanctorum communion that is moved by the Holy Spirit has to be continually actualized in a struggle against two impediments: human imperfection and sin. To rashly equate these two, either giving imperfection the weight of sin, or regarding sin as mere imperfection, means in both cases avoiding the seriousness of the Christian concept of sin" (*DBWE* 1:210).

15   See *DBWE* 1:214. Michael Mawson highlights this point when he writes, "Bonhoeffer takes care throughout his discussion to maintain a firm distinction between the Holy Spirit and the church's objective spirit. He insists that the former comes to and works in the church from above, whereas the latter is generated from below." See Mawson, "The Spirit and the Community," 464.

preaching and the celebration of the sacraments."[16] The Holy Spirit bears
the forms of preaching and the sacraments in such a way that these
forms are sanctified in the process.[17] As Michael Mawson explains, "The
Christian community is continually being actualized as a visible witness
to Christ in its own objective spirit through the sanctifying work of the
Holy Spirit."[18] The Holy Spirit works through the sinful, imperfect, and
historically contingent objective spirit of the Christian community to
make it the concrete location of God's revelation.

This is not to suggest that somehow the church's liturgical practices of preaching and celebrating the sacrament are absent of the sinful aspects of the church's objective spirit. Bonhoeffer makes clear, as
will be discussed in the next section, that the church's sacramental
life remains influenced by sinful human beings even as the Holy Spirit
works through these ecclesial forms from above. The sacrament is a
hidden form of revelation, received by faith as God's claim over the
fallen creation.[19] This hidden form of the sacrament adheres to how
Bonhoeffer talks about Christ's ongoing humiliation in the church's
liturgical practices. As he states in *Lectures on Christology*, "The sacrament is not the becoming-human of Christ but rather the ultimate
humiliation of the God-human."[20] Preaching and the sacraments are
participatory events, "the preached and preaching Christ," that incorporate the concrete sociality of the church into the life of the triune
God—"the life-creating God calling from death into life."[21] Through
the Holy Spirit, the church is united with Christ, who is sent by the
Father in the likeness of sinful flesh (Rom 8:3) yet who remains without
sin (Heb 4:15). Christ's humiliation is found in the mundane human
activity of the church's proclamation of Word and sacrament. In this
event, Barry Harvey suggests that, for Bonhoeffer, "the Christian community both bears witness to a fallen world" and "also stands in the
place in which that world should stand."[22] And in this way the church

---

16   *DBWE* 1:216.

17   *DBWE* 1:216.

18   Mawson, "The Spirit and the Community," 464.

19   In *Lectures on Christology*, Bonhoeffer states, "This is what happens in the Lord's
Supper; God hallows the elements of bread and wine by speaking the divine word" (*DBWE*
12:319).

20   *DBWE* 12:319.

21   *DBWE* 12:263.

22   Harvey, *Taking Hold of the Real*, 9.

is the humiliated form of Christ concretely given to fallen creation by the Father through the Spirit, made visible by faith.

That the church lives by faith as the form of the humiliated Christ relates to Bonhoeffer's claim in *Ethics* that the church must walk a penultimate path that prepares the way for God's ultimate word. The ultimate describes how God speaks *to* the historical church from above through the Holy Spirit to keep the church from capitulating to sinful distortions, such as the language game of whiteness. At the same time, the penultimate addresses how God speaks *through* the historical church in its reliance on Christ and the Spirit to prepare the way for the coming of the ultimate. The continuity of the historical church is upheld by the surprise of God's ultimate word, which the church lives from and toward as it participates with Christ through the Spirit in preparing the way for God to speak.

Bonhoeffer's detailed discussion of how God works through the sinful community of the church has a number of significant implications for considering the empirical church's historical and present struggle with whiteness. First, Bonhoeffer's careful distinction of how the Holy Spirit bears the church's objective spirit allows the church to acknowledge and attend to the sinfulness of the Christian community as a historical, fully human community—shaped by whiteness. Bonhoeffer's treatment of the empirical church makes it possible to confess that the church is bound up with whiteness in its objective spirit without implying that this has any comprehensive impediment on the Holy Spirit's work in the church.

Second, Bonhoeffer's insistence that the Holy Spirit works through a collective community generated from below by Christ suggests that the church-community has a relative level of human freedom that can lend itself to succumbing to whiteness or opposing it. This protects the church from fatalistically giving itself over to the bondage of whiteness and, at the same time, encourages the church to challenge whiteness as it is caught up in the movement of the Holy Spirit.

Third, Bonhoeffer's account of the Holy Spirit's sanctifying work in the church's proclamation of Word and sacrament appreciates, as Mawson suggests, how specific "sociological forms and functions" of the empirical church are constitutive of its holiness.[23] In his later writings, Bonhoeffer offers greater clarity for how this takes place when he suggests that the stumbling block of Christ's humiliation is encountered in

---

23   Mawson, "The Spirit and the Community," 465.

the sacrament. Still, this humiliation does not capitulate to human sin or death, for it is sanctified from above through the Holy Spirit—the Spirit raises Jesus from the grave. This suggests that while the language game of whiteness can influence the church's proclamation of Word and sacrament, it never has the final say. Sinful resistance to God's speaking is not excused but judged by God's ultimate word given through the church's proclamation of Word and sacrament.

Fourth, Bonhoeffer's conception of the ultimate and penultimate necessitates the church's continual participation in the fallen world with a keen sense of God's working in it. The church cannot assume that observing the sacraments constitutes all that is needed to address the language game of whiteness. Whiteness is not ignored but is dealt with in the church's preparing of the way that recognizes whiteness as unnatural, as an organized closure to Christ's coming. Thus, the church must participate with Christ through the Spirit to challenge how whiteness shapes the broader society and the church, thereby preparing the way for the coming of the ultimate in the midst of the fallen creation.

Bantum: What Is Church?

Similar to Bonhoeffer, Bantum seeks to trace the christological and pneumatological contours of the Christian church. But whereas Bonhoeffer draws these contours with specific reference to the distortions of sin, Bantum draws them in reference to the exclusionary violence of a racialized world. The christological and pneumatological contours of the church, for Bantum, are found in how the church shares in the "intermixture" of Christ's own mulatto body through the Holy Spirit. The church is called into the tragic life of the mulatto as new creatures, born of the Spirit, who join across various boundaries to render the "neither/nor [as] the basis of participation, not exclusion."[24] The church participates through the Spirit in the "neither/nor" of Christ's mulattic body, which causes a direct disruption of the exclusionary parameters of race.

Bantum locates this ecclesial response to race between two influential theological projects. He argues that in a modern world fundamentally shaped by race, the passageway of the Christian life has been bifurcated between two narrow channels: one that valorizes ideas and tradition (John Milbank) and one that valorizes the body and context (James H. Cone).[25] These channels hopelessly persist in thinking about

24   Bantum, *Redeeming Mulatto*, 130.
25   Bantum presents this dichotomy in his introduction. See *Redeeming Mulatto*, 1–6.

the church and Christ in terms of a division between bodies and ideas. In response to these approaches, Bantum claims that "accounting for Jesus cannot be articulated within the reductions of his life to ideas about him or to his body, but must be confronted by the problem of Jesus' body, the intermixture his life promises us, and the intermixture our lives must become with him and each other."[26] To be the church is to live into the intermixture given in Jesus Christ's body through the Spirit. This living into Christ's body requires both the intuitions of Milbank's Radical Orthodoxy with its emphasis on the church's worship and the instincts of Cone's Black Theology with its focus on the social concreteness of the gospel.[27] In close affinity with Carter's work, Bantum's ecclesial project can be summarized as a creative synthesis between these two approaches encapsulated in the imagery of the mulatto/a.[28]

As the central image of his book, the concept of mulatto/a requires careful consideration. Bantum suggests that the in-between existence of mixed-race persons (mulatto/a) exposes the imaginary boundaries drawn between the writings of Cone and Milbank and reveals the deeply interdependent character of their distinct approaches. Ideas are always doing work on our bodies, and our bodies shape our ideas. The mulatto/a reveals this interdependence in that mixed-race persons neatly fit neither within the simple constructs of racial ideas nor within the constitutive parameters of racialized bodies. Therefore, in the present modern context, Bantum contends that mulatto/a bodies help us grasp anew the person of Christ as we live into Christ's continued work on the world through his mulattic body. This is not simply a contextual claim, Bantum maintains, but a participatory act embodied by the church through the Holy Spirit.[29] The tension and disruption of the mulattic life in a racialized and polarized world points to the reality of a deeper tension within the "intermixture" of the divine and human natures in Jesus' own body.

26   Bantum, *Redeeming Mulatto*, 10.

27   In a like manner, Andrew Draper suggests that Carter synthesizes Milbank and Cone to push beyond both. See Draper, *A Theology of Race and Place*, 117. What Draper fails to acknowledge is the clear connection between Carter's and Bantum's projects. This is seen in that Draper is broadly appreciative of Carter's work yet dismissive of Bantum's. The claim suggested here is that Bantum offers an ecclesiology that fleshes out the trajectory set by Carter in *Race*.

28   Bantum acknowledges his indebtedness to Carter. See *Redeeming Mulatto*, 195, n. 1.

29   Here, again, Bantum's goal is to hold together the present context shaped by race and the confession of the historical church. Bantum comments, "It is at this point that this theology should be understood as markedly different from contextual Christologies and their accompanying theologies of the last forty years" (*Redeeming Mulatto*, 213, n. 29).

Bantum supports this conception of Christ as the mulatto with a distinct interpretation of the Council of Chalcedon. It is important for Bantum that Chalcedon is not simply read as an idea passed down by the historical church but as an ontological claim that is preformed through the Spirit by the church.[30] He comments, "Chalcedon's assertion regarding Christ's person is not only a rhetorical boundary, but also an ontological claim that is best interpreted within a notion of mulattic hybridity."[31] Defining Chalcedon in the ontological terms of mulattic hybridity plays directly into Bantum's concept of the church. The church is Christ's mulattic, pneumatic people who exist in the tension and disruption proceeding from Christ's own mulatto body. The church participates in the "intermixture" that Jesus' body provides in its union of flesh and Spirit.[32] Along with this, Bantum connects the church with Israel in terms of this overarching idea of mulattic hybridity. He writes, "Israel's promise was bound to the incorporation of strangers."[33] Thus, both the Christian church and Israel are distinct not in their exclusion of strangers but precisely in their inclusion of strangers as realized in Christ's mulattic body.

Based on this notion of mulattic hybridity, Bantum maintains that the church participates in the work that Christ's mulattic body performs on the world through the Holy Spirit. This Spirit-filled performance of Christ's life confounds the reductive impulses of human ideas and of demarcated peoples as given in history. The church exists in its transgressing of racial boundaries initiated in Christ's mulattic body, born of flesh and Spirit, and this is what makes the church what it is. Bantum explains,

> For the ecclesial community a mulattic identity is grounded upon the claim of one's body as bearing the image of the incarnate Word, as being people of flesh and Spirit whose very lives are the fruits of an unnatural union. This unnatural union can find no grounding

30   Bantum, *Redeeming Mulatto*, 93. Bantum offers this claim in interaction with Sarah Coakley's essay "What Does Chalcedon Solve and What Does It Not? Some Reflections on the Status and Meaning of the Chalcedonian 'Definition,'" in *The Incarnation: An Interdisciplinary Symposium on the Incarnation of the Son of God*, ed. Stephen T. Davis, Daniel Kendall S.J., and Gerald O'Collins S.J. (Oxford: Oxford University Press, 2002), 143–63. Coakley is more conservative in her interpretation of Chalcedon as she refuses to give it the same ontological status that Bantum does.

31   Bantum, *Redeeming Mulatto*, 101.

32   Bantum, *Redeeming Mulatto*, 154.

33   Bantum, *Redeeming Mulatto*, 83.

in a *history of ideas* or a *history of a people* except for their constant inter-mixture and perpetual reconstitution over time.[34]

For Bantum, the church is a dynamic reality that performs Christ's mulattic life in the world through the Holy Spirit. The church is the church precisely in its embodiment of a mulattic identity that confounds and disrupts the manner in which historical ideas or peoples may be traced clearly through history.

Bantum's understanding of the church as a lived performance of Christ's mulattic body mirrors how race functions as a lived performance of exclusionary violence that is written on and through our bodies. He offers three historical examples of how whiteness is a lived performance that vies against the "neither/nor" existence of Christ's mulattic body. The first is anti-miscegenation laws that charged white people with maintaining racial purity as the law of the land.[35] Second, Bantum portrays the public lynching of Black bodies as a liturgical act. He explains, "The material of this sacrifice was not white flesh, but a ritual of atonement where the black body was given over to death in order to reinscribe whiteness."[36] Third, Bantum addresses specifically how the white church coopted baptism into a liturgy that incorporated the baptized "into a particular institution governed and sustained by racial logic over against any gospel."[37] Rather than breaking down walls of division, the discipleship and liturgy of whiteness works on our bodies in such a way that our bodies gain meaning within the controlled partitions orchestrated by our performance of whiteness. As Bantum puts it, "These performances delimit the possibilities of personhood, becoming in themselves moments of deep idolatry, binding

---

34 Bantum, *Redeeming Mulatto*, 164 (emphasis added). It is not clear from this statement how Bantum would understand the intermixture of "a history of ideas" and "a history of a people" in relation to the church's "perpetual reconstitution over time." Bantum's main point is that these, ideas and peoples, do not constitute the church's foundation. This leaves open the question of how the church's performance relates to the church's reflection on this performance, or put otherwise, how liturgy relates to theology. For an exploration of this question, see Kevin J. Vanhoozer, *The Drama of Doctrine: A Canonical-Linguistic Approach to Christian Theology* (Louisville: Westminster John Knox Press, 2005). Vanhoozer presents doctrine as rooted in Scripture and as pertaining "to how individuals and the church can perform fittingly in the drama" (*The Drama of Doctrine*, 78).

35 See Bantum, *Redeeming Mulatto*, 31.

36 Bantum, *Redeeming Mulatto*, 34.

37 Bantum, *Redeeming Mulatto*, 35.

adherents into lives that cannot imagine their being in Christ outside of their own image."[38] Whiteness binds its adherents into corporate bodies of exclusion that are inherently disrupted through being found in Christ's mulattic body.

In sum, Bantum offers the church as a lived performance of Christ's mulattic body through the Spirit, which disrupts the embodiment and articulation of race in the modern world. The church lives into the "neither/nor" of Christ's mulattic body, born of flesh and Spirit, transgressing the illusory boundaries of race. Here, there is no space for racial existence to abide, for the church *is* Christ's mulattic body through the Holy Spirit. And the church's lived performance of Christ's mulattic body through the Spirit is inherently incompatible with the lived performance of whiteness.

Thinking Through Bonhoeffer and Bantum on "What Is Church?"

Bonhoeffer and Bantum each show sensitivity to the christological and pneumatological contours of the Christian church. For both, the church is Christ's very presence in the world through the Holy Spirit. Does this mean that Bonhoeffer's and Bantum's understandings of the church could be thought of as compatible with one another, with the former addressing sin and the latter addressing whiteness? Because the forms of their ecclesiologies offer similarities, it is important to highlight the ways their understandings of the church are divergent and the implications of these differences on how whiteness is considered within the Christian church. The uniqueness of their ecclesial approaches is illuminated through comparing Bonhoeffer's and Bantum's considerations of (1) Christ, (2) the Spirit, and (3) the inferences of both on how whiteness is addressed within the history of the Christian church.

The first distinction to be drawn between Bonhoeffer and Bantum is based on their different conceptions of Christ. Similar to Carter, Bantum's conception of Christ is based on an interpretation of Chalcedon that seeks to move beyond rhetorical boundaries and into the ontological claim of Christ's body in terms of "mulattic hybridity."[39] The "neither/nor" of Jesus Christ's mulattic body, as the "intermixture" of flesh and

---

38   Bantum, *Redeeming Mulatto*, 40.
39   Bantum, *Redeeming Mulatto*, 101.

Spirit, is embodied in the life of the church.[40] By describing Christ and the church in this way, Bantum is able to offer a clear ecclesial challenge of whiteness, but the risk, as seen in Carter's work, is that in the process Christ's person is presented in a manner that slides in the direction of an ideal. As with Carter, Bantum focuses on addressing the gap between God and humanity rather than the gap between the God-human and sin.[41] In distinction from Carter, Bantum more explicitly extends his conception of Christ onto the church when he presents the church as Christ's mulattic presence in the world.

Bonhoeffer shares Bantum's strong correspondence between Christ and the church but conceives of Christ distinctly in relation to the wonder of his bearing humanity's guilt. For Bonhoeffer Jesus Christ is revealed and known in the humiliation of his coming into a fallen world to overcome sin and death. Whereas Bantum speaks of the hybridity between divine and human, Bonhoeffer speaks of the humiliation of the God-human. This humiliation of Christ extends into the historical church and its practices of preaching and celebrating the sacraments, as observed in Bonhoeffer's *Lectures on Christology*.[42] The humilia-tion of Christ is encountered throughout time in the historical church. Whereas Bantum's project confounds the history of peoples and ideas with the dynamic performances of the church as Christ's mulattic body, Bonhoeffer upholds the historical church as God's irruption into history as the humiliated Christ. The result of Bonhoeffer's conception of Christ is that it guards against the danger of idealizing the church or Christ

40   Throughout his discussion of Jesus' mulattic hybridity, Bantum's Christology slides between the apophatic texture of language and the cataphatic material of ontology with very little explanation of how one should distinguish the one from the other. As an example of this, Bantum explains the "neither/nor existence" of hybridity by stating that "Jesus was, and he was not." Then, following this, he states, "In these boundaries we see an identity constituted through the limitations of language, a discursive identity which we can only struggle with to grasp the power of his presence and the possibility of his flesh for humani-ty" (*Redeeming Mulatto*, 97). Rather than a "neither/nor," Bonhoeffer speaks of Jesus as fully human and fully God. In *Ethics* he writes, "The name of Jesus embraces in itself the whole of humanity and the whole of God" (*DBWE* 6:85). Such a claim seems to affirm what Ban-tum means when he speaks of a "neither/nor" inclusion but reframes the concept within a positive framework.

41   Barry Harvey comments on the liability embedded within such constructions in his reflections on Bonhoeffer's understanding of Christ's relation to the world: "The theological grammar regulating the concept of incarnation does not relate the two natures as two spe-cies of being, such that uniting them creates a hybrid" (*Taking Hold of the Real*, 28).

42   See, for example, *DBWE* 12:319.

and, instead, beckons us to ask how the triune God is speaking to and through the church in its present form, here and now.

These different conceptions of Christ relate directly to the divergent ways that Bonhoeffer and Bantum discuss the Holy Spirit's working in the Christian church. Bonhoeffer's understanding of Christ's humiliation in the historical church adheres to how he sees the Holy Spirit working through the integrity of the church's objective spirit. Rather than directly identifying the church with the Holy Spirit, Bonhoeffer distinguishes how the Holy Spirit bears with the sinful community of the church from above. The Spirit works from above to sanctify a fully human community that remains a collection of willing individuals, a community established by Christ and yet shaped by the historical language game of whiteness.

Similar to Bonhoeffer, Bantum discusses how the Spirit unites the church to Christ, but he describes this union in terms of the intermixture of flesh and Spirit in Christ's body. The church is not united primarily to a humiliated Christ but to Christ's mulattic body. Bantum describes this union as "unnatural," as offered through fleshly bodies "commingling" with the Spirit.[43] While Bantum is careful not to identify the Holy Spirit with the church, his description of an "unnatural union" speaks more to how the Holy Spirit transforms the church to rise above the confines of racialized existence than it attends to how the Holy Spirit works through a sinful community troubled by whiteness. Through the Spirit, the church is distinguished from the racial existence of the modern world in its being united with Christ's mulattic body.

Bonhoeffer's and Bantum's divergent understandings of the christological and pneumatological contours of the church have real implications on how we think about whiteness being addressed in the Christian church today. From Bantum's perspective, the Christian church addresses whiteness by *disrupting* the racialized world with the "neither/nor" of Christ's mulattic existence. Identifying the church with Christ's mulattic body provides a direct challenge of whiteness, but it leaves little room to address how the violence of whiteness persists in the empirical church, here and now. Bantum places the focus on how the church contrasts the racialized world, rather than considering how God is at work in both the church and the world. The language of "disruption"

---

43   Bantum writes, "It is a commingling that does not suggest the body's equality with that which abides in it, yet the body can no longer be understood apart from it" (*Redeeming Mulatto*, 150).

that Bantum uses[44] reflects this contrastive approach in that the old is disrupted by the new without much explanation of how the old and new overlap. For this reason Bantum's understanding of the church steers us away from considering God's continual working through the historical church and in the world at large. The church is only the church, in a sense, when it is observed as performing the disruption of Christ's mulattic existence in the midst of a racialized world.

Whereas Bantum's ecclesiology presents a *disruption* of whiteness, Bonhoeffer's ecclesiology describes God's *irruptive* working in the midst of a sinful church and fallen world. From Bonhoeffer's perspective, the Christian church must rely on God's *irruptive* working in its midst to understand how whiteness is challenged by the triune God at every point in history. Bonhoeffer is able to affirm the continuity of God's speaking to and through the church with his understanding of how the Holy Spirit bears the church's objective spirit—as a fully human and sinful community—from above. The church is faced with Christ's humiliation in its own proclivities toward whiteness, and yet the church is the place where the Holy Spirit works to prepare the way for the surprise of Christ's advent. In this way Bonhoeffer's understanding of the church, in correspondence with Christ's humiliation and the Spirit's work, allows for the church to honestly look at how it has become entrenched in whiteness both today and throughout history. God's ultimate word upholds the historical church, leaving a relative space for the church to either prepare the way for God's ultimate word or obstruct its way. Thus, Bonhoeffer's ecclesiology provides a way to refuse whiteness, along with Bantum's, but in a manner that more clearly attends to how the triune God works through a historical church borne from above by the Holy Spirit.

One way of distinguishing Bonhoeffer's and Bantum's ecclesial approaches is by considering where they each place the clash between "heaven and hell," as Bonhoeffer describes it. For Bonhoeffer the clash between heaven and hell happens *in* the church. The church represents a microcosm of the whole world; "in it heaven and hell clash; in it judgment on earth takes place."[45] The church participates in Christ's humiliation on the fallen earth. In contrast, Bantum describes the clash between heaven and hell as happening not primarily *in* the church but *between* the church and the world. The church's mulattic existence clashes with the racial existence of the modern world. These two different fault lines between heaven

44   See Bantum, *Redeeming Mulatto*, 78, 107, 113, 170.
45   *DBWE* 12:263.

and hell determine two divergent ways of understanding both the church and, as we will see next, the church's sacramental life.

The Sacramental Life of the Church in the Context of Whiteness

The distinctions traced above become even more pronounced in Bonhoeffer's and Bantum's accounts of the church's sacramental life. The sacramental life of the church speaks to how the church's liturgical practices shape the distinct community of the church. Both Bonhoeffer and Bantum present the church's sacramental life as incorporating the church into God's presence in the world. They each, however, describe the sacrament in a distinctive manner. Bonhoeffer's understanding of the church as a fallen community sanctified by the Holy Spirit leads him to consider how the sacrament is both a human event influenced by sin and a divine event given from above. Bantum's understanding of the church as a Spirit-transformed, mulattic people connects with his understanding of the sacrament as an embodied performance of pneumatic existence that directly challenges the embodied performance of race in the modern world. These two different understandings of the sacrament are considered in turn and then compared to explore their implications for how whiteness is to be addressed in the life of the church.

Part of what is at stake in this comparison is how discussions of the church's sacramental life risk ensconcing God's activity within the interior volume of the church.[46] The following section seeks to illuminate how Bonhoeffer's account of the church's sacramental life avoids this risk by presenting the church's tangible worship as an opening to God's working and speaking in the fallen world.[47] Bonhoeffer's understanding

46 Romand Coles offers this critique of Hauerwas' ecclesiology in his collaborative work with Hauerwas. See Coles, "'Gentled into Being': Vanier and the Border at the Core," in Stanley Hauerwas and Romand Coles, *Christianity Democracy and the Radical Ordinary: Conversations between a Radical Democrat and a Christian* (Cambridge: Lutterworth Press, 2008), 208–28.

47 This approach of responsiveness should not be confused with current Augustinian trends that seek to affirm aspects of political liberalism. For example, see Eric Gregory, *Politics and the Order of Love* (Chicago: University of Chicago Press, 2008); and Charles Mathewes, *A Theology of Public Life* (Cambridge: Cambridge University Press, 2007). The approach developed from Bonhoeffer in this section is not concerned with an affirmation of a certain political system but with how the sacrament opens one to God's working in whatever political system one might find oneself. For similar approaches, see Tom Greggs' *Theology against Religion* and Bernd Wannenwetsch's *Political Worship*.

of the sacrament allows for this opening by connecting the life of the church with the broader world in terms of a battle between heaven and hell that is waged *in* the church as a microcosm of the world. Contrastively, Bantum's account of the church's sacramental life draws a more pronounced demarcation between the church and the world, leading to the danger of relegating God's activity within the domain of the church. Comparing Bonhoeffer's and Bantum's accounts of the church's sacramental life helps demonstrate these distinct approaches: a politics of responsiveness seen in Bonhoeffer's ecclesiology and a counter-politic observed in Bantum's.

Bonhoeffer on the Church's Sacramental Life: God's Irruption into a Fallen World

Bonhoeffer describes the church's proclamation of Word and sacrament as an ultimate word that comes from above through the Holy Spirit but that meets the gathered congregation in the midst of a fallen creation. The ultimate word given concretely in the church's liturgical practices meets human beings in the creaturely depths of the fallen world. Bonhoeffer presents the church's sacramental life, simultaneously ultimate and penultimate, divine and human, in terms of a call and response given through Christ, who is both the head of the church as its Lord and the body of the church as the one who establishes the church's objective spirit. This dual presence of Christ is signaled in Bonhoeffer's claim that Christ is the preached and the preaching, proclamation and proclaimer.[48] Bonhoeffer's considerations of (1) preaching, (2) baptism, and (3) the Lord's Supper are shown to follow this rhythm of call and response as both divine and human in a manner that links God's ultimate word given through the Spirit with the church's sociological and historical existence. In turn, Bonhoeffer's accounts of these liturgical practices as a call and response are assessed to explore how the triune God speaks to and through a historical church embedded in the language game of whiteness.

First, according to Bonhoeffer, *preaching* is God's ultimate word given from above to form a community of truth constituted by the truth of the living Word.[49] Preaching is the Spirit-proclaimed Word that forms

---

48   *DBWE* 12:263.

49   There is currently no full-length study of Bonhoeffer's approach to preaching, even though Bonhoeffer lectured on the topic. See *DBWE* 14:341–74. Isabel Best has drawn attention to Bonhoeffer as a preacher. See Best, ed., *The Collected Sermons of Dietrich Bonhoeffer*, trans. Douglas W. Stott et al. (Minneapolis: Fortress, 2012). For some articles on the

the church through God's direct, external *call*, eliciting the *response* of
faith. Bonhoeffer presents this understanding of the church's preaching as directly countering the events of the fall. The fall represents
the instance when a direct response to God's call was abandoned for
a speculative discussion about God.[50] Preaching, in contrast, is God's
external word received through Christ's response of faith that restores
the connection between God and humanity, now in the context of the
fallen creation. Bonhoeffer describes the recovery of this connection in
terms of the direct act of faith (*actus directus*), where an encounter with
God's external word meets believers in an absolute moment that is not
directly accessible to human reflection (*actus reflexes*).[51] Therefore, Bonhoeffer argues that Christ as the living Word given in the preaching is
to be distinguished from human words oriented around the discussion
of ideas (*actus reflexes*).[52] Christ is an external word that commands an
absolute human decision, acceptance or rejection; the human word is
a static idea that remains enclosed within human reflection, available
for later consideration. Because of this difference between the two, Bonhoeffer asserts that God's direct word and the indirect words of human
ideas "are mutually exclusive."[53] This is why theology with its ideas about
God, for Bonhoeffer, must always remain under the church's preaching
to protect theological thinking from becoming an idol.[54] Preaching
confronts human beings not as a timeless idea about Christ for one to
consider but as a temporal encounter with Christ that brings one to a

---

subject, see David J. Lose, "'I Believe, Help My Unbelief': Bonhoeffer on Biblical Preaching,"
Word & World 26, no. 1 (2006): 86–97; and Wes Avram, "The Work of Conscience in Bonhoeffer's Homiletic," *Homiletic* 29, no. 1 (2004): 1–14.

50   In discussing the serpent's "pious question," Bonhoeffer remarks, "The decisive point
is that through this question the idea is suggested to the human being of going behind the
word of God and now providing it with a human basis—a human understanding of the
essential nature of God" (*DBWE* 3:106).

51   For a further discussion of Bonhoeffer's understanding of the direct act of faith, see
chapter 1.

52   *DBWE* 12:316.

53   *DBWE* 12:316.

54   As noted earlier, in *Act and Being* Bonhoeffer writes, "Because theology turns revelation into something that exists, it may be practiced only where the living person of Christ
is itself present and can destroy this existing thing or acknowledge it. Therefore, theology
must be in immediate reference to preaching, helping its preparation, all the while humbly
submitting to its 'judgment'" (*DBWE* 2:131). Similarly, in *Lectures on Christology*, Bonhoeffer argues that without the external limit of preaching, ideas about God inherently turn
Christ into an idol, "directly accessible by any person at any time" (*DBWE* 12:316).

decision. Preaching is a temporal encounter with the living Christ—the church's preaching is ultimate.

And yet the church's objective spirit is incorporated into the preaching, making it simultaneously penultimate. Because the living Word comes as a historical event, preaching remains subject to the social and historical dimensions of the church. Only in this way, Bonhoeffer maintains, is the living Word truth: preaching is an event that "takes place within history."[55] While preaching is the living Word externally given from above to form a community of truth, it is proclaimed from the pulpit, out of the lips of a fallen human being found within the social concreteness of a historical community. God's Word, Bonhoeffer explains, has taken human form in Jesus Christ and "humbled itself by entering into the human word."[56] This leads Bonhoeffer to suggest that the pulpit is "the strangest place in the world."[57] The pulpit is strange because it is the place where human words are taken up as God's living Word. Bonhoeffer describes the human words of preaching as the spokes of a wheel in which the joint in the middle of the wheel is left empty.[58] The middle is filled by the wonder that it is "God who must speak on Sundays at ten o'clock if anything is to happen at all."[59] The human speaks for God in the recognition that the human cannot speak for God apart from God's Spirit. As Bonhoeffer states, "I am to speak, yet it is not I, but God—I have to confess that I am not capable of it."[60] In other words, the person who sounds God's call from the pulpit is at the very same time among the congregation responding to God's call by faith through the Spirit. The pulpit is where heaven and hell clash in the audible words preached from the pulpit, where the triune God humbly works through fallen human beings. Christ is the preached and the preaching—call and response. In being both preached and preaching, God establishes ground on the fallen earth.

As a divine event, God's concrete call and response in the church's preaching materially breaks into the life of the church to confront the

55   *DBWE* 12:316.

56   *DBWE* 12:318.

57   *DBWE* 11:227. Bonhoeffer's discussion of preaching is given here as an attempt to synthesize the insights of Troeltsch and Barth in his lecture on "The History of Twentieth-Century Theology." See *DBWE* 11:224–28.

58   *DBWE* 11:228.

59   *DBWE* 11:227–28.

60   *DBWE* 11:227. In the same passage, Bonhoeffer goes on to say, "I can only wait and pray for this."

language game of whiteness as a reflective network of meaning. The language game of whiteness is externally broken into through God's call and response enacted in the event of preaching. In terms of a response, Bonhoeffer specifies how God's external word has a material consequence in that it meets human beings concretely within the social dynamics of the historical church. This means that sermon preparation and delivery cannot ignore the historically contingent reality of whiteness that contributes to the church's objective spirit, for the Word as an event is not timeless but happens in history through human speech. In practical terms, this is not to suggest that every sermon must explicitly reference race or the problem of whiteness. Instead, the claim here is that the preacher (already influenced by the community's objective spirit) is always and already saying something about race and whiteness even when these are not explicitly referenced in the sermon. The preacher, at the very least, needs to be aware of the social dynamics that feed into the human words commandeered by the Spirit to speak to the church. With this awareness, the preacher should be continually sensitive to how the living Word confronts the social dynamics of the church.

Second, Bonhoeffer presents *baptism* as God's gift of a tangible response of faith to the proclaimed Word. In baptism, a person actively responds by the Spirit to the Word proclaimed and is passively received, once and for all, into the community of Jesus Christ. Bonhoeffer develops this understanding of baptism in his chapter on "Baptism" from *Discipleship*.[61] In this chapter Bonhoeffer argues that just as Jesus' call to his first disciples demanded the public act of turning to follow him,[62] baptism into the church constitutes the continuation of this public act in response to Jesus' call, where one is "incorporated into the visible church-community [*Gemeinde*] of Jesus Christ."[63] Baptism is God's call rightly heard through a concrete response, and for this reason it is a concretization of the preached Word. As a response baptism is not something we first offer to God but something "*Christ offers to us.*"[64] Baptism concretely gifts God's people with God's objective securing of the

---

61   See chapter 9 of *DBWE* 4:205–12.

62   For example, when Jesus calls his disciples in Matthew 4:19 or when his call is refused by the rich young ruler in Matthew 19:16–22.

63   *DBWE* 4:210. This connection between Jesus' call to his first disciples and baptism is how Bonhoeffer explains the unity between the Synoptics and Paul's epistles. He writes, "What the Synoptics describe as hearing and following the call to discipleship, Paul expresses with the concept of *baptism*" (*DBWE* 4:207, emphasis original).

64   *DBWE* 4:207 (emphasis original).

church's unity and equality through the one Spirit given in the material reality of one's baptism (Eph 4:5). "The gift received in baptism," Bonhoeffer explains, "is the Holy Spirit, and the Holy Spirit is Christ himself dwelling in the hearts of the believers."[65] In this way baptism signifies the restoration of the unity of God's call and response severed by human beings at the fall. Bonhoeffer expresses this by contending that baptism is the paradoxically passive action of "suffering Christ's call."[66] He contends that this incorporation into Christ implies a break from the chains of sin as "Christ invades the realm of Satan and lays hold of those who belong to him, thereby creating his church-community."[67] Baptism is the boundary between death and life that frees human beings to serve God materially in human creatureliness. One's whole life is hidden in Christ through the material event of baptism. Baptism places one's past, present, and future in Christ's judgment and justification of the sinner, making the church a community that lives underneath the cross. The ultimate claim that Bonhoeffer attributes to baptism, however, does not remove baptism's sociological contours.

Baptism finds one incorporated into Christ's call and response as both a divine and a *human* act. The sociological and historical character of baptism as a human act is integral to Bonhoeffer's understanding of infant baptism. Bonhoeffer maintains that the baptism of infants requires attendance to the church's objective spirit.[68] In *Sanctorum Communio* he writes, "Since the children do not themselves receive faith, even as *fides directa* [direct faith], and the sacrament nevertheless demands faith, we must conclude that the subject that receives the sacrament in faith can only be the objective spirit of the church-community."[69] Children are carried in the womb of the church's objective spirit (as both human and sinful) through which they grow into maturity until they can respond to God in the direct act of faith (*fides directa*).[70] In *Discipleship* Bonhoeffer affirms this same idea by arguing that infant baptism necessitates a "living church-community" in which the once-and-for-all justification

---

65   *DBWE* 4:209.

66   *DBWE* 4:207.

67   *DBWE* 4:207.

68   See Mawson, "The Spirit and the Community," 466.

69   *DBWE* 1:241.

70   Bonhoeffer explains that the objective spirit does this without displacing the need for personal faith. The church-community, for this reason, commits in faith to "raise and instruct the children in the Christian faith, but it cannot pledge to bring them to a free profession of their own faith" (*DBWE* 1:242).

bestowed on a child is suspended within the historical remembering of Christ's community of faith. Without the sociological form and function of the historical church, baptism, as Bonhoeffer conceives of it, loses its meaning. He proposes that those who respond to God in faith generate the objective spirit of the church from below to uphold the continuity of the baptized as included in Jesus' life, death, and resurrection. Accordingly, this suggests that *not every* person in the church-community necessarily has personal faith at the point of baptism. Baptism, however, introduces *every* person into the relative integrity of the objective spirit that the Holy Spirit works through to draw each person in the church to personal faith.

The manner in which the divine and human dimensions of baptism must be held together are illustrated in Bonhoeffer's discussion of the practice of baptizing slaves in America's early colonies. Bonhoeffer grants a relative integrity to the church's objective spirit that allows him to speak critically of the baptismal practices of slaves without dismissing the Spirit's working in them from above. In his essay "Protestantism without Reformation," Bonhoeffer presents the baptism of slaves as an enigma for human slavery. This enigma is demonstrated in the dilemma that arose when American colonialists questioned the validity of baptizing "pagan" Africans into the "pure" Christian faith. Bonhoeffer reasons that the white church resisted how the act of baptism would bring "undesirable privileges and rights to negroes [*sic*]."[71] Even in the white church's attempts to reduce baptism to a purely spiritual event, baptism itself presented a material confrontation of the slave system's network of meaning and the church's participation in this system of exclusion and violence. Baptism concretely disrupts human ideals about purity and paganism. The very act of baptism confronted Christian slave owners with the objective unity established by Christ and actualized by the Holy Spirit. Bonhoeffer argues that the church obscured this objective reality given by God through Christ when it concluded that baptism only represented an internal deliverance from sin unrelated to the removal of external fetters.[72] Thus, Bonhoeffer hints at the interdependence between God's ultimate claim on one in baptism and an attendance to obstructions like slavery that severely hinder one from hearing God's ultimate call to faith. As a result, he insinuates that the relative freedom of the church was used for the destruction of the penultimate in a way

71   *DBWE* 15:457.
72   *DBWE* 15:457.

that relentlessly impeded the coming of the ultimate. In "Ultimate and Penultimate Things," Bonhoeffer affirms the coming of grace without removing the necessity of preparing the way:

> Grace must finally clear and smooth its own way; it alone must again and again make the impossible possible. But all this does not release us from preparing the way for the coming of grace, from doing away with whatever hinders and makes it more difficult.[73]

Because God's grace has come and is coming, the church's response is to prepare the way. "The way for the word must be prepared. The word itself demands it."[74]

Bonhoeffer's attendance to the divine and human dimensions of baptism, as seen in his reflections on baptism in the early American colonies, assists the North American church in considering how God is at work through baptism to challenge the social and historical dimension of whiteness in the church. Bonhoeffer's description of baptism suggests that in this act the Spirit unites individual believers within the community of Christ through a tangible response of faith that enacts God's call and response. Baptism concretely confronts the church with its oneness in Christ through the Spirit, materially revealing the reflexive language game of whiteness as a facilitation of its own violent form of oneness. While baptism reveals the violence of whiteness, baptism does not erase the social and historical dimensions of whiteness in the church. Bonhoeffer's claim that baptism is influenced by the social concreteness of a sinful community requires that the Christian church continually attend to how whiteness obscures the wonder of receiving the divine gift of the Holy Spirit in baptism. Baptism, as a movement from death to life, leads the church into an evaluation of its sinful history, as seen through Christ, which assists in preparing the way for the ultimate by removing the hindrances of whiteness that continue to obstruct the way of God's coming.

Third, Bonhoeffer describes the *Lord's Supper* as the church's continual concretization of God's call and response through Christ's bearing of guilt extended tangibly to the church. As a continual concretization of God's call and response, the Eucharist confirms the once-and-for-all act of baptism and ensures that the preaching is not understood as a

---

73   *DBWE* 6:162.

74   *DBWE* 6:160. Bonhoeffer offers these comments about the need for preparing the way specifically in relation to the hindrance of slavery for the coming of God's grace.

wordless action. The Lord's Supper corresponds to the preaching as an "action made holy and given its meaning by the Word."[75] For this reason, similar to baptism, Bonhoeffer considers the Lord's Supper to be *"God's gift to every individual . . . and to an even greater extent, a gift to the church-community."*[76] God's gift of the Eucharist is that human beings are given the practice of a tangible act that participates in the call and response of Christ's corporeal humiliation.

The Lord's Supper is God's action in that it gains its meaning and the very content of what it is through the Word. The reality that Christ gives himself in the place of fallen humanity is concretely encountered in the Eucharist. Christ is presently given in the sacrament. Bonhoeffer emphasizes this point in his *Lectures on Christology* by steering clear of Lutheran and Reformed discussions of "how" Christ is present in the Eucharist to focus on the crucial question of "who" is present.[77] The gift and wonder of the Lord's Supper is Christ's real presence, established within the cursed earth, in the midst of the gathered church congregation. God's ultimate word is tangibly encountered in the grain and fruit of the fallen earth declared to be Christ's broken body and shed blood.

Bonhoeffer understands the Eucharist, God's tangible gift, as consisting of both divine and human action. Along with God's divine working in it, Bonhoeffer argues that the Lord's Supper must also be understood as a human action before God if it is to be understood at all.[78] Bonhoeffer accounts for this human action by arguing that the sacrament is the Word in bodily form encountering human beings in bodily form.[79] In both *Creation and Fall* and *Lectures on Christology*, Bonhoeffer describes this bodily form of the sacrament as a reversal of the fall that leaves the whole creation opaque because of sin.[80] Through the Lord's Supper, he maintains that God brings a certain transparency to a distinct piece of the fallen creation to relate human beings in their bodily nature "to the earth and to other bodies."[81] The continuity between God's call and response, Word and creature, lost at the fall is recovered through humans gathering around and partaking in Christ's broken body present in the bread and wine. The command not

---

75   *DBWE* 12:318.
76   *DBWE* 1:243 (emphasis original).
77   See *DBWE* 12:321–22.
78   *DBWE* 1:244.
79   *DBWE* 12:318.
80   See *DBWE* 3:79; *DBWE* 12:318–19
81   *DBWE* 3:79.

to eat from the tree of life given to the first humans is now met with the command given to the church to take and eat of Christ's body—the new tree of life planted in the cursed earth. The church is opened to respond to God's irruptive working in the fallen creation at all times and in all places through the church's celebration of the Eucharist.

Moreover, Bonhoeffer suggests that Christ gives not only himself in the Eucharist; the Eucharist also signals how Christ gives the church to itself. He observes that the Lord's Supper "is Christ's gift that one member is able to bear the other and to be borne by the other."[82] The Lord's Supper addresses sin not by glossing over it but by bearing it in the collective memory and expression of the church as Christ's body. As a result, each member gains the rights and obligations to act as a priest for the other on the basis of Christ's priestly work.[83] In *Life Together* Bonhoeffer practically works out this collective bearing of guilt by pairing together the confession of sin and the Eucharist.[84] Confession addresses the human dimension of sin present at the Lord's Supper and prepares the way for the joyous celebration of Christ's forgiveness of sins at the Lord's Table. That there is a need to continually address sin through direct confession to another indicates that the sacrament is not a demarcation of purity but God's working and speaking through the concrete reality of a sinful community. As Bonhoeffer explains, a church celebrating the Lord's Supper is not the "*sanctorum communio* in its pure form" but "the empirical church and nothing else."[85] Sin is addressed in the reality of Christ's humiliated body that confronts the church with its own humiliation of sin. Since the church as Christ's body remains in the realm of Adam in its objective spirit, the church-community itself represents the humiliated Christ present in the Eucharist.[86] The gracious surprise of the Lord's Supper is that Christ bears humanity's guilt so as to overcome sin through his body in the church, in which the Spirit dwells.

By accounting for the divine and human dimensions of the Lord's Supper, Bonhoeffer is able to observe how God concretely sustains and informs the historical church in the sacrament, and he is able to attend to the ways in which the clarity of God's promise of the forgiveness of sins given in the sacrament can be blurred by sinful human beings'

82   *DBWE* 1:243.
83   *DBWE* 1:243.
84   See his chapter "Confession and the Lord's Supper" in *DBWE* 5:108–18.
85   *DBWE* 1:245.
86   *DBWE* 12:323.

participation in this event. This dual approach is supported by the Apostle Paul's stern yet redemptive words against the abuses of the Lord's Supper in the Church of Corinth (1 Cor 11:17–34). Bonhoeffer's warning to the church in his own context was leveled at the danger of mistaking the personal warmth of a tightly connected church for "the flame of the true fire of Christ" kindled in the Lord's Supper.[87] The power of the Eucharist is not in what is brought to the table but in what the table does in the midst of a sinful church. Christ opens one to the sister or brother excluded by the personal warmth of whiteness.

As an extension of the baptismal moment, the Lord's Supper tangibly weaves God's objective unity and equality into the church. In coming to the Lord's Table, we bump into one another, in all of our differences and all of our sin, as we bump into Christ's humiliated flesh. But unlike Yancy's "elevator effect," where our reflexes betray our more noble sensibilities about racial diversity, at the Lord's Table we are healed in the tangible contact made in the shared space around Christ's broken body and poured-out blood. The reflexes of whiteness, buried deep within the church's history, are addressed by the even deeper wonder invoked by the call and response that confronts the church in Christ's humiliated form in the Eucharist. Christ comes in the likeness of sinful flesh to touch our leprous whiteness, and in healing us through his touch Christ fulfills the law on our behalf as the sinless one (Matt 8:2–4).[88] It is from this contact made with the fruit of the earth and other bodies through Christ that the Lord's Supper sustains and informs the church's preparation of the way. The Lord's Supper helps one better understand the reflexes of whiteness that obstruct the coming of the ultimate and moves one to bear the church's guilt not by glossing over whiteness but by attending to the ways whiteness can distort the Lord's Table. Whereas whiteness seeks to speak for God, the Lord's Table opens one to respond to the ways God is already at work in the church and throughout the fallen creation.

Bonhoeffer contends that these three together, preaching, baptism, and the Lord's Supper, give the church-community its form. Bonhoeffer states, "The presence of Christ as Word and sacrament is related to

87   *DBWE* 1:246.
88   Cheryl Townsend Gilkes describes sin in terms of the whiteness of leprosy to counter the ways sin is often depicted with allusions to darkness and blackness. See her excellent essay, "Jesus Must Needs Go through Samaria: Disestablishing the Mountains of Race and the Hegemony of Whiteness," in *Christology and Whiteness: What Would Jesus Do?*, ed. George Yancy (New York: Routledge, 2012), 59–74.

Christ as church-community, just as reality is related to form."[89] Christ's presence in the church through its tangible worship gives the church its form in the midst of the fallen creation through the Holy Spirit. Thus, Bonhoeffer presents the church's worship as the place where the church learns to negotiate the concrete material of daily life: "It is precisely in the context of everyday life that church is believed and experienced. The reality of the church is understood not in moments of spiritual exaltation, but within the routine and pains of daily life, and within the context of ordinary worship."[90] Bonhoeffer's account of the church as formed by its worship affirms God's irruptive working in the fallen world through the historical church without excusing the church's participation in whiteness. It is Christ's real presence in the church's Spirit-filled worship that gives the church its form in the midst of its continued struggle with whiteness. In turn, the church's form attunes the discernment of the church, assisting it in preparing the way for the wonder of Christ's advent.

Bantum on the Church's Sacramental Life: God's Disruption of a Racialized World

In *Redeeming Mulatto* Brian Bantum addresses the problem of whiteness with the embodied response of the church's sacramental life.[91] His ecclesial challenge of whiteness reflects a combination of the ecclesial sensibilities of Stanley Hauerwas and the theological insights of Jennings and Carter. By focusing on the church's worship as the locus where whiteness is fundamentally addressed, Bantum extends Hauerwas' work in his own distinct way to address questions that Hauerwas largely leaves unaddressed.[92] On the other hand, Bantum's ecclesial approach sets his work apart from the works of Jennings and Carter discussed in chapters 3 and 4. It is Bantum's mixture of Hauerwas' ecclesial approach and

89   *DBWE* 12:323.

90   *DBWE* 1:281.

91   In Bantum's more recent publication *Death of Race*, he offers a powerful discussion about the daily struggle of addressing race. See Brian Bantum, *The Death of Race: Building a New Christianity in a Racial World* (Minneapolis: Fortress, 2016). However, because this book does not clearly connect these struggles with the church's liturgical practices, the comparison between Bantum and Bonhoeffer offered here relies primarily on Bantum's account of the church's sacramental life and Christian discipleship from *Redeeming Mulatto*.

92   For a reflection on Hauerwas' interactions with race, see Jonathan Tran, "Time for Hauerwas' Racism," in *Unsettling Arguments: A Festschrift on the Occasion of Stanley Hauerwas' 70th Birthday*, ed. Charles R. Pinches, Kelly S. Johnson, and Charles M. Collier (Eugene: Cascade Books, 2010), 246–61.

Jennings and Carter's work on whiteness that makes his work an interesting point of comparison to the ecclesial proposal suggested in this study.

Bantum presents baptism, the Lord's Supper, and Christian discipleship as concretely countering the modern world's lived performance of race. Bantum's views on baptism and the Lord's Supper have been selected for analysis here because the role of preaching and the significance of the external word in relation to the sacrament is largely left unaddressed in Bantum's account of the sacraments in *Redeeming Mulatto*. This absence of the preached word indicates how Bantum is working within a broadly Catholic understanding of sacrament, while Bonhoeffer's emphasis on the preached word in conjunction with the sacraments aligns him more with Lutheran sensibilities.[93]

For Bantum, baptism and the Lord's Supper are performative events that embody a newly given, pneumatic existence found in one's union with Christ's body, a body that intrinsically challenges race through the intermixture of flesh and Spirit. In this way baptism and the Eucharist constitute the mulattic existence of the church, signaling an eschatological break from the racial existence of the modern world. This mulattic existence is lived out, according to Bantum, through the church's life of discipleship as the continuance of the Spirit's presence given in the sacrament. Discipleship is to participate with Christ in transgressing and challenging the racial boundaries persistently upheld through the modern world's performances of racial purity. Thus, Bantum's ecclesial approach to race lifts up the church's liturgical practices and discipleship as a lived performance of the intermixture of Christ's mulattic body that directly challenges the modern world's performances of race.

Based on his conception of Christ as the mulatto, Bantum presents baptism as the reception of mulattic existence in being united to Christ through the Holy Spirit. This mulattic existence is understood as a sharing in Christ's "hybridity" that confronts and disrupts one's

---

93 The differences between Catholic and Protestant approaches to the sacrament can be observed by comparing works like William T. Cavanaugh's *Torture and Eucharist* and Bernd Wannenwetsch's *Political Worship*. See Cavanaugh, *Torture and Eucharist: Theology, Politics, and the Body of Christ* (New York: Wiley-Blackwell, 1998); and Wannenwetsch, *Political Worship*. Cavanaugh's account works from a more substance-oriented understanding of the sacrament that offers the church as distinct from the broader society, while Wannenwetsch works from a Lutheran word-act understanding of the sacrament that leads to a responsiveness to God's working in all of creation. This same divergence is highlighted through the comparison of Bonhoeffer and Bantum offered here.

existence in a world of race. Baptism is a rebirth through the Holy
Spirit that initiates one into Christ's person by participating in Christ's
performance of baptism on our behalf.[94] In entering into and performing this distinct mulattic being in Christ, Bantum explains, baptism
"requires a departure from the racial economy of the West and its
children."[95] Baptism makes this departure by ushering the ecclesial
community into the radical presence of God, which transforms those
in church into something they "once were not."[96] Bantum goes on to
pronounce the sharp break initiated through baptism by arguing that
it constitutes an "unnatural" transformation of rebirth in the Spirit
that lifts one "out of the confines of humanity."[97] Bantum here employs
the classical idea of deification to challenge modern ideas about race.[98]
He suggests that deification confounds biologically quantifiable definitions about humanity. In baptism one is joined to the divine life of the
church through the Spirit. Baptism speaks of the new, breaking one
out of the confines of the old. The modern world's racial existence is
disrupted and challenged by a pneumatic existence initiated through
being baptized into Christ's mulattic body.

This description of baptism helpfully unveils the dangers of a
church that uses baptism to initiate people into a system of whiteness. In
theologically narrating the baptism of slaves, Bantum explores how baptism in the early American colonies was employed to organize Black and
white bodies into the exclusionary violence of whiteness. The subservi-
ence of slaves was secured through a practice of baptism that invoked
God "in order to concretize one's participation in a racialized community."[99] Bantum suggests that this practice of baptism enveloped its
participants, both Black and white, into a racialized existence that over-
shadowed and displaced baptism as a concretization of pneumatic existence wrought in Christ's mulattic body. He writes, "Here the church, as

---

94   See Bantum, *Redeeming Mulatto*, 142.
95   Bantum, *Redeeming Mulatto*, 142.
96   Bantum, *Redeeming Mulatto*, 142.
97   Bantum, *Redeeming Mulatto*, 154.
98   See Bantum, *Redeeming Mulatto*, 146, 157. As seen with Carter, Bantum draws from
a patristic understanding of deification to undergird his conception of being as an intermixture received in baptism. From the Eastern Orthodox theologian John Zizioulas, for
example, he borrows the concept of "ecclesial hypostasis," which suggests baptism is the
identification of one's hypostasis "with the hypostasis of the Son of God." See John Zizioulas, *Being as Communion: Studies in Personhood and the Church* (Crestwood: St. Vladimir's
Seminary Press, 1985), 56.
99   Bantum, *Redeeming Mulatto*, 35.

well as the presence of God, are but tools that fortify a reality far deeper and more profound than God and the church—race."[100] In other words, the actual presence of God and God's church are exchanged for an idea of race expressed through an act of baptism that concretizes people into a racialized world. This reflects how Bantum portrays the lived performance of race and the lived performance of pneumatic existence as countering one another, as mutually exclusive. The negotiation between old and new is a negotiation between concrete practices that embody Christ's mulattic body and those that do not.

In the case of slave Christianity, Bantum reasons that the most profound moment of transformation in baptism had no "impact upon the embodied life of the participant."[101] Because slave Christianity reconfigured this act of transformation into an act of oppression, Bantum argues that its baptismal practices were "ultimately idolatrous."[102] The difficulty here that Bantum must work out is what this meant for the slaves receiving this baptism. He resolves this question by suggesting that, while the church may not have been living into the transformation of Christ's mulattic body, the slaves themselves were still radically transformed in their being baptized.[103] Similar to Bonhoeffer, Bantum suggests that the resistance of the church could not thwart the Holy Spirit's transformative power in baptism. While there are difficulties that remain to be worked out with regard to the complex problem of slave baptism, what is clear is that there is an existential threat to the form of baptism, according to Bantum, when it is used to affirm the modern world's racial existence rather than the pneumatic existence offered by Christ's mulattic body.

Bantum's treatment of the Lord's Supper follows a similar trajectory to his account of baptism. He suggests that the Lord's Supper extends the baptismal moment into the weekly rhythms of the church's sacramental life. The Lord's Supper is a concrete enactment of the church's mulattic existence originating in baptism. This is illustrated in Bantum's suggestion

100 Bantum, *Redeeming Mulatto*, 35. Bantum's engagement of slave baptism does not examine the perplexing question of how African traditions are integrated with European expressions of Christianity through the practice of baptism. For a discussion of this, see Albert J. Raboteau, *Slave Religion: The "Invisible Institution" in the Antebellum South* (Oxford: Oxford University Press, 1978), 57–58; and Carter's discussion of Raboteau on the topic in *Race*, 137–38.

101 Bantum, *Redeeming Mulatto*, 154.

102 Bantum, *Redeeming Mulatto*, 154.

103 Bantum writes, "Yet, even in the attempts of slave Christianity to police the transformative power of these practices we see the baptismal moment being a moment of radical transformation in the lives of Christian slaves themselves" (*Redeeming Mulatto*, 154).

that the Lord's Supper is an exceeding of "our nature and our failures."[104] This moment of eating together becomes the marker of what the church is and what the church is to become. The breaking of bread together allows the church to participate with Christ in the call to continually enter into a life of faith marked by contamination, transgression, and transformation. The Eucharist, Bantum contends, is a receiving of the church's identity as those who "do not exhibit physical demarcations of racial logic, but defy them through their union with bodies of difference among them."[105] The Lord's Supper constitutes a disruption to racial existence with one's new pneumatic existence in a mulatto Christ. Through being stitched together by this meal, the church becomes an eschatological image of the interwoven differences given in Christ's person. Bantum declares, "They become a burning bush . . . whose fearsome aberrant beauty declares the glory of God and disrupts all assertions of identity and purity in its midst."[106]

This dramatic inclusion into something new, emphasized in Bantum's description of baptism and the Lord's Supper, helpfully challenges the defined categories of race. Yet it moves in the direction of setting up an eschatological end that displaces the fallen creation. Bantum is aware of this danger and accounts for it by arguing that the church is the historical expression of Christ's person and work, requiring a negotiation between one's new and old identity. Bantum warns that the "notion of a mulattic personhood" given in the church's liturgical life should not be seen as a clever device for imagining a particular people or as a way of imaging Christian existence but rather "encapsulates the negotiation of identity inherent in our claim to be 'in Christ.'"[107] How Bantum practically works out this negotiation between new and old is seen in his discussion of discipleship.

Bantum describes discipleship as a performance of pneumatic existence in direct opposition to racial existence.[108] Discipleship requires

104 Bantum, *Redeeming Mulatto*, 164.
105 Bantum, *Redeeming Mulatto*, 165.
106 Bantum, *Redeeming Mulatto*, 164–65.
107 Bantum, *Redeeming Mulatto*, 142.
108 Bantum's newer book *The Death of Race* offers an extension of his discussion of discipleship from *Redeeming Mulatto*. He states the purpose of the book as follows: "In this book I do not offer steps to reconciliation or a radical new world . . . I hope this book is a way of helping us to see our unfaithfulness, but also begin to see the beauty and gift of what it means to be made in the image of God" (*The Death of Race*, 19). *The Death of Race* offers a deeper exploration of the lasting impact of race on Christians' daily lives and explores how to navigate these challenges. *The Death of Race* helpfully compliments Bantum's *Redeeming Mulatto*.

one to negotiate the world of one's natural birth into race that conflicts with the unnatural birth of one's pneumatic existence. Those born of the Spirit are not confronted with the world of their blessed birth, Bantum asserts, "but with the world of their death."[109] Because discipleship is an extension of the baptismal moment, one's negotiation of the world of race is already determined by one's baptism, where racial existence is fundamentally challenged. Bantum argues that baptism is an initiation into an *already given* reality in Christ's body and performance. Still, this transformation is "not an existence where the salvific work of Christ is complete within the life of the one cleansed."[110] One must continue to work out one's salvation through discipleship. Bantum portrays this continual sanctification of discipleship as the struggle to overcome the confines and limits of racial existence. Disciples participate in the world from a new life in Christ that disrupts the racial orders of the world. The disciple does this by confounding the racial boundaries of the world by becoming present to strange peoples and becoming a stranger among his or her own people.[111] Discipleship, thus, is the continuation of one's transformation through the mixture of those in the church as Christ's mulattic people.

Bantum's ecclesial response to whiteness offers a potent disruption of the racial demarcations of the modern world. His approach to race moves beyond many of the current approaches presented in theological race studies because it specifically examines how the church as a concrete embodiment of Christ's presence opposes the divisions of race in general and the hegemony of whiteness in particular. Nevertheless, Bantum's intense focus on how the church counters racial boundaries largely removes the space for considering how the church remains influenced by whiteness even as God works in and through it. Bantum's intention to challenge and counter whiteness with the reality of Christ's presence in the church must not be abandoned, but the crucial theological task is to articulate how this challenge comes through the reality of God's working in and through the empirical church, here and now.

---

109 Bantum, *Redeeming Mulatto*, 167.

110 Bantum, *Redeeming Mulatto*, 150. Bantum elsewhere describes it this way: "In the baptismal moment there is full work within us that we must still yet live into" (*Redeeming Mulatto*, 153).

111 Bantum, *Redeeming Mulatto*, 168.

Thinking Through Bonhoeffer and Bantum on the Church's Sacramental Life in the Context of Whiteness

Because Bantum does not discuss the preached word and because the Lord's Supper has been touched upon in previous chapters, the following comparison of Bonhoeffer and Bantum focuses on their accounts of baptism. The sacrament of baptism seems to be the most appropriate place to compare Bonhoeffer and Bantum because both address it at length.[112] Baptism also represents an interesting point of discussion because both Bonhoeffer and Bantum discuss the baptismal practices of slave Christianity, offering a specific case study for considering the sacrament in the context of an explicit expression of the Christian church's facilitation of whiteness.[113] It has been demonstrated how both Bonhoeffer and Bantum maintain that baptism is an event given from above through the Spirit. The distinction to be made between the two concerns how Bonhoeffer connects the Spirit's work from above in baptism with the Christian church's placement in the fallen creation, while Bantum describes how the Spirit's work of baptism transforms the church to directly disrupt the racial existence of the modern world. Bonhoeffer presents the church's sacramental life as God's *irruption* into the fallen world; Bantum presents the church's sacramental life as God's *disruption* of a racialized world. Bonhoeffer's approach presents the church's politic as one that is responsive to the ways God is already working in all times and places; Bantum's approach presents the church as a counter-politic oriented around Christ's mulattic body, which sharply contrasts the modern world of race.

Bonhoeffer's emphasis on how baptism connects the Christian church to its history in the fallen creation is poignantly illustrated in his baptismal homily written from Tegel prison for little Dietrich Bethge.[114] In this homily Bonhoeffer connects the spiritual hope of little Dietrich's new life with the historical continuity of his being born into the soil of a time and place in which he must actively participate. Bonhoeffer writes that "to be deeply rooted in the soil of the past makes life harder, but also

112 Bantum dedicates chapter 5 of *Redeeming Mulatto* to the sacrament of baptism. Bonhoeffer discusses baptism throughout his writings. For example, see *DBWE* 1:240–47, 260–64; 2:159–60; 4:205–12; 8:383–90.

113 For Bantum's account of the baptismal practices of slave Christianity, see Bantum, *Redeeming Mulatto*, 35–37, 154–55. For Bonhoeffer's account, see his reflections on the Black church in "Protestantism without Reformation," *DBWE* 15:456–58.

114 See *DBWE* 8:383–90.

richer and more vigorous."[115] The Spirit's work from above in baptism is connected to the objective spirit of the historical church established by Christ, where community is generated from below. This connection to history is not to discount how Bonhoeffer, like Bantum, will speak of baptism as an absolute "break with the world" requiring and causing "our *death*."[116] Baptism is absolute, for Bonhoeffer, in that it is God's work from above, but it meets one in the midst of a fallen world in which the church stands.

Bantum, in contrast, focuses on how the mulatto Christ is realized in the "intermixture" carried out in baptism. This eschatological description of baptism is presented by Bantum as an "unnatural" birth that lifts one "out of the confines of humanity."[117] In accordance with this unnatural birth, Bantum claims that one's spiritual ties to the church require a departure from one's biological family and one's racial affinity groups. In this way Bantum seems to emphasize eschatology in a manner that overshadows protology—our connection to the earth, history, and God's preservation of creation. While it is true that one must hate one's father and mother to follow Christ (Luke 14:26), this does not remove the command to obey one's parents (Eph 6:1).[118] Bantum's overall discussion of the mulatto as an in-between existence offers the texture to fit within this tension of eschatology and protology. The difficulty is in how Bantum connects this concept of the mulatto to his specific eschatological discussion of baptism.

Bantum speaks of baptism as an unnatural birth into a pneumatic existence that directly challenges one's racial existence in the modern world; Bonhoeffer speaks of baptism as incorporating the whole of one's life, earthly and divine, sinful and righteous, into God's work in the

115 *DBWE* 8:385.

116 *DBWE* 4:208.

117 Bantum, *Redeeming Mulatto*, 154. There are points where Bantum softens this radical, eschatological break between the new community and the old. For example, when speaking of being baptized into Christ, he writes, "To do this is not to move beyond the slave ship or the encyclopedia. Rather, to enter into Christ is to recognize ourselves as bound to both, as children of enslavement and conquerors of knowledge" (*Redeeming Mulatto*, 163). While at points Bantum draws out the continuity of the church's history, his overall proposal accentuates an eschatological break. Even here Bantum goes on to say that the waters of baptism bring "profound confusion" as we are grafted into realities that "once seemed foreign" (*Redeeming Mulatto*, 163).

118 Bantum shows more care in how he discusses one's connection to one's biological family in his discussion of marriage in *The Death of Race*. See Bantum, *The Death of Race*, 28–31.

fallen world. God's working is not against the fallen creation, primarily, but for it and from within it. This important distinction of how God is for the world is seen in the connection Bonhoeffer draws between the ultimate and penultimate. The penultimate is preserved by the ultimate for the sake of the ultimate. The church can obscure God's ultimate word in enacting the modality of whiteness in its baptizing, but God's ultimate word cannot be altogether blocked. Where Bonhoeffer speaks of a relative struggle upheld by God's ultimate word, Bantum speaks of how a pneumatic existence received in baptism directly counters one's racial existence. Thus, Bantum's description of baptism offers a disruptive counter-politic that challenges the modern world of race, while Bonhoeffer's description of baptism offers God's irruptive working in the fallen world as opening one to respond in new ways to God's present work in the world through persons and places.[119] Irruption signals how the triune God burrows God's self in the cursed earth to bring new life through the endurance of a Christian church found in history. It is through God's irruption into the midst of the church's struggle with whiteness that whiteness itself is not only disrupted but also fundamentally challenged by the material continuity of the historical church through its preparing of the way.

The disparity between Bonhoeffer's approach of responsiveness and Bantum's approach of the church as a counter-politic is aptly illustrated in their divergent accounts of slave baptism. Bantum's narration of slave Christianity draws attention to precisely how the church is marked by whiteness but not to how God is at work in its midst. Bantum's understanding of the church's sacramental life rests decidedly upon how the Christian church can distinguish itself from the broader world in its sacramental practices. For Bantum, the liturgical practices of slave baptism are diametrically opposed to his own understanding of being baptized into Christ's mulattic body. As a result, baptism into Christ's mulattic body presents a counter-politic that directly challenges a racialized

---

119 The suggestion, made throughout this study, that Bonhoeffer's account of the church's proclamation of Word and sacrament should be understood as open to the world rather than closed to the world is to be distinguished from recent attempts to relate Bonhoeffer's ethic to an ethics of virtue and formation. For examples of this, see Lisa E. Dahill, *Reading from the Underside of Selfhood: Bonhoeffer and Spiritual Formation* (Eugene: Wipf & Stock, 2009); and Jennifer Mobley, *The Virtue of Bonhoeffer's Ethics: A Study of Dietrich Bonhoeffer's Ethics in Relation to Virtue Ethics* (Eugene: Wipf & Stock, 2013). For a contrasting view to these studies, as offered in the present project, see Wannenwetsch, "'Responsible Living' or 'Responsible Self'?"

world. This direct challenge creates the difficulty of connecting Bantum's eschatological vision of the sacraments with the actual state of the historical church's liturgical practices on the ground. Bonhoeffer's motif of the ultimate and penultimate assists in making this connection between God's eschatological inbreaking and the historical continuity of the church.

Bonhoeffer's narration of the baptism of slaves attends to God's irruption in history through the sinful church to address obstructions that hinder the way of Christ's coming. Bonhoeffer's conception of the ultimate and penultimate would allow him to say that slave Christianity, and its practices that oppressed baptized slaves, was a destruction of the penultimate that seriously obstructed the ultimate and, for that reason, needed (and needs) human reform.[120] At the same time, Bonhoeffer can also stipulate that God's ultimate word given in baptism continues to uphold the humanity of both slave and master in the midst of the slaveholder's dehumanization of both slave and master. The irruptive power of God's presence allows Bonhoeffer to strongly challenge the baptismal practices of slave Christianity as "unnatural" (i.e. not open to Christ's coming) without ever placing the baptisms themselves in question. This reflects Bonhoeffer's approach to the sacrament as a responsive listening for God's word that is spoken over the fallen world. The sacrament of baptism presents God's direct claim over the bodies entering the waters of baptism, opening the church's attentiveness to how God speaks over all of the fallen creation. Bonhoeffer's novel approach offers the church hope in God's irruptive working that challenges whiteness both from above (an ultimate challenge) and, at the same time, always from within the fallen earth (a penultimate challenge) on which the historical and empirical church stands.

One may worry whether the relative freedom Bonhoeffer attributes to humanity permits slavery and racism to exist in the church and world in a way that Bantum's proposal refuses at least for the church. Bonhoeffer's assertion, however, is not permissive but attentive to the reality of a sinful world as it is. For it is this sinful world to which Christ comes in the likeness of sinful flesh (Rom 8:3). This highlights the need for the church to participate with Christ in preparing the way through a repentance that takes the sinful church and world seriously. From Bonhoeffer's perspective, Christians oppose obstructions

---

120 Bonhoeffer suggests that the "destruction of the penultimate seriously harms the ultimate" (*DBWE* 6:160).

to Christ's coming in the broader society for the same reasons they must resist these same obstructions in the church, not primarily with the aim of making the world or church an ideal place but with the aim of preparing the way for the ultimate coming of Christ.[121] Bonhoeffer's proposal of preparing the way begins with the church but necessitates that the church's life and work is representative of and extends to the whole world. Preparing the way "is not only an inward process, but a visible, creative activity on the greatest scale."[122] The goal of the church's preparing of the way, then, is not to distinguish itself from the world, but to attend and respond to how the triune God is already speaking in the fallen earth.

Preparing the Way in the Midst of Whiteness

Throughout the preceding discussion support has been given for the importance of Bonhoeffer's proposal of preparing the way. In particular, the above comparison highlighted how Bonhoeffer's ecclesial approach of responsiveness leaves a relative space open for the Christian church to either obstruct or prepare the way for the ultimate. The final task that remains is to examine what this proposal specifically means for the Christian church's preparing of the way in the midst of whiteness. How does the Christian church wrestle with its own participation in the language game of whiteness to prepare the way for the surprise of God's ultimate word? In *Life Together* Bonhoeffer offers an account of the church's discernment that helps answer this question.[123] He suggests that the church prepares the way by carefully discerning its place in God's working in the fallen world. The Christian church prepares the way for God's ultimate word not by overcoming whiteness but by discerning how the triune God remains at work precisely in the church's repentant struggle with whiteness.

---

121 See the conclusion of Bonhoeffer's lecture "On the Theological Foundation of the Work of the World Alliance" in *DBWE* 11:369.

122 *DBWE* 6:161.

123 In fact, *Life Together* is not only a presentation of the church's discernment as a preparing of the way but also an enactment of it. It begins with Bonhoeffer's reflections on community, the day alone, the day together, and service, all as preparatory for the culminating chapter on "Confession and the Lord's Supper." For Bonhoeffer the church's daily life is encompassed by and oriented toward its incorporation in Christ through tangible worship.

The Church's Discernment as a Preparing of the Way

With the struggle of the Confessing Church at the forefront of his mind, Bonhoeffer wrote *Life Together* to offer the church alarm bells for when a spiritual yearning after Christ might become tainted with desires for something other than the church already established by Christ.[124] In his own historical moment, Bonhoeffer sought to warn his seminarians of the danger of defecting to the German Christian church that had already been condemned in the confession given at Dahlem and Barmen.[125] When human beings reach beyond the church as already given (in Bonhoeffer's case as defined by the Dahlem synod), the alarm sounds:

> Precisely at this point Christian community is most often threatened from the very outset by the greatest danger, the danger of internal poisoning, the danger of confusing Christian community with some wishful image of pious community, the danger of blending the devout heart's natural desire for community with the spiritual reality of Christian community.[126]

Bonhoeffer reminds the church to remain sensitive to its natural desires for community that can supplant the community established by Christ—the empirical church, here and now. These natural desires are not necessarily wrong but must be distinguished from and remain subject to Christ as the community's limit and mediator, its Lord and brother.[127]

In *Life Together* Bonhoeffer contrasts the ideal, psychic community of Adam with the real, spiritual community of Christ. What is important to note is that Bonhoeffer sees both of these, Adam and Christ, as present in the empirical church. This means the church's discernment is not an attempt to move past being an ideal, psychic community so it can become a real, spiritual community. Instead, the church's discernment addresses the challenge of remaining attentive

124 For more background on the context of *Life Together*, see Stephen Plant's "Theological Education and Christian Formation in Conversation with Dietrich Bonhoeffer's *Life Together*," *Colloquium* 47, no. 2 (2015): 180–94.

125 See Bonhoeffer's essay "Lecture on the Path of the Young Illegal Theologians" in *DBWE* 15:421–22.

126 *DBWE* 5:34–35.

127 Christ as Lord and brother corresponds to Bonhoeffer's belief in the dual presence of Christ as both the church's head and its body, governing and communal. See *DBWE* 1:147 and the discussion of this point in chapter 4.

to the present struggle between the two, Adam and Christ, within the given community of the church.

Bonhoeffer's distinctions between the ideal and real and between the psychic and spiritual each offer insights for the church's discernment. These two distinctions are especially instructive for providing churches in the United States with a continual check on ideals and controls perniciously put forth by the language game of whiteness. The church cannot eradicate or erase its historical indebtedness to whiteness, but it must discern how Christ struggles within its midst, and in the fallen world, to offer a repentance that prepares the way for the coming of the ultimate.

The Christian community remains *real* by receiving the reality given to it in Christ that counters urges to become an *ideal* community. The reality of Christ, in the social concreteness of the empirical church, limits and confronts human dreams and visions of a perfect community. Fictitious dreams are tamed by the given community, here and now, received as a gift from God. As Bonhoeffer poetically expresses it, "The bright day of Christian community dawns wherever the early morning mists of dreamy visions are lifting."[128] Idyllic images of community must be shattered by the reality of Christ because these ideals destroy Christian community by making unrealistic demands on the community rather than thankfully receiving what Christ has already given.

Bonhoeffer warns that ideals may come from personal intentions that are "honest, earnest, and sacrificial," but they remain a hindrance to the real community established by Christ.[129] These ideals are a hindrance because they evacuate the reality of sin and imperfections that the humiliated Christ took on and continues to bear in the church.[130] The endurance of the church is not established on subjective human yearnings that come and go, and that capitulate to whiteness, but on the reality of the eternal Christ present in the empirical church. Bonhoeffer argues that the more the church is secured by Christ as the ground, strength, and promise of the community, the more it can approach its daily life with the calm assurance to pray for and discern God's working in the midst of the fallen creation.[131]

128 *DBWE* 5:37.

129 *DBWE* 5:36.

130 Bonhoeffer asks, "Even when sin and misunderstanding burden the common life, is not the one who sins still a person with whom I too stand under the word of Christ?" (*DBWE* 5:36).

131 See *DBWE* 5:38.

Along with the trappings of idealizing the church, there is the danger of defaulting to the impulses of the psychic community, which comports itself as being for God, yet does so apart from God (much like the Christianity of slave baptism described by Bantum). In contrast, the spiritual community refers to the reassertion of God's power in the fallen world given in Christ's mediation of persons through the Spirit. The psychic community seeks to leverage power through relationships mediated from one's own resources. Instead, the spiritual community is leveraged through Christ's mediation of persons in the power of the Holy Spirit. Bonhoeffer explains that "there is never, in any way whatsoever, an 'immediate' relationship of one to another."[132] In trying to make community, the instinctive powers of self-centered love seek unmediated control of the other. Here "strong persons enjoy life to the full, securing for themselves the admiration, the love, or the fear of the weak."[133] Inherent in this description of the psychic community is Bonhoeffer's sensitivity to the way human power is always in play in the church, and how human power seeks to control through seemingly good intentions (e.g., slave baptism as offering salvation). The psychic community, he explains, may go to great lengths for others, even surpassing what is expressed in the genuine service given through the love of Christ.[134] Yet, apart from the love of Christ, the great lengths traveled for others remain self-affirming (1 Cor 13:1–3). These seemingly sacrificial acts are embedded within one's own desires to control the other by recreating one's self in the other.

In contrast, Christ's objective spirit given to the church allows human beings to generate community through a constructive struggle with one another. This is what Bonhoeffer means in *Life Together*, when he simply states, "Christ stands between me and others."[135] Only Christ is the mediator of genuine community, because only Christ fully encounters the other. Bonhoeffer expresses this point in the beginning of *Life Together* by arguing that Christ's Lordship is a ruling imparted among his enemies: "Jesus Christ lived in the midst of his enemies."[136] The struggle for power occurring after the fall is reoriented by Christ's

132 *DBWE* 5:41. Bonhoeffer substantiates this claim based on his understanding of the sinful condition of human beings. See *DBWE* 1:107–21; 2:136–50 (discussed in chapter 2).

133 *DBWE* 5:41.

134 *DBWE* 5:42.

135 *DBWE* 5:43.

136 *DBWE* 5:27.

humiliation in the fallen world through the power of the Holy Spirit. The mediation of Christ in the spiritual community inherently challenges the abuses of power in the psychic community. For this reason the church must be discerning of the ways it seeks unmediated relationships (as performed constantly by whiteness) and of how Christ's mediation challenges abuses of power in the church and in its celebration of the sacraments.

God's Continual Call to Prepare the Way

Bonhoeffer's attention to the church's discernment of ideals and psychic controls highlights many of the difficulties congregations face when they seek to address a pervasive problem like whiteness. Often in our seemingly good intentions to address whiteness in the church, we only find ourselves capitulating to new configurations of whiteness (as is the case with many multicultural churches). This leads many of us to apathy with the church or anger at the church. On the other hand, when we do experience breakthrough in our churches around racial issues, there is the temptation of presenting the church as an antidote for the world's racial woes. This sentiment easily falls into an idealizing of the church. If the Christian church is to have a true reckoning with whiteness, it must grow in its awareness of the intensity of the battle and, more so, of the intensity of God's gracious love for the fallen creation. Bonhoeffer's proposal of preparing the way suggests that it is precisely in the church that the struggles with sinful enclosures, such as whiteness, rage with the most ferocity. The clash between heaven and hell takes place *in* the church. The only way to sustain such a struggle with whiteness is in reliance on God's irruptive working in fallen creation.

While Bantum presents the church's sacramental life in a way that explicitly challenges whiteness, this explicit challenge is predicated upon a stark contrast that he draws between the church's liturgical practices of pneumatic existence and the worldly practices of racial existence. This contrast creates two risks. First, it tempts the church with closing itself off to God's working in the world rather than seeing the sacrament as opening the church to discern God's working in both the church and world. Second, it moves in the direction of assessing our churches based on ideals rather than discerning how God is at work in the church in which we find ourselves—whether it be multiracial, cross-cultural, homogenous, or otherwise.

Bonhoeffer's *Life Together* presents the need to discern how our ideals for the church can stand in the way of attending to God's present working in the church. Bonhoeffer's proposal of preparing the way holds open a relative space for the church's responsive discernment in distinguishing between its own ideals and the reality of the given church as established by Christ. The church must repent of both its ideals of whiteness and its ideals that subtly seek to evacuate the ongoing struggle with whiteness in the church. This does not mean, however, that Bonhoeffer settles for a sinful church that has no form of visibility in the world. Bonhoeffer is not interested in a visibility originating from human ideals or human desires to control but one given in the reality of Christ's humiliation in the world. The church looks only to the wonder of the humiliated Christ that vanquishes every attempt to idealize the church.

Along with the need to address the danger of idealizing the church, there is an urgent necessity to challenge the psychic controls of whiteness in the Christian church of the West. Bantum's discussion of slave baptism offers a description of how the psychic controls of whiteness distorted God's gift of baptism into a concretization of racial existence in the churches of the American colonies. In such an extreme situation as that of slave baptism, Bonhoeffer's concept of the church holds open the possibility of present-day church councils (such as the one convened in Dahlem), which may offer a judgment for God that seeks to be in coherence with previous church councils. These types of judgments are reserved for extreme cases and are offered, as Bonhoeffer writes, "where the church knows the guilt of its ruptured knowledge of the truth, and where it thinks that it nevertheless must speak under God's commandment."[137] Bonhoeffer's premise that a judgment of this proportion is made with the church's acknowledgment of "guilt" and of its owned "ruptured knowledge" reflects what he would see as the grounds for making such a judgment. As discussed in chapter 3 in dialogue with Jennings, Bonhoeffer's claim against the German Christian church was not that it was sinful but that it portrayed its sin as righteousness—it was unrepentant. The real danger is not the psychic community, but rather mistaking the psychic community for the spiritual community, which is precisely what Bonhoeffer sought to address in *Life Together*. In Bonhoeffer's case, the measure of a final judgment was made to form the Confessing Church,

---

137 *DBWE* 11:369.

and such a judgment seems to have similar applicability in the case of slave baptism.[138]

The potency in Bantum's treatment of slave baptism is in how he dissects the psychic controls of whiteness in the early American church, but his analysis does not specifically handle how these psychic controls could have or should have been addressed within the empirical reality of the racialized church of the early colonies. Bonhoeffer's understanding of the church's sacramental life both dissects psychic controls in the church's liturgical practices and directs the church toward a preparing of the way that challenges these psychic controls within the empirical church. It is in this struggle to prepare the way that there may be a time to make a final judgment of sorts, as made in Dahlem, to affirm the boundaries of the empirical church. This judgment must recognize that the ultimate danger is not the psychic community that persists within the Christian church, but the temptation to portray the psychic community as Christ's spiritual community. Bantum's proposal rightly seeks to reform the liturgical practices of slave baptism. But Bonhoeffer takes this one step further by seeking to discern how God is already at work in the church's distorted liturgy to challenge it to prepare the way for God's ultimate word.

This is where Bonhoeffer's proposal of preparing the way is desperately needed today. Bonhoeffer's account of the church's discernment draws attention to how the psychic community persists within the historical church and continues to threaten diverse congregations in the present moment. In *Life Together* Bonhoeffer suggests that "extraordinary vigilance and clear thinking are called for" in diverse congregations, because diverse congregations are even more susceptible than homogenous ones to emotional manipulation.[139] Diversity does not remove the constant threat of the facilitation of whiteness but makes this threat all the more real with increased proximity (as seen in the "multiracial churches" of the early colonies that baptized slaves). In his book *The Next Evangelicalism*, Soong-Chan Rah addresses how the threat of

138 One of the difficulties of making such a judgment in the American context is that the Protestant church, at least, in the early American colonies began in a splintered state that made it difficult to actually form a church council. Bonhoeffer discusses the difficulties of the American church's fragmentation in his essay "Protestantism Without Reformation." He writes, "*The denominations in America* are faced from the start with an unimaginable variety of Christian communities. None of them can dare to make the claim to be the one church" (*DBWE* 15:443, emphasis original).

139 *DBWE* 5:47.

the manipulative controls of whiteness occurs in multiracial congregations.[140] He likens most multiracial churches to a mixed salad drenched
in ranch dressing.[141] Unaware of the configurations of whiteness undergirding the church historically, those from diverse backgrounds are
gathered together into a whiteness that facilitates diversity.[142] To address
this danger, Rah argues that the church must recognize that embedded
in multiracial gatherings are significant historical and ongoing disparities related to race that must not be swept under the rug but encountered unashamedly.[143] The constant threat of white facilitation is one of
the reasons why there is an appropriate place at times for predominately
African American churches and non-English-speaking churches. Even
in these cases, however, the power of whiteness can linger in significant
ways that must be challenged through a preparing of the way that moves
toward equitable integration.

To be clear, Bantum powerfully disputes the facilitation of diversity by
whiteness, as seen in his clear challenge of slave Christianity. It is precisely,
however, in the strength of Bantum's direct challenge of whiteness that the
thrust of his project steers from offering the necessary space for exploring
how whiteness persists within the Christian church of the West and how
whiteness must be continually addressed through a preparing of the way.
Recognition that Christ is the ground, strength, and promise of the church
secures the community, allowing it to deal seriously with its disparate history and the psychic manipulation resulting from this history. The church
must not disregard how the psychic controls of whiteness will continually
present themselves in the church, and therefore the church must continually prepare the way through a repentance that is discerning of how whiteness resists the surprise of Christ's coming.

Conclusion

The divergent implications of Bonhoeffer's and Bantum's ecclesiologies
are revealed in how each of their proposals accounts for the church's
historical continuity and the church's openness to the world. Whereas

---

140 Rah, *The Next Evangelicalism*. See especially 86–87.

141 Rah, *The Next Evangelicalism*, 86.

142 Gerardo Marti's *Mosaic of Believers* is one representative example of how this approach is endorsed. Marti argues that his church demonstrates that "membership in a religious community can suspend or supersede ethnic identity and become the basis for a new
type of status" (*A Mosaic of Believers*, 16–17).

143 Rah, *The Next Evangelicalism*, 87.

Bantum presents God's working in the modern world as a disruption that offers a counter-politic, Bonhoeffer presents God's working in the fallen world as an irruption found in the historical and empirical church that offers a politic of responsiveness. Bantum's vision of the mulatto church provides a direct disruption to the lived performance of race in the modern world, but this vision does not address how God works in the midst of the fallen world through the historical church. This is where Bonhoeffer's ecclesiology offers a distinct contribution to contemporary theologies of race. Bonhoeffer's understanding of the church attends to how God's irruption within history challenges sinful enclosures through the historical church's responsiveness to God's working in the fallen world. Whiteness must be not only disrupted; it must also be overcome through God's working throughout history. For this reason, to truly address whiteness, one must retain the continuity of the historical church and its open relation to the fallen world. This retention of the historical church and its openness to God's working in the fallen world is what Bonhoeffer's theology uniquely offers. While Bonhoeffer's theology may have its shortcomings, its promise is found in his novel explanation of how God works through a sinful church to challenge sinful enclosures as seen in the language game of whiteness.

Bonhoeffer presents the church's proclamation of Word and sacrament as God's irruptive working in the fallen world that opens the church up to encounter neighbors and the earth. In the center of the fallen world, "from the wood of the cross, the fountain of life springs up."[144] Bonhoeffer's ecclesiology is significant for theological race discourse because it accounts for God's material working through the historical church in the midst of the fallen world. God's working through the continuity of the historical church indicates the concrete defeat of whiteness in history. While the historical church may be marked by whiteness, it is not overcome by whiteness because God is at work in the historical church. Jesus has the final word.

144 *DBWE* 3:146.

Conclusion

Throughout this book I have sought to hold together two seemingly incongruent realities in the Western Christian church. The Christian church of the West has been historically formed within a fatal facilitation of whiteness. At the same time, the Western Christian church has been upheld by the life-giving loquaciousness of the triune God. God speaks through Christ's presence in the Christian church, precisely in the face of the church's resistance to this very speaking. Such a conclusion has led me to propose that what is needed in theological discussions of race is not a *problem/solution* approach to the Christian church's entrenchment in whiteness but a *discernment/surprise* approach that remains attentive to how God continues to speak in the midst of our resistance. This approach was substantiated through exploring how Bonhoeffer's proposal of an ecclesial preparing of the way allows for a candid assessment of the Christian church's troubled disfigurement in whiteness from the perspective that the church has been carried and is kept in existence by God's gracious speaking. Here the question is not how to overcome whiteness but how to discern God's active working in the midst of a community shaped by whiteness, so to join with the living Christ through a repentance that prepares the way for the surprise of God's gracious invocation.

In response to this overarching inquiry, the conclusion drawn by this study was that Bonhoeffer's motif of the ultimate and penultimate assists in linking a temporal challenge of whiteness, directly offered through repentance, with the surprise of God's ultimate word. The theological grammar of ultimate and penultimate was shown to be crucial in that it avoids giving human beings the power to thwart God's speaking throughout history, now, and into the future. Whiteness offers a resistance to God's ultimate word, but it cannot refuse God's coming in Jesus Christ that is already in full tilt to revive and rescue this tired earth and all its inhabitants, human and nonhuman. Within the freedom created by God's ultimate speaking, God's people are invited to embrace creaturely time to participate with Jesus Christ in preparing the way for his coming (Isa 40:3). And in this way, God speaks into and through a Christian church disfigured by whiteness without ever capitulating to the devastating reflexes of whiteness.

For those acutely involved in a local congregation, the suggestion that the Christian church is both a profound miracle orchestrated by the triune God and a desperate mess of human relationships should come as no major revelation. What hopefully this study has supplied is a glimpse into the wonder of God's gracious invocation that found us in the Christian church in the first place and that drives us further into a church marred by whiteness, a fallen body to which Christ is bound. Engaging in a continual struggle with the overwhelming breadth and depth of whiteness has a way of wearing us down and tempting us to evade or resolve the struggle. Comfort is to be taken in the reality that it is Christ who calls us into the struggle with whiteness and that we are joined with Christ and one another in preparing the way for the surprise of God's speaking, here and now. Thus, the aim of this study has not been to say something new or to offer a new solution but to repeat again what has already been said: "Repent, for the kingdom of heaven has come near" (Matt 4:17). This invocation from our living Lord is a challenge that confronts us, but more than this, it is an invitation that heals us.

Lamentably, the Western Christian church has a long history of muffling God's ultimate call through participating in configurations of whiteness that resist the surprise of God's speaking rather than responding with a repentance that anticipates the advent of Christ. Entering into the violent history of the church's compromise with whiteness is to offer a lament that prepares the way for the wonder of how God speaks in the midst of our resistance. It was to this end that I presented a history of whiteness in chapter 2 and engaged the thoughtful theological provocations of Jennings, Carter, and Bantum in chapters 3, 4, and 5. These explorations were based on the belief that all the experiences of those within the Christian church are borne by Christ through time. Bonhoeffer reflects on this point in his discussion of the prayers of lament from the Psalms: "No single human being can pray the psalms of lamentation out of his or her own experience. Spread out before us here is the anguish of the entire Christian community throughout all time, as Jesus Christ has wholly experienced it."[1] While the focus of this book has been on repentance, lament is an equally important response to God's speaking that deserves further attention with relation to the historical and continued violence of whiteness in the Christian church.[2]

Along with this, I must acknowledge that this book is woefully inadequate in relation to where much of the discussions about race are headed. As mentioned in the introduction, Womanist voices are leading the charge in delving into the complex interrelation between race, gender, and sexuality. Women of color are quickly charting theological discussions of race into new territory, requiring a repentance that goes beyond the scope of this book. This trailblazing offered by women of color is not new, as it has always been women of color at the forefront of realizing justice in our broken nation and in the Christian church. Women of color are leading not only the discussion but also the implementation of new possibilities of ministry in service to the church and world.[3] Contemporary theological discussions of race remain open, requiring continual repentance. It is to this end that this book has sought to foster and reflect a posture of repentance that prepares the way for the hearing of God's gracious word. The following final reflections are directed primarily to white Christians who may read this book and ask, "What would you have us do?"

Remaining in Repentance to Prepare the Way

Discussions of whiteness and its inequitable impact are often hastily received by white people with practical questions of "What should we do?" and "How can we make things right?" As promising and repentant as these questions may seem, they can reiterate whiteness in subtle

1 DBWE 5:169.
2 As a starting point, see Soong-Chan Rah, Prophetic Lament: A Call for Justice in Troubled Times (Downers Grove: InterVarsity Press, 2015).
3 For example, see the creative work of Latasha Morrison through Be the Bridge and her recently published book Be the Bridge: Pursuing God's Heart for Racial Reconciliation (Colorado Springs: WaterBrooks, 2019). See, as well, the Truth's Table podcast hosted by Christina Edmondson, Ekemini Uwan, and Michelle Higgins.

yet powerful ways. Whiteness is about being in control, about having the correct answers at one's disposal. Questions such as these can easily evacuate sitting with and owning a history that unjustly elevates us above others, leading us into a paternalism that reiterates whiteness. Repentance is not a means for solving whiteness or an answer booklet for working toward reconciliation.

It is with a wariness of how repentance can be distorted in relation to whiteness that this book has suggested that repentance is not a turning to a new way but the continual and concrete process of being found on the path Jesus walks—the way the suffering God comes as Israel's Messiah.[4] John the Baptist's call to repentance is not its own end, in terms of a new way, but a way already given in reference to the "Lamb of God who takes away the sins of the world" (John 1:29).[5] Repentance is oriented toward and from the wonder of God's gracious suffering, encountered in the tangible worship of the church. Repentance as a preparing of the way is not a clearing of the way for Jesus to come. As Bonhoeffer explains, "Christ comes, to be sure, clearing the way for this coming, whether one is ready for it or not."[6] Preparing the way pertains to our readiness for the surprise of God's gracious coming in the suffering servant of Israel (Isa 53).

The violence of whiteness opposes Christ's coming by subjecting us to an unequal share in the sufferings of a fallen creation. Preparing the way requires a redistribution of suffering found in our collective sharing in God's suffering in the fallen creation. We must recognize that remaining in the church of the West often exacts a higher cost on people of color and has led to what some have called a "quiet exodus" of Black worshipers from white Evangelical churches.[7] Preparing the way requires a redistribution of suffering through white people becoming

4   Jennifer McBride insightfully explains how repentance in terms of a confession of sin should not be understood simply as an apology. Instead, gleaning from Bonhoeffer's understanding of repentance and responsibility, she argues that confession of sin requires an accepting of responsibility and acknowledgment of complicity in specific sins. See McBride, *The Church for the World*, 17.

5   In his letter from July 18, 1944, Bonhoeffer expresses a similar point in his discussion of repentance as "walking the path that Jesus walks" (*DBWE* 8:480).

6   *DBWE* 6:162.

7   See Campbell Robertson, "A Quiet Exodus: Why Black Worshipers Are Leaving White Evangelical Churches," *New York Times*, March 9, 2018, https://www.nytimes.com/2018/03/09/us/blacks-evangelical-churches.html. See also William E. Pannell's account of the difficulty of remaining in the evangelical church from over five decades ago, *My Friend, the Enemy* (Waco: World Books, 1968).

more concerned with the pain exacted on people of color than with our own fears, questions, and needs.

So what can white Christians do? We can begin by working on ourselves and with one another to enter the pain of our racial past without trying to alleviate it or solve it. One lesson I learned through our church's intensive discussions of race is that most white Christians have preparatory work to do before entering into discussions of race with people of color. We must grow in our awareness of our whiteness and how it constantly buffers us from encountering others so that we are better prepared to discuss whiteness in diverse groups. This preparation also helps to minimize the inevitable pain we will exact on people of color willing to have the conversation with us.

Additionally, rather than looking for a new church, we should begin the repentant work of challenging whiteness where we find ourselves. One of the main proposals offered in this book is that the language game of whiteness is a game that is always in play and is always informing our words, gestures, and gazes. The premise that whiteness is always in play suggests that there is a struggle with whiteness through which each local congregation must work, whether it be homogenous or multiracial. Whiteness shapes our churches in such a way that our communities are welcoming to some and unapproachable to others. Rather than seeking diversity, a better aim is to grow in our discernment of how our churches are often mediated by whiteness instead of the living Christ. Adding diversity to a local congregation does not address configurations of whiteness but only complicates them. Diversity or not, repentance requires an attunement to how Christ is already at work in our local congregations to prepare the way for God's promise that "all flesh shall see the salvation of God" (Luke 3:6).

Reparations *Now* to Prepare the Way

For those enacting a continual posture of repentance, the question is not whether reparations are necessary, but how we can repentantly participate *now* in repairing the racial injustices that have compounded over centuries of our country's and church's history.[8] God's gracious call

---

8   For a general discussion of reparations, see Ta-Nehisi Coates' article "The Case for Reparations" in *We Were Eight Years in Power*, 163–210. For a discussion of the need for reparation now and its applicability for the Christian church, see Christina Edmondson, Ekemini Uwan, and Michelle Higgins, hosts, "Reparations Now: Repent and Repair," *Truth's Table*, season 2, episode 1, Soundcloud, 2018, https://soundcloud.com/truthstable/reparations-now-repent-and-repair.

leads to a repentant response of reparations that must be offered again and again to address the compounding interest of racial disparity that has accrued over time. In the same way that whiteness has been enacted again and again to privilege and benefit those deemed white, the repentant response of reparations must be enacted again and again to bring repair. Reparations is more than an act; it is a way of life with systemic repercussions. By understanding reparations as a continual practice and as a response oriented by and toward God's address, we avoid the risk of turning reparations into a solution applied by white people to fix and resolve the problem of whiteness. Reparations is not a one-time solution but a journey into the surprise of a forgotten place.

From the perspective of the Christian church, the repentant response of reparations is participation in the work already initiated by Christ through the Spirit to clear away each and every hindrance that stands in the way of God's ultimate word being heard. Reparation is not an end in itself but an opening to the wonder of God's gracious summons to a tired and weary world. The wisdom required in applying reparations must be fueled by a childlike hope in the triune God who holds the future in Jesus Christ. Our imagination about what could be is limited by the fact that very little effort or thought has gone into offering reparations in the context of the Christian church. The call that came out of the Black Economic Development Conference, requesting $500 million in reparations, remains waiting for a response.

What would it look like to consider reparations at every level of the Christian church, from the denominational level to the local congregation to our personal lives? How might God be calling us to administer reparations as part of church discipline? How might God be calling us to apply reparations in our resourcing of churches at a denominational level to offset gentrification? How might God be calling us to offer reparations in our church's giving, our worship, and our preaching? How might God be calling each of us to repair the imbalances in power, control, and resources caused by whiteness that buffer us each and every day from others? If we are not asking questions like these continually and persistently, how will reparations ever become a preparing of the way for God's ultimate word to be heard? As Bonhoeffer writes, "The way of the word must be prepared. The word itself demands it."[9] Again, if we understand reparations as a preparing of the way for the surprise of God's address, then pursuing these questions

9   *DBWE* 6:160.

must not be offered as a solution but as an opening into better questions and more opportunities for repair.

Our failure to ask questions such as these reflects how we continue to operate within the reflexes of whiteness that resist God's gracious word to God's creation. As a result, we miss the invitation to participate with Christ in preparing the way for the advent of God's coming.

Hope Endures

Nestled within one of his prison letters from July 16, 1944, Bonhoeffer supplies his closest friend, Eberhard Bethge, with the possible content for a future sermon. After citing a handful of passages,[10] texts that proclaim how God is with us in the bleak silence of ominous days, Bonhoeffer expresses the thrust of the message as confined to a simple thought: "One has to live in a congregation for a while to understand how 'Christ is formed' in it (Gal 4:19)."[11]

The claim that the triune God speaks to and through Christian congregations, which are already speaking the language game of whiteness, is not a verifiable theory but an audacious conviction that requires one "live in a congregation for a while to understand." The face value foolishness of such a belief is that it calls one into the exclusion and violence of whiteness, present in the communal life of our Christian congregations. Not only must we endure the negative impacts of whiteness, but we must also confess our own participation in speaking whiteness into existence with each new day. The hope found in the church is not that it is free from the inequities of whiteness permeating the Western world, but that it constitutes a community sustained by Christ where these inequities can be honestly confessed, explored, and challenged. Christ lifts the church through the Spirit to prepare the way for the pending moment of his arrival, an arrival that always takes us by surprise. In turn, this preparing of the way incorporates the church into the humiliated Christ to discover the surprise of God's gracious care for all of creation. May we endure with a childlike hope that allows us the necessary time in a congregation and a Christian church to discover the surprise of witnessing "Christ formed in it!"

10   Bonhoeffer lists the following verses: "Pss. 62:2[1]; 119:94a; 42:6[5], Jer. 31:3; Isa. 41:10; 43:1; Matt. 28:20b" (*DBWE* 8:475).

11   *DBWE* 8:475. Galatians 4:19 reads, "My little children, for whom I am again in the pain of childbirth until Christ is formed in you."

Bibliography

Adams, Nicholas. "Reparative Reasoning." *Modern Theology* 24, no. 3 (2008): 447–57.

Allen, Theodore. *Racial Oppression and Social Contract.* Volume 1 of *The Invention of the White Race.* New York: Verso Books, 1994.

———. *The Origin of Racial Oppression in Anglo-America.* Volume 2 of *The Invention of the White Race.* New York: Verso Books, 1997.

Anderson, Victor. *Beyond Ontological Blackness: An Essay on African American Religious and Cultural Criticism.* New York: Continuum, 1995.

Avram, Wes. "The Work of Conscience in Bonhoeffer's Homiletic." *Homiletic* 29, no. 1 (2004): 1–14.

Baldwin, James. *The Price of the Ticket: Collected Nonfiction, 1948–1985.* New York: St. Martin's Press, 1985.

Bantum, Brian. *The Death of Race: Building a New Christianity in a Racial World.* Minneapolis: Fortress, 2016.

———. *Redeeming Mulatto: A Theology of Race and Christian Hybridity.* Waco: Baylor University Press, 2010.

Barnes, Kenneth C. "Dietrich Bonhoeffer and Hitler's Persecution of the Jews." In *Betrayal: German Churches and the Holocaust*, edited by Robert Ericksen and Susannah Heschel, 110–28. Minneapolis: Fortress, 1999.

Barth, Karl. "Fate and Idea in Theology." In *The Way of Theology in Karl Barth: Essay and Comments*, edited by H. Martin Rumscheidt, 25–62. Eugene: Pickwick, 1986.

Benesh, Sean. "The Appeal of Gentrification." In *Vespas, Cafes, Singlespeed Bikes, and Urban Hipsters: Gentrification, Urban Mission, and Church*

Planting, edited by Sean Benesh, 95–110. Portland: Urban Loft Publishers, 2014.

Berry, Wendell. *The Hidden Wound*. Farrar: North Point Press, 1989.

Best, Isabel, ed. *The Collected Sermons of Dietrich Bonhoeffer*. Translated by Douglas W. Stott, Anne Schmidt-Lange, Isabel Best, Scott A. Moore, and Claudia D. Bergmann. Minneapolis: Fortress, 2012.

Bethge, Eberhard. *Dietrich Bonhoeffer: A Biography*. Rev. ed. Edited by Victoria Barnett. Minneapolis: Fortress, 2000.

Brock, Brian. *Singing the Ethos of God: On the Place of Christian Ethics in Scripture*. Grand Rapids: Eerdmans, 2007.

Brodkin, Karen. *How Jews Became White Folks and What That Says about Race in America*. New Brunswick: Rutgers University Press, 1998.

Canon, Katie. *Black Womanist Ethics*. Eugene: Wipf & Stock, 1988.

Carter, J. Kameron. *Race: A Theological Account*. Oxford: Oxford University Press, 2008.

Cavanaugh, William T. *Torture and Eucharist: Theology, Politics, and the Body of Christ*. New York: Wiley-Blackwell, 1998.

Cimino, Richard. "Neighborhoods, Niches, and Networks: The Religious Ecology of Gentrification," *City & Community* 10, no. 2 (2011): 157–81.

Clements, Keith. "Ecumenical Witness for Peace." In *The Cambridge Companion to Dietrich Bonhoeffer*, edited by John W. de Gruchy, 154–89. Cambridge: Cambridge University Press, 1999.

Coakley, Sarah. "What Does Chalcedon Solve and What Does It Not? Some Reflections on the Status and Meaning of the Chalcedonian 'Definition.'" In *The Incarnation: An Interdisciplinary Symposium on the Incarnation of the Son of God*, edited by Stephen T. Davis, Daniel Kendall S.J., and Gerald O'Collins S.J., 143–63. Oxford: Oxford University Press, 2002.

Coates, Ta-Nehisi. *We Were Eight Years in Power: An American Tragedy*. New York: One World Publishing, 2017.

Cone, James H. *A Black Theology of Liberation*. Maryknoll: Orbis Books, 1970.

———. *Black Theology and Black Power*. Maryknoll: Orbis Books, 1969.

———. *The Cross and the Lynching Tree*. Maryknoll: Orbis Books, 2011.

Conn, Harvie M. *The American City and the Evangelical Church: A Historical Overview*. Grand Rapids: Baker Books, 1994.

Copeland, M. Shawn. *Enfleshing Freedom: Body, Race, and Being*. Minneapolis: Fortress, 2010.

Dahill, Lisa E. *Reading from the Underside of Selfhood: Bonhoeffer and Spiritual Formation*. Eugene: Wipf & Stock, 2009.

Davis, Angela Y. *The Meaning of Freedom*. San Francisco: City Light Books, 2012.

Day, Thomas. "Conviviality and Common Sense: The Meaning of Christian Community for Dietrich Bonhoeffer." Ph.D. diss. Union Theological Seminary, 1975.

De Gruchy, John W. *Bonhoeffer and South Africa: Theology in Dialogue.* Grand Rapids: Eerdmans, 1984.

DeJonge, Michael. *Bonhoeffer's Theological Formation: Berlin, Barth, and Protestant Theology.* Oxford: Oxford University Press, 2012.

Deloria, Vine, Jr. *Custer Died for Your Sins: An Indian Manifesto.* New York: Macmillan, 1969.

———. *For This Land: Writings on Religion in America.* New York: Routledge, 1999.

DeSalvo, Louise. *Crazy in the Kitchen: Foods, Feuds, and Forgiveness in an Italian American Family.* New York: Bloomsbury, 2004.

DeYoung, Curtis Paul, Michael O. Emerson, George Yancey, and Karen Chai Kim. *United by Faith: The Multiracial Congregation as an Answer to the Problem of Race.* Oxford: Oxford University Press, 2003.

DiAngelo, Robin. *White Fragility: Why It's So Hard for White People to Talk about Racism.* Boston: Beacon Press, 2018.

Douglas, Kelly Brown. *Sexuality and the Black Church: A Womanist Perspective.* Maryknoll: Orbis Books, 1999.

Draper, Andrew. *A Theology of Race and Place: Liberation and Reconciliation in the Works of Jennings and Carter.* Eugene: Pickwick, 2016.

Dudley, Carl. "Churches in Changing Communities." In *Metro-Ministry: Ways and Means for the Urban Church,* edited by David Frenchak and Sharrel Keyes, 78–89. Eglin: David C. Cook, 1979.

Dumas, André. *Dietrich Bonhoeffer: Theologian of Reality.* Translated by Robert McAfee Brown. London: SCM Press, 1971.

Dussel, Enrique. *The Underside of Modernity: Apel, Ricoeur, Rorty, Taylor, and the Philosophy of Liberation.* Translated by Eduardo Mendieta. Atlantic Highlands: Humanities, 1996.

Edmondson, Christina, Ekemini Uwan, and Michelle Higgins, hosts. "Reparations Now: Repent and Repair." *Truth's Table,* season 2, episode 1, Soundcloud, 2018. https://soundcloud.com/truthstable/reparations-now -repent-and-repair.

Ellingsen, Mark. "Bonhoeffer, Racism, and a Communal Model for Healing." *Journal of Church and State* 43, no. 2 (2001): 235–49.

Feil, Ernst. *The Theology of Dietrich Bonhoeffer.* Translated by Martin Rumscheidt. Minneapolis: Fortress, 1985.

Floyd, Wayne W., Jr. *Theology and the Dialectics of Otherness: On Reading Bonhoeffer and Adorno.* Lanham: University Press of America, 1988.

Friedlander, Albert H. "Bonhoeffer and Baeck: Theology after Auschwitz." *European Judaism* 14 (1980): 23–32.

Gilkes, Cheryl Townsend. "Jesus Must Needs Go through Samaria: Disestablishing the Mountains of Race and the Hegemony of Whiteness." In *Christology and Whiteness: What Would Jesus Do?*, edited by George Yancy, 59–74. New York: Routledge, 2012.

Gillard, Dominique Dubois. *Rethinking Incarceration: Advocating for Justice That Restores.* Downers Grove: InterVarsity Press, 2018.

Givens, Tommy. *We the People: Israel and the Catholicity of Jesus.* Minneapolis: Fortress, 2014.

Godsey, John. *The Theology of Dietrich Bonhoeffer.* London: SCM Press, 1960.

Green, Clifford J. "Editor's Introduction to the English Edition." In *DBWE* 6, 1–44.

Greggs, Tom. *Theology against Religion: Constructive Dialogues with Bonhoeffer and Barth.* London: T&T Clark, 2011.

Gregory, Eric. *Politics and the Order of Love.* Chicago: University of Chicago Press, 2008.

Gregory of Nyssa, "Homilies on Ecclesiastes." In *Gregory of Nyssa, Homilies on Ecclesiastes: An English Version with Supporting Studies*, edited by Stuart G. Hall, 31–144. New York: de Gruyter, 1993.

Harnack, Adolf von. *Outlines of the History of Dogma.* Translated by Edwin Knox Mitchell. New York: Funk & Wagnalls, 1893.

Harris, Cheryl. "Whiteness as Property," *Harvard Law Review* 106, no. 8 (1993): 1707–91.

Harvey, Barry. *Taking Hold of the Real: Dietrich Bonhoeffer and the Profound Worldliness of Christianity.* Eugene: Cascade Books, 2015.

Harvey, Jennifer. *Dear White Christians: For Those Still Longing for Racial Reconciliation.* Grand Rapids: Eerdmans, 2014.

Hauerwas, Stanley, and Romand Coles. *Christianity, Democracy and the Radical Ordinary: Conversations between a Radical Democrat and a Christian.* Cambridge: Lutterworth Press, 2008.

Haynes, Stephen R. *The Bonhoeffer Legacy: Post-Holocaust Perspectives.* Minneapolis: Fortress, 2006.

———. *The Bonhoeffer Phenomenon: Portraits of a Protestant Saint.* Minneapolis: Fortress, 2004.

Headley, Cleavis. "Delegitimizing the Normativity of 'Whiteness': A Critical Africana Philosophical Study of the Metaphoricity of 'Whiteness.'" In *What White Looks Like: African-American Philosophers on the Whiteness Question*, edited by George Yancy, 87–106. New York: Routledge, 2004.

Heschel, Susannah. *The Aryan Jesus: Christian Theologians and the Bible in Nazi Germany*. Princeton: Princeton University Press, 2008.

Hinchliff, Peter. *Holiness and Politics*. Grand Rapids: Eerdmans, 1979.

Ignatiev, Noel. *How the Irish Became White*. New York: Routledge, 1995.

Jacobson, Matthew Frye. *Roots Too: White Ethnic Revival in Post-Civil Rights America*. Cambridge: Harvard University Press, 2006.

———. *Whiteness of a Different Color: European Immigrants and the Alchemy of Race*. Cambridge: Harvard University Press, 1998.

Jager, Michael. "Class Definition and the Esthetics of Gentrification: Victoriana in Melbourne." In *Gentrification of the City*, edited by Neil Smith and Peter Williams, 78–91. Boston: Allen and Unwin, 1986.

Jennings, Willie James. *Acts*. Louisville: Westminster John Knox Press, 2017.

———. *The Christian Imagination: Theology and the Origins of Race*. New Haven: Yale University Press, 2010.

Kaiser, Joshua A. *Becoming Simple and Wise: Moral Discernment in Dietrich Bonhoeffer's Vision of Christian Ethics*. Eugene: Pickwick, 2015.

Katznelson, Ira. *When Affirmative Action Was White: An Untold History of Racial Inequality in Twentieth-Century America*. New York: W. W. Norton, 2005.

Kendi, Ibram X. *How to Be an Antiracist*. New York: Random House, 2019.

Lees, Loretta, Tom Slater, and Elvin K. Wyly. *Gentrification*. New York: Routledge, 2007.

Liguš, Ján. "Dietrich Bonhoeffer: Ultimate, Penultimate and Their Impact. The Origin and Essence of Ethics." In *Bonhoeffer's Ethics: Old Europe and New Frontiers*, edited by Guy Christopher Carter, René van Eyden, Hans-Dirk van Hoogstraten, and Jurjen Wiersma, 59–77. Kampen: Kok Pharos, 1991.

Lose, David J. "'I Believe, Help My Unbelief': Bonhoeffer on Biblical Preaching." *Word & World* 26, no. 1 (2006): 86–97.

Luther, Martin. *Lecture on Romans*, edited by Hilton C. Oswald. St. Louis: Concordia, 1971.

———. "Psalm 111." In *Luther's Works*. American ed., vol. 13, edited by Jaroslav Pelikan and Helmut T. Lehmann, 351–87. Philadelphia: Muehlenberg and Fortress, and St. Louis: Concordia, 1955–1986.

Ma, Sheng-Mei. *The Deathly Embrace: Orientalism and Asian American Identity*. Minneapolis: University of Minnesota Press, 2000.

MacIntyre, Alasdair. *After Virtue: A Study in Moral Theory*. Notre Dame: University of Notre Dame Press, 1981.

Manoussakis, John. "'At the Recurrent End of the Unending': Bonhoeffer's Eschatology of the Penultimate." In *Bonhoeffer and Continental Thought:*

Cruciform Philosophy, edited by Brian Gregor and Jens Zimmermann, 228–29. Bloomington: Indiana University Press, 2009.

Marsh, Charles. *Reclaiming Dietrich Bonhoeffer: The Promise of His Theology*. Oxford: Oxford University Press, 1996.

————. *Strange Glory: A Life of Dietrich Bonhoeffer*. New York: Vintage, 2014.

Marti, Gerardo. *A Mosaic of Believers: Diversity and Innovation in a Multiethnic Church*. Bloomington: Indiana University Press, 2005.

Mathewes, Charles. *A Theology of Public Life*. Cambridge: Cambridge University Press, 2007.

Mawson, Michael. *Christ Existing as Community: Bonhoeffer's Early Ecclesiology*. Oxford: Oxford University Press, 2018.

————. "The Spirit and the Community: Pneumatology and Ecclesiology in Jenson, Hütter and Bonhoeffer." *International Journal of Systematic Theology* 15, no. 4 (2013): 453–68.

McBride, Jennifer M. *The Church for the World: A Theology of Public Witness*. Oxford: Oxford University Press, 2012.

Metzger, Paul Louis. *Consuming Jesus: Beyond Race and Class Divisions in a Consumer Church*. Grand Rapids: Eerdmans, 2007.

Milbank, John. *Theology and Social Theory: Beyond Secular Reason*. Oxford: Blackwell, 1992.

Mobley, Jennifer. *The Virtue of Bonhoeffer's Ethics: A Study of Dietrich Bonhoeffer's Ethics in Relation to Virtue Ethics*. Eugene: Wipf & Stock, 2013.

Moltmann, Jürgen and Jürgen Weissbach. *Two Studies in the Theology of Bonhoeffer*, translated by Reginald H. Fuller and Ilse Fuller. New York: Charles Scribner's Sons, 1967.

Morrison, Latasha. *Be the Bridge: Pursuing God's Heart for Racial Reconciliation*. Colorado Springs: WaterBrooks, 2019.

Nielsen, Kirsten Busch. "Community Turned Inside Out: Dietrich Bonhoeffer's Concept of the Church and of Humanity Reconsidered." In *Being Human, Becoming Human: Dietrich Bonhoeffer and Social Thought*, edited by Jen Zimmermann and Brian Gregor, 91–101. Eugene: Wipf & Stock, 2010.

Northcott, Michael. "'Who Am I?' Human Identity and the Spiritual Disciplines in the Witness of Dietrich Bonhoeffer." In *Who Am I?: Bonhoeffer's Theology through His Poetry*, edited by Bernd Wannenwetsch, 11–29. London: T&T Clark, 2009.

Novak, Michael. *The Rise of the Unmeltable Ethnics: Politics and Culture in the Seventies*. New York: Macmillan, 1971.

Painter, Nell Irvin. *The History of White People*. New York: W. W. Norton, 2010.

Pangritz, Andreas. "Who Is Christ, for Us, Today?" In *The Cambridge Companion to Dietrich Bonhoeffer*, edited by John W. de Gruchy, 134–53. Cambridge: Cambridge University Press, 1999.

Pannell, William E. *My Friend, the Enemy.* Waco: World Books, 1968.

Perkinson, James W. *White Theology: Outing Supremacy in Modernity.* New York: Palgrave Macmillan, 2004.

Phillips, Jon. *Christ for Us in the Theology of Dietrich Bonhoeffer.* San Francisco: Harper & Row, 1967.

Piper, John. *Bloodlines: Race, Cross, and the Christian Church.* Wheaton: Crossway, 2011.

Plant, Stephen. "Theological Education and Christian Formation in Conversation with Dietrich Bonhoeffer's *Life Together.*" *Colloquium* 47, no. 2 (2015): 180–94.

Puffer, Matthew. "Bonhoeffer's Ethics of Election: Discerning a Late Revision." *International Journal of Systematic Theology* 14 (2012): 255–76.

Raboteau, Albert J. *A Fire in the Bones: Reflections on African-American Religious History.* Boston: Beacon Press, 1995.

———. *Slave Religion: The "Invisible Institution" in the Antebellum South.* Oxford: Oxford University Press, 1978.

Rah, Soong-Chan. *The Next Evangelicalism: Freeing the Church from Western Cultural Captivity.* Downers Grove: InterVarsity Press, 2009.

———. *Prophetic Lament: A Call for Justice in Troubled Times.* Downers Grove: InterVarsity Press, 2015.

Ray, Stephen G., Jr. *Do No Harm: Social Sin and Christian Responsibility.* Minneapolis: Fortress, 2003.

Ripley, William Z. "Race Progress and Immigration," *Annals of the American Academy of Political and Social Science* 34, no. 1 (1909): 130–38.

———. *The Races of Europe: A Sociological Study.* New York: D. Appleton, 1899.

Roberts, J. Deotis. *A Black Political Theology.* Philadelphia: Westminster, 1974.

Robertson, Campbell. "A Quiet Exodus: Why Black Worshipers are Leaving White Evangelical Churches." *New York Times.* March 9, 2018, https://www.nytimes.com/2018/03/09/us/blacks-evangelical-churches.html.

Roediger, David R. *The Wages of Whiteness: Race and the Making of the American Working Class.* New York: Verso Books, 1991.

Rofe, Matthew. "'I Want to Be Global': Theorising the Gentrifying Class as an Emergent Elite Global Community," *Urban Studies* 40, no. 12 (2003): 2511–26.

Rosenbaum, Stanley R. "Dietrich Bonhoeffer: A Jewish View." *Journal of Ecumenical Studies* 18, no. 2 (1981): 301–7.

Schwartz, Bernard. *Behind Bakke: Affirmative Action and the Supreme Court.* New York: New York University Press, 1988.

Smith, Ted A. *Weird John Brown: Divine Violence and the Limits of Ethics.* Stanford: Stanford University Press, 2015.

Soosten, Joachim von. "Editor's Afterword to the German Edition." In *DBWE* 1, 290–306.

Stevens, David E. *God's New Humanity: A Biblical Theology of Multiethnicity for the Church.* Eugene: Wipf & Stock, 2012.

Tietz, Christiane. "The Mysteries of Knowledge, Sin, and Shame." In *Mysteries in the Theology of Dietrich Bonhoeffer: A Copenhagen Bonhoeffer Symposium*, edited by Kirsten Busch Nielsen and Christiane Tietz, 27–48. Göttingen: Vandenhoeck & Ruprecht, 2007.

Tisby, Jemar. *The Color of Compromise: The Truth about the American Church's Complicity in Racism.* Grand Rapids: Zondervan, 2019.

Tran, Jonathan. "Time for Hauerwas' Racism." In *Unsettling Arguments: A Festschrift on the Occasion of Stanley Hauerwas' 70th Birthday*, edited by Charles R. Pinches, Kelly S. Johnson, and Charles M. Collier, 246–61. Eugene: Cascade Books, 2010.

———. *The Vietnam War and Theologies of Memory: Time and Eternity in the Far Country.* West Sussex: Wiley-Blackwell, 2010.

Vanhoozer, Kevin J. *The Drama of Doctrine: A Canonical-Linguistic Approach to Christian Theology.* Louisville: Westminster John Knox Press, 2005.

Volf, Miroslav. *The End of Memory: Remembering Rightly in a Violent World.* Grand Rapids: Eerdmans, 2006.

———. *Exclusion and Embrace: A Theological Exploration of Identity, Otherness, and Reconciliation.* Nashville: Abingdon Press, 1996.

Wannenwetsch, Bernd. *Political Worship: Ethics for Christian Citizens.* Translated by Margaret Kohl. Oxford: Oxford University Press, 2004.

———. "'Responsible Living' or 'Responsible Self'? Bonhoefferian Reflections on a Vexed Moral Notion." *Studies in Christian Ethics* 18, no. 3 (2005): 125–40.

West, Charles C. "Ground under Our Feet." In *New Studies in Bonhoeffer's Ethics*, edited by William J. Peck, 235–73. Lewiston: Edwin Mellen Press, 1987.

Williams, A. N. *The Architecture of Theology: Structure, System, and Ratio.* Oxford: Oxford University Press, 2011.

Williams, Delores S. *Sisters in the Wilderness: The Challenge of Womanist God-Talk.* Maryknoll: Orbis Books, 1993.

Williams, Reggie L. *Bonhoeffer's Black Jesus: Harlem Renaissance Theology and an Ethic of Resistance.* Waco: Baylor University Press, 2014.

Wittgenstein, Ludwig. *Philosophical Investigations*. Translated by G. E. M. Anscombe, P. M. S. Hacker, and Joachim Schulte. Oxford: Wiley-Blackwell, 2009.

Wytsma, Ken. *The Myth of Equality: Uncovering the Roots of Injustice and Privilege*. Downers Grove: InterVarsity Press, 2017.

Yancy, George. *Black Bodies, White Gazes: The Continuing Significance of Race*. Lanham: Rowman & Littlefield, 2008.

——, ed. *Christology and Whiteness: What Would Jesus Do?* New York: Routledge, 2012.

Young, Josiah Ulysses. "'Is the White Christ, Too, Distraught by These Dark Sins His Father Wrought?': Dietrich Bonhoeffer and the Problem of the White Christ." *Religious Studies* 26, no. 3 (1999): 317–330.

——. *No Difference in the Fare: Dietrich Bonhoeffer and the Problem of Racism*. Grand Rapids: Eerdmans, 1998.

——. "Nobody Knows but Jesus." *The Living Pulpit* 4, no. 2 (1995): 12–13.

——. "Who Belongs to Christ?" In *Christology and Whiteness: What Would Jesus Do?*, edited by George Yancy, 128–35. New York: Routledge, 2012.

Zerner, Ruth. "Dietrich Bonhoeffer's American Experiences: People, Letters, and Papers from Union Seminary." *Union Seminary Quarterly Review* 31, no. 4 (1976): 261–82.

Zizioulas, John. *Being as Communion: Studies in Personhood and the Church*. Crestwood: St. Vladimir's Seminary Press, 1985.

Zukin, Sharon. *Loft Living: Culture and Capital in Urban Change*. New Brunswick: Rutgers University Press, 1989.

Index

Abraham, 6, 51n116, 108n58, 116, 144–45, 157, 168
actus directus: see direct act of faith
actus reflexus, 94, 96, 96n14; *see also* theological knowledge
Adam, 95, 111, 117, 118n100, 137–42, 146, 149, 150, 202, 215, 216; *see also* creation
advent, 49, 58, 100, 122, 124, 154, 162, 192, 204, 224, 229; *see also* surprise
analogia entis, 96

baptism, 5–6, 53, 57n1, 194, 197–200, 205–7; slave, 188–89, 210–13, 219–20
Barth, Karl, 94–95, 95n10, 96n14, 158, 159, 196n57
Berry, Wendell, 67–68, 71n38
Bethge, Eberhard, 8n7, 25n15, 31, 147n42, 174n146, 229
Black Manifesto, 70–71

cantus firmus, 142, 175
Civil Rights Movement, 54, 72–80, 126

Coates, Ta-Nehisi, 83, 227n8
communicatio idiomatum, 156
Cone, James, 23, 45n103, 46, 158, 160, 185, 186, 186n27
contingent, 32, 36–37, 40, 43, 49, 52, 53, 55, 93, 94–99, 102, 106, 114, 130, 163, 183, 197
creation, 10, 11, 14, 16, 29–30, 34–43, 92, 136–37, 179, 229; and Christology, 4, 137–49, 156–57, 174; ex nihilo, 6; fallen, 11, 14, 38, 41–42, 49, 53–54, 64, 93–100, 113–18, 132–33, 152, 171, 179–81, 174, 179, 212–13, 216, 218, 226; orders of, 9; and place, 67, 101–3, 120–21; and sacrament, 128–29, 183–85, 195, 201–4, 208, 210; temporal, 8, 32–34, 38, 170; and whiteness, 65, 91–134; *see also* natural and unnatural

De Gruchy, John W., 22n1, 108n60, 131n146
DeJonge, Michael, 95n10